Jim Peters: Texas Ranger

Jim Peters:

Texas Ranger

BY LEE PAUL

JONA BOOKS
Bedford, IN

Published by JONA Books
P. O. Box 336
Bedford, IN 47421
Manufactured in the U.S.A.
First Edition

CONTENTS

INTRODUCTION

My decision to write this book on Texas Ranger Jim Peters came about through a chance meeting with a grizzled, old ex-Ranger at the Gage Motel in the tiny West Texas town of Marathon. It was early April, 1993, and although it was only mid-morning, the temperature was already 74 degrees and promising to sizzle near the 100 mark. I was hungry and thirsty, and the shaded veranda of the hotel's porch was positively inviting. The old man sat in one of the hotel's comfortable leather chairs just inside the doorway under a ceiling fan, sipping a mug of steaming coffee between puffs on his cigarette, greeting everyone who stepped through the screen door with a wide smile and friendly wave of his hand as if they were old friends of many years. It was obvious that he enjoyed himself. It was also just as obvious that welcoming visitors was not a new pastime for him, that he had greeted people in that fashion for ages---probably forever-tolerated by the friendly staff of the hotel.

I smiled at him, turned toward the Branding Iron dining room and an eagerly anticipated late breakfast or early lunch---whichever I could get---when the rasping voice stopped me in mid-stride. "Writing about the hotel? Or the area?" I knew it was he before I even turned around. He grinned, pointing to the camera slung around my neck and the small notebook tucked into my shirt pocket. Motioning for me to join him, he took a sip of his coffee and then neatly wiped his mustache with a blue bandana he magically produced from under the table. Deciding food could wait, I ordered iced tea and pulled up another chair to join him.

Marathon is not much more than a community rest stop on Highway 90 at the gateway to Big Bend National Park. It has a smattering of buildings, a gas station, and a small grocery store, but it attracts tourists like flies because of its historic Gage Hotel. The two-story structure hasn't changed much since Alfred Gage opened it in 1927 as a waystation for scores of travelers in the sparsely populated grazing and mining land. It even has the original old hitching rail out front, as well as several proverbial rocking chairs on the front porch. In fact, it is so unique that it has been designated a historical treasure. The friendly staff treats everyone like royalty.

"Name's Ed," the old man said, extending a bony hand with the look and feel of rough leather. "Seen a lot of you folks since that news fella came through on his hunting trip a while back. This place

7

has been right popular since then."

I learned a few moments later that the "news fella" was none other than Dan Rather of CBS television fame. Rather had been born and raised around Wharton and often hunted in the Big Bend area with friends he still had in that part of the State. Mister Ed said that in years past, he himself had helped around the camp---until he had gotten too old for the chores and his arthritis had started acting up.

I also learned that the hotel was making improvements on its western side, improvements which required the addition of more than 80,000 adobe tiles, tiles the hotel insisted be made the old-fashioned Mexican way---by back-breaking, hand labor. Television, newspaper, and magazine reporters, as well as historians from all across America, had been flocking to Marathon for months to record the process.

I explained to Mr. Ed that my reason for being in West Texas didn't include any of his theories. I just happen to like that part of Texas and take advantage of every opportunity to visit. I didn't know about the adobe tiles---my project had been the Black Seminole Scouts of Fort Clark fame. After a week of following the Scouts' trail from Fort Clark through the Seminole Canyon to Fort Davis, snapping pictures by the score, I was finally headed home to Corpus Christi. I had only stopped by the Gage because I had taken a detour to witness the greatest living legend in Texas the night before---the Marfa Lights. Instead of spending the night in Alpine as I had originally planned, I had stayed in Marfa, and the added twenty-five miles, coupled with a little later start than my usual crack of dawn departures, put me in Marathon around my regular eating time.

Edward Charles Kimberley was the most perfect example of an old-time Texas cowboy I have ever seen. His skin was the color of tree bark and all wrinkly-smooth and leathery from too many days in the hot sun. He had grey-yellow hair which curled in tiny ringlets under his shirt collar as if it had been perspiration-soaked from mending fences all morning. Drooping at the outer corners of his mouth, the silvery-white moustache lay thick and slightly in need of trimming over his upper lip. In contrast to his unruly hair and moustache, his face was clean-shaven, although full of wrinkles and dimples and just plain laugh lines. Under the sweat-stained red ball cap that he preferred to a cowboy hat, his blue eyes danced with mischief. I had the distinct impression that he was a true scamp in disguise.

He wore no jewelry of any kind, not even a watch, but the

8

pearlized snaps of his light-colored, flowered-print, western shirt gleamed like mirrors in the morning sunlight. His faded denim jeans were cinched in tight at the thin waist with a black belt which sported a variety of flowers and cattle brands nicely tooled along the grain of the leather. The jeans were also so faded as to be almost white down the thighs. A brass buckle bearing some sort of writing on it completed the effect.

If his garb wasn't enough to convince me that he was the genuine article, his boots certainly were. They were the ugliest pair of scroll-topped, hand-tooled, brown cowboy boots in the world. Each looked like it had come through the wrong end of cactus and mesquite thorns, been rolled over a half dozen rocks for a month, and then suffered all the indignities of West Texas dust storms. I fully expected them to contain a little cow pasture in the seams. Even the narrow, pointed toes curled rakishly back to meet the sky.

Mister Ed grinned when he saw me staring at his boots. "Had 'em made in Presidio about twenty years ago. Wore the soles out two times. Yes sir, been through a lot together, we have." He patted the right one, which lay on top his left knee, with pride or affection, maybe both. It was hard to tell.

Mister Ed said he was eighty-eight years old and that he lived alone in Alpine, his wife having died a decade earlier. Every morning right after sunrise, he drove the forty miles to Marathon in his old, beat-up pickup truck "to check the roads and see if any stock had got out in the night." It was partly the truth. He did check the highway for loose stock for the local ranchers, but mostly he drove over to visit his daughter who worked in the Marathon bank. He always went straight to the Gage for his coffee while waiting for the bank to open. He's now such a fixture around the place that the staff just treats him like one of the family.

We got to talking, and with one thing leading to another, I discovered Mr. Ed had once been a Texas Ranger---not a full-fledged Ranger like the men of today, but a "Special Ranger" from the days of yore. He said that he had spent his entire life as a law enforcement officer of one kind or another, mostly in the Houston area, before retiring and moving to Alpine. He then whipped out various identification cards from his wallet to prove it. This piqued my interest because I had been trying to trace the career of a great-grandfather who had been a Ranger back in the 1860's or 1870's---no one in my family knew for sure when---and in doing my research about the Rangers of that era, I had acquired a reverence for the organization almost bordering on awe. I eagerly asked Mr. Ed question after question, and we ended up spending the remainder of the morning talking about nothing but Texas Rangers.

"You know," Mr. Ed said, almost as an afterthought, as I was preparing to leave for lunch, "you got a good one there in Corpus. Name's Peters. A right interesting character. Might want to write about him someday."

Mister Ed stood up to leave with me, and I noticed for the first time that his belt buckle said "TEXAS RANGER" in block letters. We walked out to the porch, and he waved a friendly farewell, before heading around the side of the building in the general direction of the bank, slightly bowlegged and arthritic, but otherwise regal and erect.

And that's how it began. Mister Ed's parting words haunted me for months. "You got a good one there in Corpus," he had said. "Might want to write about him someday." Right. But how to go about meeting the man? Was he really as interesting as Mr. Ed claimed? And how did "Name's Peters," as a modern-day Ranger, compare to the Rangers of legend? How could he possibly be as interesting as "Big Foot" Wallace, Bill McDonald, Lee McNelly, Jack Hays, or any of the others who gave their lifetimes to taming the frontier?

I began by asking a Corpus Christi police reserve officer friend of mine if he had ever met the local Texas Ranger. "Nah," he replied with a sad shake of his head. "He ain't like the other one."

"What do you mean?" I asked, taken aback. "What other one?" Was the local Ranger named Peters, or not? If not, was there ever a Peters, and what happened to him?

"Well...," my reserve police officer friend drawled, unsure how to explain it, "Ranger Peters was here, all right, but this new guy's just not like him. What else can I say? Ranger Peters was part of the old school where being a Ranger meant something more than pinning a badge on your chest. He was the best this place ever had. And I've been around since the early 70's. That doesn't mean that the new guy ain't no good---he is or he wouldn't be here. It just means that he ain't no Ranger Peters."

My friend went on to explain that Jim Peters was always available, always friendly and courteous, always willing to be part of anything at any time, anywhere, day or night. He said that 'he was a no-nonsense, don't-mess-with-me-type Ranger. No one could pull the wool over his eyes. And he never forgot anything. It was almost spooky the way he could recall people and places...things like that. Know what I mean? Everyone admired him, including the criminals. It was sure a sad day when he retired."

So that was it! Jim Peters had retired from the Rangers. Not only that, he lived right around the corner, practically in the same neighborhood as myself. All I had to do was to find a way to meet him and that turned out to be a piece of cake. My veterinarian, Dr. Henry A. "Cap" Hodges of the Annaville Animal Hospital, has known Jim Peters for many, many years. The two of them, along with former Ranger Captain and United States Marshal Clint Peoples, used to go hunting and fishing together all the time before Clint Peoples died in a car wreck in 1992. Now, it's mostly just the two of them. Jim Peters is also godfather to one of Dr. Hodges' daughters. Since I've known Dr. Hodges for more than twenty years, he not only offered to help me with material on his friend, he offered to introduce me the next time I dropped by the clinic.

And that's how it all began. Jim Peters and I met, sized each other up, and this book began. I also had to change my preconceived impression of him. After learning about some of his famous cases, about how he's stood toe-to-toe facing down armed and dangerous criminals, about his sleuthing exploits all over South Texas and in the Gulf of Mexico, I had built up a character so out of proportion, so intimidating, so larger-than-life, that I was sure he needed a flatbed just to get himself home at night.

But Jim Peters is not like that. Yes, he does have a "larger-than-life" reputation, but it is also well-deserved. And he's not larger-than-life--just large in life. He stands six feet, five inches tall and weighs 220 pounds-all tough, lean, muscle and grit. Although Jim Peters has provided me with most of the material in this book, it is not totally his story from his point of view. He is far too modest for that. "I like to give credit where credit is due," he keeps telling me when I want to change things. "A lot of good people worked with me, and I'd like for them to get recognition for it."

Be that as it may, this is the story of Jim Peters, one of the most famous Texas Rangers in South Texas history. Where it doesn't seem to matter, names have been omitted. However, no slight is intended. Each of you know who you are, and you know what you did. And Texas is grateful.

I'm grateful, too---to Ed Kimberley and his "You got a good one there in Corpus." He was so right. If it wasn't for that chance meeting in Marathon, I might never have found out---and then, neither would you.

This book is dedicated to my husband, Jim Sturdivant, for all his understanding and support in "getting the job done," to Jim Peters for giving me the opportunity, to my wonderful in-laws, J. Allen and Evalena Sturdivant, for their encouragement, and to my wonderful parents, Jim and Jackie Paul, for being there.

ACKNOWLEDGEMENTS

When a book is true, as this one is, I am totally dependant on facts, documentation, and the keen memories of other people. It is also a challenge to gather photographs, especially from sources *other* than Jim Peters, from people who trusted me to give their *originals* back. There are also my friends and critics who read the manuscript as it was written, offering suggestions and criticism by the score. To each of you I give my thanks.

Special thanks go to Jim Peters for his meticulous file system which he generously opened to me for research, to Lydia Peters for added insight on the openly generous and deeply complicated man she married, and to Dr. H. A. "Cap" Hodges for the humorous, often hilarious, anecdotes on his friend. Thank you to Commander Lou Villagomez, Captains John Wood and Jack Dean, Judy and Bruce Brown, Sharon and Carl Mullen, Jim Stephenson, and Lynn Patten.

Special thanks to go to Janice Reece of the Texas Ranger Moody Research Library and Charles Schreiner III of the Y-O Ranch. To Kevin Saunders, Best All-Around Wheelchair Champion of the World and Olympic Gold Medalist, goes my deepest thanks for his motivational encouragement to "Don't give up. Keep going. Live your dream." And special thanks to my publisher and friend, Joe Glasgow, for having the patience of Job. Bless you all!

Jim Peters in his first Ranger photo 1969.

PROLOGUE

It was Friday night, August 14, 1987, and Jim Peters fidgeted ever so slightly in his chair at the head table in the banquet room, listening as others recalled his career. He was uncomfortable. And it wasn't the heat, either---although the room could stand to be a few degrees cooler to accommodate the extra-large crowd. No, his discomfort stemmed totally from being the center of attention. It violated his code of ethics, his number one rule, the one he called, "KEEP A LOW PROFILE." He'd lived and breathed it for years, ever since he had joined the Texas Ranger force.

His rule had never been an easy one to enforce. As a Ranger, people just naturally tended to put him up on a pedestal, thrust him forward into the spotlight. He knew it was more from the Ranger mystic, more from the incredible fables and myths and legends attributed to the men who had shaped the force and made it what it is today than with him as a person. Rangers were special. No doubt about it. No other law enforcement organization anywhere in the world came close to approximating them for bringing criminals to justice, and he'd done his best to prove it. Still, it had taken all his resolve, all his wits to control the publicity, the hero worship. The only time he thought he really had a handle on it was the day he overheard a disgruntled reporter grumble that posterity would read, "HE KEPT A LOW PROFILE," carved on his tombstone.

He squirmed, running a finger around his collar to loosen his tie, as he listened to the stories and jokes told on his behalf. It was his retirement party, and 350 people had shown up to roast and toast him for the occasion. He listened as tales lauded his courage, his bravery in face of death. Others regaled his empathy for the victims, his compassion for the families left behind. But mostly, the anecdotes were funny: his snake stomping days with the Highway Patrol, the Ranger retreats at the Y-O Ranch, hunting and fishing hilarity all over South Texas...personal fun, things like that.

Squinting out on the sea of faces before him, he tried to see all the people through the low lighting, but it was impossible. The place was crammed full of city, county, state, and federal law enforcement officials, not to mention the mayor, a few lawyers, judges, and political figures thrown in for good measure. His family was there, as were many of his close friends. Maybe if he looked hard enough, he might even find one or two police informers tucked neatly away into the dark recesses at the back. He was rich in friends, poor in enemies, the way his father had always been...the way his father had wanted him to be. He wished his father could have lived to see this. The old man would have been proud.

Applause jerked him to attention, and he turned his head slightly to better see Betty Turner, Mayor of Corpus Christi. She was saying something about him being more than an asset to the community. Seeing her made him wonder how many mayors from how many different communities he had known. What about Governors? Which one had made him the "Honorary Texan?" How many Sheriffs, Chiefs of Police, FBI Agents? He mentally ticked off names, trying to place the officials in some sort of chronological order, but it was impossible. The truth was that he didn't know. He had touched so many lives in his career, been so many places, solved so many crimes. All he had ever wanted to be was a Texas Ranger....

Author's Note:

The names of all law enforcement officers, witnesses, and prepetrators are real. In some instances, however, names were changed to protect the privacy of the victims and witnesses. Whenever this occurs, the changes are indicated with an asterisk (*).

PART ONE:
THE EARLY YEARS

Former Ranger Sergeant James Buchanan Gillett once wrote that 'truth never makes very interesting reading.' It was Ranger humor, of course, since Ranger exploits on the frontier were far more astonishing than anything the fiction writers could dream up. Yet, he understood only too well the hypnotic hold that the Rangers have on the people of Texas. Millions of words have been written about the elite organization, yet precious little has come directly from Ranger lips. It's not entirely due to lack of spontaneity on the part of the Rangers. It's just that the vast distances over which they rode, the harshness of the terrain in which they lived, and the sheer meanness of their adversaries precluded any kind of formal reporting. Most Rangers were so brief about their accomplishments that people had to read between the lines for the details---"Shot all to pieces, but not serious," James Dunaway wired to Governor Thomas M. Campbell in 1907, *after* he had been drilled with seventeen bullet holes and left for dead in an ambush on the streets of Grovetown while trying to bring order to a hotly contested, local election.

It's this type of "formal" reporting which keeps the Ranger legend alive. Although the environment has greatly improved for today's Ranger, he is still not much different from his predecessor. Even with every modern communication vehicle at his disposal, his coverage is only as detailed or as brief as his individual character. Nowhere will he ever brag or gloat about personal achievements. It's always been this way and probably always will be.

Jim Peters is no exception. Cut smartly from the same mold that forged other Ranger legends, he is noticeably uncomfortable when talking about himself, preferring instead to say, "we did this" or "we did that." He has a keen, analytical mind that is near-photographic in memory, recalling events and details years after the happening, yet he insists on downplaying his role in the proceedings. His neatly typed pages sent weekly to Ranger Headquarters in Austin contain little essence of him, which makes later reconstruction almost impossible. In reading his reports, one gets no feel for the danger, satisfaction, and disappointments of being "JIM PETERS, TEXAS RANGER."

Jim's Ranger reports are all impersonal. Nowhere did he reveal his glee at bringing a surly Coast Guard seaman to justice for murder, or express his sigh of relief at rescuing a kidnap victim from a hot car trunk in the middle of a sweltering July. Nowhere does one read of his tenacity in pursuing robbery suspects into Mexico, or of his Wild West tracking technique in recovering stolen farm property. There's not even any mention of his bitter disappointment when an child molester's case was thrown out of court because the Statute of Limitations had expired.

In one typical week in 1985, he travelled 690 miles---more than thirteen hours---on the highways of South Texas. He also spent twenty-nine hours investigating murder, burglary, kidnapping, conspiracy, and conducted two hypnosis sessions. He then spent another two hours in a conference with Aransas County Sheriff Bob Hewes. During this same week, he obtained an artist's sketch of an arson suspect in Corpus Christi, recovered a gun taken in a burglary in Aransas County, and obtained artist's sketches of murder suspects in Nueces County. Although his travels took him from Rio Grande City in southernmost Texas to Rockport two hundred miles away on the Gulf Coast, his assistance covered requests from Houston to the Mexican border. Take his name off the report, however, and it could be any Ranger in Texas. Maybe that's the way it is supposed to be.

When Jim first became a member of the elite organization, he wanted only to do his job the best way he knew how. At that time, there were just eighty-two Rangers for the whole State of Texas, and the job carried enormous responsibility. The best Jim could hope for was not to make a fool of himself in the eyes of the adoring public. Yet, barely a year after he pinned on the distinctive badge, he came to the attention of Texans in a big way with the investigation of a murder involving jurisdiction in four counties, several Federal agencies, and two states. Right on the heels of that crime came one of the biggest investigations in modern Texas history, the murder of Randy Farenthold, millionaire playboy step-son of gubernatorial candidate Frances "Sissy" Farenthold, on the eve of runoff elections. In fact, in a few short years, he became such a success story, earned such a reputation for investigative excellence, that the Governor made him an "Honorary Texan," something that is practically unheard of even for the most prestigious of visitors. In Texan lingo, "if you aren't born in the State, you're a transplant all your life."

Although it's not widely known, Jim has always wanted to be a Texas Ranger, ever since playing cowboys and Indians as a child in San Benito. He has on the mantle in his den, a small framed picture of himself as a child of about eight holding a toy pistol. "That was my first Ranger picture," he says with a big grin, and one can believe it or not, since he didn't arrive in Texas until the summer of 1938, when he was eleven. "When choosing up sides for cowboys and Indians, nobody wanted to be the bad guy. Everybody always wanted to be a Ranger, like the Lone Ranger, which was popular on the radio then. Of course, we didn't know there really were real people called Texas Rangers...."

It wasn't long before Jim learned the truth. San Benito lay in the heart of some of the most fierce skirmishes in Ranger history. The whole area owes its very existence to that selfless breed of men. The Rangers, under the leadership of Leander McNelly, brought peace to the Valley by eradicating the Mexican cattle thieves and bandits, who almost doomed settlement by murdering entire ranch families.

It wasn't long before hunting and fishing replaced the cowboys and Indians as Jim's favorite pastime, but he never forgot that Texas Rangers were always the good guys in white hats, that they never quit until they got their man, that THEY WERE TEXAS. He vowed that one day he would become a member of the team.

Blond-haired, blue-eyed, James Richard Peters, like many famous Rangers before him, began his formative years in another state. Born October 2, 1927, in Chicago, Illinois, he was the oldest son of a footloose auto mechanic and his wife, Chester and Anna Mae (Shoestek) Peters. Brother Marvin, nicknamed "Bud," arrived nine years later.

Chester Peters knew automobiles like the back of his hand. Back then, the Ford Model T was the hottest selling car in the world. It came crated in a box, and Chester put it together. Because he could get work anywhere, he travelled whenever he got wanderlust fever. Even at the height of the Depression, when jobs became scarce and having work of any kind was a valued commodity, Chester was restless. It suited Anna just fine. She thrived on travel. Whenever the yearning for adventure seized either one of them, the whole family picked up and headed out.

"My father was a traveling man," Jim said in explaining it. "When he got the urge to move on, he'd pack everybody in the car, drive to the edge of town, and ask Mother which way she wanted to go. She'd look around as if deciding, then point and say, 'That way,' and off we'd go. By the time I'd graduated from high school, we'd lived in eight states."

Jim spent his entire youth moving around the country. He lived in small towns and big towns and even places where the nearest town was several miles away. Since he had a natural aptitude for getting along with people, it never bothered him that his family moved a lot. He looked upon everything as a great new adventure and a magnificent way of getting more friends. Moving, however, did have some drawbacks. By his own admittance, he attended so many schools that he no longer remembers them all. He also admits to being a somewhat indifferent student, preferring extracurricular activities, like hunting and fishing, to his scholastic studies.

After living in the lush Rio Grande Valley for three years, Jim and his family moved to a small farm in Southton, a tiny community on the southwest side of San Antonio. Southton no longer exists as a separate entity, having long ago become part of the "River City," but the old water tower is still there, along with an exit off Interstate 37 when driving north from Corpus Christi to San Antonio. It was here in Southton that Jim perfected his skills of tracking, hunting, and fishing. It was also here as a student in Harlandale High School that he really learned all about Texas history and lore, an education that included a healthy dose of the legendary Texas Rangers.

Before Jim could graduate from Harlandale High School, his father once again headed out. This time, it was south, to the Deep South and the palm-tree environment of Florida. It was in Florida where Jim graduated from Duncan Fletcher High School in Jacksonville at the age of seventeen. He then promptly left home to join the United States Merchant Marine, attending the United States Maritime Academy in St. Petersburg, Florida. By this time, he was nearly six feet, five inches tall, but he only weighed a mere 160 pounds. In an effort to "beef" himself up, he took up boxing as a sport, and soon discovered that he had a natural coordination and agility in the ring. It wasn't long before he became the Academy's champion boxer, winning so many boxing events that he competed in numerous Golden Glove tournaments. He brushes this accomplishment aside by stating that his arms were so long, no one could touch him, but he understates the facts. His achievements in the ring were destiny in the making for his later career.

After graduating from the Maritime Academy, Jim sailed for one year on the Great Lakes---until he was old enough to become a member of the United States Marine Corps, which was his original intention in the first place. When he turned eighteen in 1945, he enlisted, spending his first two years of service in China. His duties were with a Marine detachment assigned to disarming and repatriating the defeated Japanese Army, while at the same time preventing a Communist takeover by the Red Chinese.

As a Marine, in typical military fashion, he had "other duties as assigned." Some of these other duties included guard duty, where he guarded both prisoners and supplies, supply duty, where he drove all kinds of motor transports hauling supplies all over China, and ultimately, the difficult motor patrol duty, where he acted as lawman for practically everything and everyone. Being a "motor policeman" was his first introduction to the rigors and responsibilities of law enforcement, and he found out he liked it.

His last year of enlistment brought him back to Texas---to Naval Air Station Corpus Christi, where he pulled guard duty at the North Gate. His hobbies were still hunting and fishing, which the surrounding area offered in abundance, and he took every advantage of it. In pursuit of his hobby, he easily learned every little back road and waterway in the South Texas area. Although he couldn't know it at the time, that knowledge would later serve him tremendously as an officer of the law. Also, as an expert tracker and shrewd fisherman, his advice was highly sought by many avid sportsmen in the areas surrounding the Base.

Jim received his discharge in 1948. He still dreamed of becoming a Texas Ranger, only he had no earthly idea how, or where, to begin. Deciding to launch his civilian career by investigating something familiar from his past, he took a job as a Cadillac mechanic in Austin. It was a job he would have for nine years, before he found himself on the right road toward fulfilling his dream.

At the time Jim began work in Austin as a mechanic, his parents were once again living in Texas---this time, in the San Antonio area, only eighty miles distant. Although Jim still hunted and fished in his spare time, his favorite pastime now became working the stock car circuit around Austin with his father and brother. With Chester Peters in the pits designing and maintaining the engines, Jim and Bud climbed behind the wheel. The threesome were an unbeatable combination, setting driving, fuel, and speed records which thrilled audiences for years.

Jim enjoyed all his years driving in the stock car circuit, and he even began designing and building engines with his father, but when younger brother Bud joined the Texas Department of Public Safety, Jim once again began thinking of his Texas Ranger dream. He knew the only way to become a Texas Ranger was through a career in law enforcement, but he did not want the restrictions associated with city and country police efforts. In October 1957, Jim took the entrance examination to become a member of the difficult Highway Patrol segment of the Texas Department of Public Safety.

PART TWO
DEPARTMENT OF PUBLIC SAFETY YEARS

In Texas, as in other states, every law enforcement officer candidate must meet a morass of requirements before being hired. For Jim, the hardest of all was the oral exam. He had to sit before a board of ranking brass and answer questions, sweating all the time and wondering if there *was* a right answer, or if they were throwing trick questions at him. All the while, his stone-faced questioners only nodded and checked their grading sheets. Jim was judged on his appearance, enunciation, manner, emotional control, comprehension, logic, and coherency.

Jim passed everything at the top of the list, and he entered the Department of Public Safety Academy in Austin, where he went to class from eight to five, five days a week, and most of Saturday. His schooling was intense and packed with information that might save his life---or someone else's life---when he would be out on the road. He learned everything from First Aid to Human Behavior, from Arrest Techniques to Courtroom Demeanor, from Criminal Law to Crimes Against Persons. He learned how to gather and preserve evidence, how to lift fingerprints, and how to interview and interrogate. He had radar and other speed measurement devices to master, and of course, accident investigation. Defensive driving, firearms, criminal investigation, criminal law---all had to be mastered before the graduation ceremony in March 1958. Jim absorbed everything like a sponge.

After graduation, Jim's first duty assignment became South Texas, where he was to patrol the giant chunk of country in Jim Wells and Duval Counties. He couldn't have asked for a better place to begin his law enforcement career. The area lay smack dab in the middle of his old hunting and fishing haunts from his youth.

His patrol headquarters was the small, oil-mad town of Alice, and Alice was the largest city in Jim Wells County, having around 2,500 population at the time. In fact, it was the largest city in BOTH counties, as that part of Texas was mostly ranching and farming land. Only forty miles away lay the big metropolis of Corpus Christi, with a population approaching 100,000, where he had served as a Marine. Jim was so acquainted with the roads and tributaries in the area that he could practically act as scout for the rest of the highway patrol department.

In those years, Alice was in the middle of an oil boom, and the ever-increasing drilling frenzy left the landscape littered with derricks and pumpers scattered everywhere. It was also a major stop on the highway system of the State, lying halfway between the north-south traffic of San Antonio to McAllen and the east-west traffic of Corpus Christi to Freer.

The north-south highway, U.S. Highway 281, was one of only two arteries to the entire Rio Grande Valley---the other being U.S. Highway 77 to the east, which has the historical distinction of once being known as the "Old Taylor Trail," after General Zachary Taylor's route to Mexico in the United States war with that country in 1846.

Jim presented quite a picture in his DPS uniform. Tall and lean with the tanned, healthy look of one who lived in the rugged outdoors, he looked the part of a typical Texas lawman. He was now full-grown at six feet, five inches tall, and still thin as a toothpick at 160 pounds. But with his revolver worn Wild West style, his ten-gallon felt cowboy hat parked squarely on his blond head, and dark sunglasses shielding his blue eyes, he was most intimidating when he stepped from his patrol car. Before everyone learned to respect him for his savvy and authority, they respected him for his size. Even his slow Texan drawl worked to his advantage. Men in the Alice area averaged five feet, eight inches in height, and spoke with thick, Mexican accents. If they didn't know what to make of the new "gringo" when he first came to town, it didn't take them long to learn.

Since Jim was so tall and so thin, people dubbed him "Hummingbird," after the tiny, little creatures that migrated into the area each year. And like the hummingbird, he often had to contend with birds nearly twice his weight in the performance of his duties. He seemed to be everywhere, and lawbreakers soon learned that he wasn't the type to let anyone push him around. Time and again, he demonstrated that he had the "right stuff" to become a top lawman---a Texas Ranger---which was his ultimate goal.

As with most highway patrol officers, Jim's main duties were to enforce the driving safety of everyone on Texas highways, something that was a never-ending challenge in his part of the State. The whole South Texas area is a most unique stretch of territory. Hot and humid, it's dotted with stirrup-high grassland stretching as far as the eye can see. In the early 1800's, local folks called it the "Wild Horse Desert" because of the large herds of wild mustangs that roamed there. The people who tried to tame it and make it produce called it the "Desert of the Dead." The soil has never been really fertile, and all that has ever managed to grow is sparse vegetation.

The area is also sandy, and the sand is constantly shifting northeastward by the prevailing winds off the Gulf of Mexico. It creates great dunes of blazing whiteness in some areas spotted with sea oats, moss rose, and Spanish dagger plants. There are low-lying tidal flats with shallow lakes of brackish water surrounded on higher ground by a cover of "sacahuiste" or salt grass. Some places have clumps of live oak thickets called "mottes," a few mesquites, and the black-barked, native huisache trees. Some parts of the area have very little drinking water, as there are no live creeks and few natural basins to capture water from the rains. The arroyos and gullies cutting across the landscape only fill during torrential downpours and just as suddenly dry up again. In fact, it is even difficult to ranch, although that is what is currently being done with the Texas longhorn, the Santa Gertrudis, and other short-horned cattle. But wildlife is abundant, and with salt water fishing a prime attraction, the area draws tourists by the thousands.

Since people could see for miles in all directions with an unobstructed view in Jim's territory, the temptation to exceed the speed limit was a constant invitation. Everyone also seemed to know exactly where his patrol car was most likely to be at any given moment, especially the area youths and local ranchers, who knew all the back roads and used them to the best of their advantage with speeds often approaching liftoff.

It took about six months, but Jim methodically put an end to all that. What the speed freaks didn't know, couldn't know, was that he was an expert driver, having honed his skill to perfection in a decade on the stock car circuit. He took corners on four wheels at high speeds, bounced over washboard back roads in grand style, and expertly maneuvered in driving rain and high winds without once losing sight of his quarry or control of his car. He was such a terror on wheels that everyone quickly learned to live in complete awe of him---or fear him.

Jim also changed his patrol routine to suit his own whim. If going east or west one moment, he'd turn north or south, or double back over ground he had just covered. He'd even drive down dirt roads through pasture lands, stirring up dust like a rooster plume in his wake. It was cornbread hell for potential violators. They never knew where he would turn up next.

According to Jim, there were only two highway patrol officers and one patrol car for the whole area when he first arrived in 1958, and it involved a tremendous amount of driving. The area is gigantic in size. Sometimes, he'd no sooner get off duty, get home, tumble into bed and be almost on the verge of sleep, when he'd have to get up and drive sixty or seventy miles to investigate an accident scene.

One such accident happened around 1963 when Jim was just getting off duty. In the black of night, at a place where one of the ranch roads emptied onto a Farm to Market road about six miles south of Mathis, a pickup truck and a passenger car collided. It was a Saturday night, and two teenage boys, Keith and Danny, ran a stop sign while travelling at a high rate of speed. Their pickup truck hit a car at the intersection, scrunching the car off the road and into a field. Both vehicles were total wrecks.

The boys had spent the day drinking and partying with a group of friends at Lake Corpus Christi in Mathis. They had originally intended to spend the night with their friends at the lake, but with all the beer they had consumed, Keith was feeling a little sick and wanted to go home. Danny decided to drive Keith home in Keith's new truck. Danny helped the sick boy into the passenger seat and took off with a squeal of rubber on the dark pavement.

As with most accidents, this one happened a few miles from home for both drivers. The boys were speeding along the back road, and in their intoxicated condition, failed to make the stop sign at the end of the road. They plowed into a car driven by a thirty-two year old Orange Grove woman. Their speed was later estimated at seventy miles per hour. Keith died on the way to the hospital. Danny eventually recovered, but only after he spent nearly a month in the hospital with massive head injuries.

The woman sustained only a badly bruised forehead and a broken wrist. She was disoriented and staggering around in the dark pasture when Jim found her, and she remembered thinking that she had died and gone to heaven because he looked like a giant white ghost coming toward her out of the blackness. After carrying her over to his car, Jim sat her down in the back seat and made sure she was able to manage before returning to the horrors of the truck.

Most accident investigations were routine, but Jim also remembers aggravating incidents. They didn't happen often, but when one did, it left him with a foul taste about the ethics of some law enforcement officers. It was not the main reason he was so professional and conscientious in his own performance, but it did play a major role. The stupidity and total lack of regard for others in the same profession gave him much food for thought. He vowed he'd never be calloused to another officer as long as he lived.

The one incident that really irritated him the most occurred right after he had just finished investigating an accident thirty miles into Jim Wells County. He was hot, and tired, and looking forward to a nice relaxing evening at home for a change. But when he got back to Alice, he barely had time to sit down before receiving word that there had been an accident in Duval County, forty miles away, that needed his immediate attention.

Thinking the worst, that somebody had been killed or badly hurt, Jim raced to the scene, only to discover that a cow had been hit. Not only that, two Deputy Sheriffs were sitting idly by on the hood of their patrol car, talking and laughing, waiting for HIM to come along and take down the man's name and address and write up the report on it!

It was when Jim was in pursuit that he was sheer poetry in motion. He chased his quarry through ranch land, down back roads, across gullies, into towns, and down side streets like a hound from hell. He never let up---

25

just pressed onward and onward until each and every one of the violators became too tired or too scared to go any further. He never lost one, and he just wouldn't quit. "Quit's only a four-letter word for people who don't know better," he once said, shrugging his shoulders in explaining his persistence behind the wheel. Where it had once been a rite of passage to brag about losing the highway patrol, it soon became routine to admit, "Yeah, Mr. Peters got me." In all the years he worked as a highway patrol officer, no one ever escaped his pursuit---no one, that is, except the mighty Duke of Duval, and that was only because the Duke had a few seconds head start.

THE MIDNIGHT RIDE OF GEORGE PARR

George Berham Parr (1901-1975) was the uncontested ruler of Duval County, the large chunk of country situated 95 miles to the south of San Antonio "like a loincloth at the groin of Texas." Not only was the County in the grip of a politically powerful dictator, it was two centuries, perhaps three, to the rear of Jeffersonian Democracy, a situation found mostly in feudal Mexico and not in modern-day America. George Parr inherited the Duval political machine from his father, the infamous Archie Parr (1860-1942). Altogether, the Parr political machine spanned more than sixty years.

Everyone in Duval County knew George Parr on sight, and every law officer tried to tame him, but the mighty Duke was too savvy to be caught. The only time he was ever in any real danger of losing control---indeed, his life---was when Ranger Captain Alfred Young Allee, Sr., almost shot him in a face-to-face confrontation in the Jim Wells County Courthouse. The only thing that saved the Duke was that he recognized the wisdom of Captain Allee's big .45 automatic. George Parr bowed in submission.

The highway patrol night chase occurred when Jim and his partner were working an accident scene just east of Freer in 1960. A drunk driver had lost control and had run his car off the road. That sort of accident was commonplace on the little travelled roads in the two counties where drinking and driving usually went hand in glove, along with driving without a license. Although running a car off the road normally never really amounted to much more than a banged head and bruised body, it still had to be given the thorough investigation required of a collision or serious accident. On this particular night, the car lay rolled over onto its side in the bar ditch just past the old drive-in theater on the east side of town. The driver was bloody and cut in several places from the broken window glass, but otherwise unhurt.

In those days, cars were built tough. Even if a driver did lose control and ran his vehicle out in the ranch land or smashed it against a telephone pole, the heavy frame of the vehicle withstood a little more pounding, provided a little more shock absorption than the lighter cars of today. With the bloody driver sitting in the dirt next to the wrecked car awaiting the arrival of the ambulance and with his partner administering first aid, Jim went out in the street and stepped off the skid marks. He also directed the occasional traffic.

Suddenly, from the direction of Freer, a black car sped into view, and Jim tried to slow it down with his flashlight. Now, most people coming upon an accident scene slow down and gawk, but not this driver. He took one look at the situation and stomped the accelerator, swerving his big car around the wreck with a squeal of tires that missed Jim only by inches. As he sped past, Jim recognized the car as that of George Parr's. It was a big, black Chrysler 300, and everyone in Duval County knew it on sight. The car was Parr's trademark, and he never let anyone drive it---except maybe his wife, and even that's doubtful.

At that time, Jim's father, Chester Peters, was with Jim and his partner as a "ride-along passenger" in the back seat of the patrol car. Most police agencies still do this. It allows the general public to fully appreciate what everyday life is like for the lawman. While Jim and his partner worked the accident scene, Chester remained safe near the patrol car and out of the way.

If it had been anybody else, Jim may not have done it, but the ride-along passenger was his father, and his father had worked the stock car circuit around Austin for years. Chester was totally familiar with cars and high-speed driving---not to mention that Jim was a wizard behind the wheel.

As soon as the Chrysler roared past, Jim made sure his partner could handle the accident situation, and then yelled, "Come on, Dad! Let's get him!" Jim jumped behind the wheel, his father took the passenger seat, and the chase was on. They sped east down the blacktop toward the direction of San Diego, the tiny county seat of Duval County...and George Parr's home.

Although mostly flat and otherwise unobstructed, some of the country between Freer and San Diego is hilly, as it winds through canyons of ranchland. The Chrysler was practically out of sight by the time Jim started his pursuit. He floored the accelerator on his 1959 Ford Interceptor, sending the red tip of the needle clear past the highest marking on the speedometer gauge. With his siren screaming like a banshee from hell and his lights flashing with the brilliance of a star going nova, he managed to slowly creep up behind the speeding car---only to watch it zoom away on the first uphill slope.

Cresting the hill, Jim again began to catch up on the down grade, but the big Chrysler thundered off again on the next hill. It went on this way for twenty-six miles with speeds estimated at more than 130 miles per hour. The Chrysler became tantalizingly close on the downhills and irritatingly far on the uphills, as each driver determined to outwit the other. Neither one would admit defeat. All the while, they were drawing closer and closer to San Diego---and safety for George Parr.

About seven or eight miles from San Diego, one of the valves in Jim's interceptor started floating from overheating, and he had to back off his pursuit. As he radioed ahead for Sergeant Bill McCoy at patrol headquarters in Alice to set up a road block, he watched in frustration as the tiny, red tail lights of George Parr's car disappeared down the road. The roadblock didn't work because Parr somehow managed to avoid it. By the time Jim reached San Diego, George Parr and his car were nowhere to be seen. Jim and the local authorities drove their vehicles to Parr's house, where they spotted the black Chrysler all safely tucked away inside the garage with the overhead door almost all the way closed. There was nothing anyone could do, so they decided to park across the street and watch for awhile. It had been a vexing chase; maybe something would still come of it.

The garage was detached from the main house by a short breezeway which used a lattice network as walls. As Jim watched, a trouser clad figure walked to the trunk of the car, unloaded a package, and walked it to the house. The person, which everyone present took to be George Parr, then returned, retrieved another parcel and carried it into the house. This went on for nearly fifteen minutes until the trunk of the car was presumably empty of parcels.

There's no telling exactly what George Parr had in his trunk, but he was notorious for hunting out of season, and it was DEFINITELY out of season---by several months. George Parr lived by his own rules, which proclaimed that anything he wanted to do was okay, as long as he didn't get caught. If he was hunting out of season and hurrying home with the carcass, he knew better than to let Jim get a good look at the inside of the Chrysler, which Jim definitely would have done while working the accident scene. Jim is no fool; he would have arrested Parr on the spot.

The irony is that George Parr always insisted that his people cooperated with the police and highway patrol, and they always did. When asked later about the incident, Parr replied, "Oh, it must have been my wife driving the car. I'll speak to her about it. It won't happen again." And it never did---at least, not while Jim was on duty.

RANGER WALT RUSSELL AND THE DRILL BIT CAPER

Throughout Jim's highway patrol days, he had several occasions to work alongside various Texas Rangers. And it was an opportunity he never wasted. He studied everything they did. Through them, he learned that people respect an officer only if he's fit to be respected. He learned to never flinch, never bluff, never waste a word or movement. He also learned that every Ranger is just as idiosyncratic as Judge Roy Bean. Being an unique individual himself, Ranger life continued to tease and torment him just out of reach. With more determination than ever, he vowed to join the organization at the first opportunity.

Jim read somewhere that no other law enforcement organization could ever approximate the Texas Rangers, except maybe the Canadian Mounties, for getting their man. By openly admiring the Rangers, absorbing their vast investigative knowledge, studying their various techniques, and asking lots of intelligent questions, Jim gradually accumulated a wealth of information not found in any book or in any classroom instruction. It seems mundane, then, that one of the best "classroom" encounters happened the day Ranger Walter Russell decided to help bust an oil-field theft ring.

It was 1959 or 1960, Jim's not really sure of the exact date, that Ranger Russell got asked to participate in the recovery of stolen oil field drill bits. And the experience left an indelible impression in Jim's mind about the Texas Ranger organization in general and old-time Rangers in particular. He still laughs when he talks about it.

Oil field drill bits are huge, heavy, three-sided, diamond-tipped chunks of tempered steel used for coring through the hard rock and geological formations of the earth. Because of their rugged construction and diamond tips, they are always very expensive, costing anywhere from tens of thousands of dollars upwards to hundreds of thousands, depending on their size. At that time, many of the stolen bits originated in West Texas, which was in the middle of a gigantic drilling frenzy with derricks and drilling equipment all over the landscape. The stolen bits were then trucked all over Texas following the oil booms. When Alice began booming, so did the thieves. One of the hardest hit companies was Hughes Equipment. Their oil field investigator had traced a load of stolen bits and two crooks all over West Texas before the thieves had headed southward to the Alice area.

The Alice oil fields were just as busy as those in West Texas with wells being drilled left and right, and any kind of oil field drill bit was a prime commodity on the black market. Knowing where two of the crooks were, the Hughes investigator approached Bill Miller, Chief Deputy Sheriff of Jim Wells County in Alice, to help with the stakeout.

The Hughes investigator said he had a tall, skinny informer who drove an old, slope-backed 1949 Buick, and this man had made contact with two men having drill bits to sell. According to the informer, the two crooks were supposed to be located in a small clearing surrounded by dense brush, mesquite trees, and cactus about six miles south of San Diego on Highway 1329.

San Diego, however, wasn't in Jim Wells County, and since Deputy Sheriff Bill Miller didn't want to get the Sheriff of Duval County involved, he asked Jim Peters and Sergeant Bill McCoy of the Texas Highway Patrol if they wanted to come along. Jim knew the area well, having travelled Highway 1329 thousands of times. The clearing was about three miles past George Parr's house and off to the side of the road a little ways. The idea was for the lawmen to surround the clearing, the informer would make arrangements to purchase the drill bits, and then the lawmen would arrest the crooks.

On the day of the arranged "buy," the lawmen headed out. They had a little time to kill, so they sat along the side of the highway, smoked cigarettes, and whiled away the minutes. Presently, Jim spied Texas Ranger Walter Russell driving by.

"Sarge, there goes Walter Russell," Jim said, and Sergeant McCoy immediately called the Ranger on the radio and asked if he would like to go with them. It was an informal invitation not sent through official channels, but that's the way a lot of Rangers work. Jim himself would adopt that method when he became a Ranger years later.

"Yeah," said the Ranger---the catch phrase in Russell's vocabulary was always the word "yeah"---and he whipped his car back around to join the other lawmen.

Walter Russell was from the old school of Rangers---the kind of man who meant exactly what he said, each and every time he said it. And, he expected everyone to immediately follow his orders without any hesitation or questions being asked. If he issued instructions, one either did exactly what he said---or suffered the consequences. And some of his consequences could be really drastic. Everyone who knew him NEVER called his bluff.

He was born at an encampment near Presidio, Texas, on August 23, 1903. As a boy, he lived on a horse ranch in Oregon before moving to the Double Zero Ranch in Arizona. In the early 1920's, he became an Arizona Ranger, eventually working for the Chiricahua Cattle Company. He came back to Texas in 1930 and went to work for Central Power and Light Company as the security officer. World War II found him as a civilian investigator for the United States Government. He became a Texas Ranger in 1952, serving under Captain Alfred Allee's Company "D" with

31

headquarters in Alice. At one time his territory ran from El Paso to Brownsville, and he was a familiar sight riding the river in the Big Bend. He was known as the last of the active horseback rangers with a law career spanning more than forty years.

Russell led the glamorized life of a Western lawman, riding his horse along the Rio Grande, mixing with Hollywood legends like Tom Mix and Walter Brennan, and butting heads with the powerful Duke of Duval County, George Parr on several occasions. One night when Parr and Russell were alone in the jail, Russell decided he'd had just about enough of Parr's shenanigans. He threw two guns down on the table and said, "George, let's just settle this right now. Go for that pistol!" Parr jumped back clear to the wall and said, "No, sir. I'm not going to reach for that gun. Why, you're nothing but an assassin." Walter Russell often rode as a scout for Zane Grey when the author would come to Texas researching one of his Western novels. Russell said that Graves Peeler broke him in as a young Ranger. One time with Peeler, they were out scouting the countryside and came upon rustlers altering the brands on some stock in a canyon. Graves instructed Russell to ride into the canyon and inform the stock thieves that they were under arrest. Russell did as he was instructed, but the rustlers both reached for their rifles. Graves shot them both right between the eyes and closed that case real quick. Russell said he figured out right then that his main duty was to get them to go for their guns.

Russell was first deputized as a state ranger in New Mexico. In issuing the commission, the governor said, "I want you men to enforce the laws, show proper respect for womankind and if anybody calls you a sonofabitch, shoot him." During his Ranger career, he lived by those words and had many a run-in with border bad men, his stern system of law enforcement prevailing at all times. He was the last of the old-time lawmen.

Upon receiving the radio call, Walter Russell joined the other lawmen, and they explained the whole situation to him. They described the informer, stating that he was a thin man about six feet tall, that he would be driving his own vehicle, which was the old Buick, that he would be the one purchasing the bits from the two crooks, that they were out to arrest the other two men and not the informer, and so on.

"Yeah," said the old Ranger, "let's go do that."

The lawmen hid themselves in the thick brush surrounding the clearing. A few minutes later, the old Buick drove into the brushy area where the drill bits had been stashed, and three men got out. The informer began negotiating with the other two men, and when the details were ironed out to the satisfaction of everyone, the informer began loading the big, heavy bits into the trunk of his car. He was in the process of loading one heavy bit by himself, staggering around somewhat with bent knees, when all the lawmen stepped out of the brush.

Walter Russell shoots left-handed, and he's an expert shot, once complaining that the sight was a little off on a new pistol someone had given him when the target showed he had shot a pattern of five bullet holes bunched up about the size of a quarter about two inches to the right of the bull's eye. He had his big .45 automatic weapon strapped to his waist when the lawmen got ready to move in on the transaction. He pulled it out, and along with the other law officers, shouted, "Everybody stay where you are! Put your hands up! You're under arrest!"

The two crooks instantly threw their hands into the air and surrendered peacefully, but the informer paid no attention to the law officers commands. After all, he was on THEIR side. He just kept struggling with the big, heavy drill bit, loading it into the trunk.

BLAAAMM!

Walter Russell shot off a round from his big .45 automatic. The sound was like a cannon explosion. Birds screamed in alarm and flew from the trees, and cattle in the next pasture stampeded in terror. The bullet just missed the informer, as it whizzed right through the side of the old Buick.

"Walter, Walter!" yelled Jim and the other lawmen in unison, ears ringing from the loudness of the shot which seemed to hang in the air like fine dust. "That's our man! Don't shoot him!"

"Well, by god," said the old Ranger in his no-nonsense tone of voice, "I tell a man to put his hands up, he'd better put them up. I don't care who he is. Yeah."

Shortly after that occasion, Walter Russell told Jim how to instruct people to surrender in South Texas. Unlike other states and even North Texas where guns are the preferred weapons of choice, South Texans, and especially the Mexican contingent, seem to prefer knives, which can be easily concealed on the body.

"Yeah," the old Ranger said to Jim one day in one of his most constructive 'do as I say and you'll live' moods, "a lot of those old sorries out there, when you go to arrest them, you just say, 'You're under arrest. Hand me your knife.' One time a guy pulled a knife on me, and I had to kill him. Yeah."

Walter Russell died at his home in Kingsville when he was 83.

33

HIGHWAY PATROL HUMOR

It was with the highway patrol that Jim began to make his presence felt. A reasonable man, he tolerated most infractions on his turf probably better than another patrol officer would, mainly because he had lived in so many places that he knew how to expertly handle people. Also, most of the violators weren't violent by nature, just a little drunk or reckless after too much partying. Many of them lived in the two counties or were visitors from the neighboring ones. They sometimes gave him a little bellicose trouble, and he had to master a little Spanish to communicate with others, but for the most part, he was the master and they were the slaves, and they knew it.

"I made over 500 DUI's when I was in Alice, and I never once had to hit a man," Jim said in reminisce of those days. "I had to pick a few up and set them down a few times...put them where I wanted them to be, but I never had to hit one."

Like all Highway Patrol officers, Jim never knew what he would find as he drove the highways of the State. Pulling someone over today can be extremely dangerous or completely laughable, and today's officers have to be prepared for either event. But back when Jim was driving the roads, most highway patrol officers usually either had accident days, routine days, or days with completely outrageous episodes that stick in mind long after the incident is over---like the time an officer patrolling Interstate 20 near Sweetwater pulled an old, battered Chevrolet to the side of the road for speeding. The officer approached the elderly driver and routinely asked, "What's the big hurry?" as he adjusted the elderly man's driver's license on the clipboard. He then noticed that the man's license proclaimed that the man was ninety-two years old. The officer bent down and took a long look at the driver.

Describing the incident later, the officer said the man was extremely old with wrinkled skin and liver spots. He was missing several front teeth, showed tobacco stains between the two first fingers of the left hand, and wore hearing aids in both ears. But his hands were steady---even if he did look like he could totter over at any minute. He also wore no glasses, and when the officer tested his vision, he found the old man could see everything perfectly.

"Are you really ninety-two years old?" the officer asked, totally amazed.

"Yessir," the man said in a short, slightly wheezing breath.

"Well, where are you going in such a hurry?"

"I'm going to the nursing home in Sweetwater...." the man took a breath.

34

Good, thought the officer.

"....to see my mother," the old man finished.

"What else could I do," the officer said, shrugging his shoulders and throwing his hands in the air. "He said his mother was fourteen years older than he was and that he was driving to the nursing home to help her celebrate her 107th birthday. I gave him a ticket and let him go, with the advice to slow down."

It was this sort of situation that Jim ran into time and again on the blacktops around Alice. The one he remembers best, and which was probably one of the funniest, occurred one summer in the early 1960's.

It was a beautiful, fresh summer day with lots of sunshine and clear skies, the kind of day people would rather be lazing away than having to work. Jim was with his partner, Willie Stafford, and they were patrolling Highway 281 south of Alice with Jim at the wheel. That area is monotonous country with the low sage and buffalo grass of ranch land. The officers could see for miles in all directions, and the only things they found stirring were a few head of cattle off to the right and a couple of hawks soaring in the warm air currents overhead.

They had gone several miles without seeing much of anything, prattling nonchalantly with each other about what they were going to do after their shift was over, when a black speck suddenly appeared in the distance. It grew slowly into a big, shiny new Cadillac, and as it whizzed past toward the direction of Alice, Jim could see a little old lady hunched up behind the wheel. He turned the cruiser around and gave chase, finally managing to overtake the speeding car five miles further down the road. He motioned it over to the side of the highway.

Collecting his clip board and ticket book, he unfolded from behind the seat of the patrol car and stretched his long legs a moment before walking up to the other vehicle. He did this every time he got out of the car because even with the seat all the way back, there was never enough room for his height.

When he got to the other driver's window, he bent his tall, skinny frame at the waist, peered inside, and was humored to see that the woman driver was about ninety years old---all prim and proper in her Sunday best. Even though she had the seat all the way forward, she could barely see over the top of the steering wheel. Jim rapped lightly on the window and motioned for her to roll down the glass.

The little woman peered at him a moment through her spectacles, wisps of gray hair fluttering in the car's air-conditioning, before reaching a dainty, gloved hand down to her electric window buttons. "Zzzzzz." The little motor hummed as she lowered the window about two inches.

"Good afternoon, Ma'am," Jim said into the crack in his best,

35

professional voice. "The reason that I pulled you over is that you are exceeding the speed limit."

"Thank you," she responded in her high, fluttered voice. Her hand moved to the window buttons. "Zzzzzz." The motor hummed again as the window went up. Off she went, leaving Jim standing in the road with his mouth open.

Jim stood silently in the highway for a few moments, collecting his wits, watching as the black car disappeared into a speck in the distance. Returning to the patrol car, he found Willie slouched in the seat, leaning against the door with his arm crooked up behind his head, a huge, open-mouthed grin spread across his face. Willie was positively enjoying the situation.

Ignoring his partner, Jim climbed behind the wheel, patiently put away the clip board, and returned to routine patrol without saying one word.

The silence was too much for Willie. "Aren't you going after her?" he demanded in mock indignation.

"Naw," drawled Jim, eyes crinkling at the outer corners. "She's been warned." They both burst into laughter.

Like all law enforcement agencies, sometimes the humorous episodes just couldn't involve the general public. It's not that the general public couldn't appreciate the situation, it's just that the very nature of the job dictated otherwise. One that is still talked about today in the Alice office happened to a young "wannabe" highway patrol officer the day he decided to tag along in Jim's cruiser.

It was about 1963, and before his highway patrol captain put a stop to it, Jim and Willie Stafford used to sharpen their pistol skills shooting the rattlesnakes that curled up on the highways in the late afternoon and early evenings in the area. Duval and Jim Wells Counties are thick with snakes, and probably ninety-five percent of them are rattlesnakes. In fact, the Freer rattlesnake roundup each spring in Duval County is a major tourist draw with thousands of the deadly creatures being captured and barbecued---many of them more than four feet in length and bigger around than a man's arm.

At the time that Jim and Willie shot snakes, it was actually possible to kill fifteen or twenty of the slithery reptiles in one night, especially since the snakes flocked to the roadway to lounge on the warm highway surface. Ninety-nine percent of the snakes would also be eighteen to twenty inches long, and since the object of the target practice was to shoot off the snake's head, their smaller size usually guaranteed that they would be difficult targets. Whoever missed had to buy supper that night.

After shooting snakes for several months, Captain Herbert Weeks, who was then Captain of the Texas Highway Patrol of Region 3 in Corpus Christi, which had jurisdiction in the Alice area, called Jim and Willie into his office. He said, "No more shooting snakes. That's against the law. You're out there to catch speeders, and even though you're on a long stretch of deserted highway where no one can see you, you're still not supposed to be doing that."

Jim and Willie agreed to stop shooting snakes, but as the days passed, the snake problem became worse than ever. It seemed that every time they stopped someone on the highway, a big snake would be either underfoot or slithering off into the grass. And, it was downright dangerous to walk around in the dark. "What can we do?" Jim and Willie mulled it over between themselves. "The Captain says we can't shoot snakes."

They finally decided that although their captain said they couldn't SHOOT snakes, nowhere did he say they couldn't KILL snakes. With typical Texan, country-boy ingenuity, they devised another method of ridding the area of the deadly creatures. They began stomping snake heads, which was definitely more dangerous because of the soft earth and tall grass---if the snake wasn't killed on the first stomp, it was apt to turn and strike. Whoever killed the smallest snake had to buy dinner.

There was at that time a young driver's license trooper who came to work in Alice, and he wanted to be a highway patrolman just as soon as he put in his mandatory year in the driver's license bureau. It was all he ever talked about, and he was forever pestering Jim and Willie to let him ride along on their patrols. Jim no longer remembers the man's name, but he was tall and skinny with blond hair, and just as green as it was possible to get about the highway patrol---and South Texas snakes.

One night, the young trooper asked again if he could ride with Jim and Willie and get a feel for the highway patrol. Jim looked over at Willie--and saw Willie grinning back. Each of them had the same idea. They would take the greenhorn out and introduce him to snake stomping. Jim turned back to the young trooper and magnanimously motioned him into the back seat.

The young trooped was thrilled, and as they rode down the highway, he eagerly listened as Jim and Willie explained that it was part of the highway patrolman's responsibility to kill snakes. Snakes got out on the highway, the two veterans said, and people stopping for any reason---flat tires, tickets, rest stops, whatever---were in danger of being bitten and killed. It was the highway patrol officer's duty to protect the public by killing the snakes.

"We used to shoot their heads off," Jim explained, "but Captain Weeks doesn't want us doing that any more. Here's how we do it now."

He pulled the patrol car to the side of the road, and all three men got out. Sure enough, a huge snake slithered off into the grass. Jim raced into the grass after it, and after kicking the brush around with his boot for a few moments, he paused, completely dismayed at the size of the thing. It was every bit as long as six feet with a head that looked as huge as his hand. And, there was no way of getting out of what he had planned because the greenhorn was watching his every move with something akin to worship written all over his face. "Come on down here," Jim finally called to the young trooper.

The young man gingerly walked down the grassy slope over to where Jim had corralled the gigantic rattlesnake, and he watched in shocked disbelief and horror as Jim stomped on the snake's head. After turning several shades of white, the man wheeled around and made a beeline for the patrol car. "Hell," he said, "I'm not being a highway patrolman for nothing. I wouldn't do that for anything in the world."

It wasn't until later, after Jim's nerves had steadied and he and Willie had wiped the tears from their eyes, that they told the young trooper the truth.

Jim and Willie shared a lot of adventures together as troopers for the highway patrol. Usually, the days were routine and without any special significance, but occasionally something happened to change the mundane into madness---like the cold Sunday night in late November 1964 when Jim got himself chewed out by a drunk.

Jim was always an exceptionally tall, thin officer all during his highway patrol days, keeping his weight around 160 or so pounds. It wasn't that he didn't like to eat, because he did. He just burned the weight off with his activities. He wasn't married at the time, and consequently, he had no regular schedule set aside for meals. He ate when and if he thought about it, and if he happened to be busy at the time, he skipped the meal altogether. It was a magnificent way to keep trim.

Still, although he was tall and rangy, he was never overtly ungainly---until that November night. He usually just folded himself up behind the wheel and pretended that the cramped space didn't bother him. Willie knew better, though. Jim's long legs demanded a good stretch each and every time they stopped a car for infractions on their patrol. And if Willie judged the time frame too long between stops, he made sure Jim worked out all the kinks on the next stop before once again sliding behind the wheel. After all, that's what partners were for, right?

At the time of the irate drunk incident, it had been a typical weekend for the patrol officers in the Alice area, with the usual array of drunk drivers, speeders, and fender benders. Jim and Willie knew they could look forward to more of the same before getting off duty and hitting the hay. Many people thought of Alice as the "boonies," and the locals did everything possible to spice up life on the weekends. The small town started partying at sunset on Friday and usually didn't let up until the sun rose on Monday morning.

Around eleven o'clock that cold Sunday evening, the two patrol officers flashed their lights and pulled another weaving car over to the side of the road. They arrested an amiable drunk driver named Juan. Juan was all chatter and smiles as the two lawmen took him into custody and drove him to the Alice Police Station for processing. After booking Juan on a charge of "driving while under the influence," Willie let Jim escort the prisoner out the back door of city hall, down the back stairs, and toward the city jail which was located right next door, thus giving Jim the welcomed opportunity to really stretch his legs on the short, routine walk.

But it wasn't to be a routine escort to the jail. On the way down the back steps, Jim suddenly spied someone outside the jail, talking to a prisoner inside. He immediately challenged the stranger.

"Hey! Hold it right there!" he yelled.

The suspect, spying Jim in uniform, turned tail and ran around the side of the building, totally ignoring Jim's order to halt. Jim promptly sat Juan down on the bottom step of the back stairs of city hall and gave chase.

Right next door to the jail was a large house. The fleeing man careened around the corner of the house and zoomed across the back yard, never once breaking stride. But when Jim galloped around the corner of the house in hot pursuit after the suspect, his feet lost their footing in the loose gravel of the driveway. With his legs and feet in a hopeless tangle, he crashed to the ground with a thud, almost knocking the wind out of himself. As he fell, he pulled his revolver and fired one round into the air.

The revolver shot brought immediate attention from the police. Sergeant Ramon Falcon reached the gravel driveway just as Jim, his long legs and feet finally unwound, was getting up. Both officers then gave chase to the running man, firing their pistols into the air, trying to get him to stop. The fugitive, however, only ran faster. Jim and Sergeant Falcon chased the fleeing suspect around another building, through the yard, and across a street where the running man then turned and made a mad dash to a nearby alley. Sergeant Falcon pounded down the alley as Jim galloped down the block in front of the houses. The two lawmen finally corralled the suspect at the far end of the alley. Seeing that he had no further escape, the suspect surrendered peacefully and was later fined $25 in corporation court on drunk charges.

And Juan? Well, when Willie Stafford heard all the commotion, he rushed out the back door and found Juan still sitting on the back steps where Jim had left him, shaking like a leaf in the November air. And it was cold. South Texas lay in the grip of a blue norther---the kind area residents

39

hadn't seen in decades. The temperature was in the mid-20s, and with a 15-knot North wind, the wind chill factor felt like it was around zero degrees or below.

"Where's my partner?" demanded Willie.

"I don't know." The words struggled from Juan's mouth as his teeth clattered in the icy blast. He was all huddled over, his arms wrapped together, trying to keep warm. He was also cold sober and totally furious. "He shoot his gun and go that way." Instead of pointing, he threw his head in the general direction of the jail house next door.

Willie got Juan to his feet and back inside the building to warm up. And this is where Jim found the drunk when he returned.

Spying Jim, Juan demanded, "How come you leave me in the cold?"

Although it's funny now, at the time Jim couldn't figure out why Juan was so mad at him. After all, Jim had just run across half the town of Alice chasing a suspect, and he didn't think it was so cold. He was sweating up a storm!

When Alice became a larger community---it's population now is around 5,900---the highway patrol added more officers and additional cars for patrol. Being one of the most experienced, Jim had occasion to patrol by himself. When he made an arrest, like lawmen everywhere, he normally put the prisoner in the back seat of the patrol car. But sometimes, he had occasion to place the prisoner in the front seat. When that happened, he always moved his gun over to his left side and out of the way of temptation.

On one arrest, the prisoner was a friendly, sotted fool. Fearing the man would throw up all over the back seat of the cruiser if put back there where he would lie down, Jim made the decision to sit the drunk in the front seat beside himself. As usual, Jim moved his gun to his left side.

The fool was totally intoxicated and had trouble sitting upright in the seat. As Jim drove the short distance to the jail, the drunk swayed back and forth, ultimately ending with his head lolling on Jim's shoulder. There, the drunk would belch streams of foul-smelling whiskey breath into Jim's face. If it wasn't for the belching, Jim would have left the sot alone to sleep on his shoulder until they arrived at the police station, but the man's breath was more than Jim could take in the close confines of the car. Each time the fool fell over, Jim pushed him back upright and straight-armed him over to the passenger side of the car. This went on every few seconds for two miles.

Finally, Jim reached the end of his patience. He decided that the next time the drunk fell over, no matter where they were, even if it was two feet from the jail's parking lot, he was going to stop the car and throw the guy into the back seat. He'd worry about cleaning up the mess later.

Sure enough, a few seconds after Jim made his decision, the fool fell over again. This time, however, the drunk poked Jim in the arm with one fat finger. It so shocked Jim that he looked down to see what the drunk wanted.

"Say," the man slurred into Jim's face with a wide, toothy grin, "you lost your gun." He pointed down to Jim's empty holster.

Jim had many amusing incidents in his years with the highway patrol around Alice. It wasn't that Alice had something special going for it in the levity department; it was just that the South Texas region was more prone to humorous incidents. The area is, for the most part, flat farmland with little character, and the major crops are low-growing maize and cotton. Even the native trees of huisache and mesquite, ebony and live oak have small, fairy-wing leaves. One can see for miles in all directions, and the open remoteness leaves an impression of being alone in the universe. Sometimes, drivers take this feeling literally, and they end up doing outlandish things when behind the wheel. Always, when this happens, it creates levity in an otherwise routine, sometimes boring, patrol.

One laughable incident happened when Jim and his father, Chester Peters, were on patrol about two years after the "little old lady in the big Cadillac" episode. It was a pitch black night with no moon, and it involved three young women in their early twenties out for a Saturday night on the town---the "town" being the strip between the two small communities of Alice and Orange Grove.

The two towns of Alice and Orange Grove were nowhere near the same size in population. Alice had around 2,500 people, but tiny, little Orange Grove was practically non-existent at around 300. The town was, however, a very convenient highway stop at the intersection of Farm to Market Road 624 from Corpus Christi to Highway 359, which shuttled between Alice and Mathis.

At the time, there were only two really popular hangouts in Jim's jurisdiction: the VFW Hall in Alice, where there was always a big dance, and the Rifle Club in Orange Grove, which also had a big dance. People came from surrounding counties to attend the affairs, and it was common belief that each club was in friendly competition with the other. They each hired the best local bands and tried to lure the most area youths to the dances. Usually, though, all that ever really happened was that people began the evening at one establishment and ended at the other, making the road between the two a fun-loving drag-strip on Saturday nights.

Jim and his daddy were travelling between the two hot spots when Jim noticed a car leaving the VFW Hall headed toward Orange Grove. It wasn't speeding or anything like that, but it did have a headlight out, and he thought he should make the driver aware of the infraction, especially since the two-lane highway was so dark and so many cars travelled it between the two dance halls. Anyone chancing upon the one-eyed car might mistake it for a motorcycle, and all sorts of things could happen.

As the other car passed him, Jim turned his cruiser around, intending to stop and issue a warning, only when he started his turn, the other car raced off into the darkness. He immediately turned on his red lights and bright headlights and began his pursuit.

About a mile down the road, the other driver suddenly swerved into a beer joint's parking lot. The bar sat slightly back off the road, and as the other driver skidded sideways into the graveled lot, the sliding tires spewed rocks and dust in all directions. Jim pulled in behind the other vehicle and sat for a moment watching three heads bob around in the front seat of the other car.

"'Uh-huh,' I told my dad, 'they're changing drivers,'" Jim said, shaking his head as he recalled the scene. Changing drivers was a common enough occurrence when someone wasn't old enough to be driving, and Jim had witnessed the same "bobbing head" routine many times in his career. The area youths were notorious for driving while under age.

Reaching for his clipboard and flashlight, Jim got out of his car, walked over to the other vehicle, and shone the light in on three of the cutest girls he had ever seen in all of South Texas. They had long, flowing hair, flushed cheeks, beautiful smiles, and all were dressed up for a party. They were also giggling nervously as they sat with their miniskirts hiked high on their thighs.

"What is it, officer?" the beauty behind the wheel asked, her voice all innocent, her eyes opened wide in nervous surprise. She laughed anxiously and fidgeted in her seat, her fingers constantly twisting and clasping.

"Good evening, little lady," Jim said pleasantly. "The reason I stopped you is that you have a headlight out. May I see your license, please?"

"Yes, sir," the beauty said, relief in her voice, as she reached for her purse and shakily handed Jim her driver's license.

Jim examined it carefully before handing it back . He then said, "Now, I want to see the driver's license of the little lady sitting next to you." He pointed to the young woman in the middle. It confused the girl behind the wheel, and scared the one in the middle.

"But, I wasn't driving," the middle one stammered, fear creeping into her voice. The beauty behind the wheel echoed it.

"Look," said Jim in his best, paternal voice. "Let me explain something to you. When I turned around, you raced off like you had something to hide. Then you came sliding in here, and I watched as your heads bobbed around. I've been doing this job a long time, and I think you were switching drivers. Now, may I see your license, please?"

"No-o-o, officer," the girl in the middle squeaked with just a trace of relieved embarrassment in her voice. She then laughed nervously. "We've been to the VFW club in Alice, and we were on our way to the Orange Grove Rifle Club to dance up there. I was right in the middle of taking off my garter belt when you turned around on us." She reached down beside her, grabbed the offending garment and dangled it nervously in the air for him to see. "I had to finish getting it off before we could stop and let you see us."

Jim said he was suddenly struck dumb, which is a rarity for him because he can always find something to say. He remembers mumbling something about fixing the headlight and then warning them to stop the next time a patrol officer requested it, before walking stiffly back to his cruiser, and getting in. After answering his father's questions, and peeling with laughter, he resumed his patrol. The rest of the night was without further incident.

LIFE SAVING

Most of Jim's years with the highway patrol involved ticket chasing where, with siren blasting and lights flashing, he chased cars and issued tickets. But there were times when he became involved in life or death struggles, struggles which surely would have ended in tragedy had he not been there. The one that brought him to the attention of his superiors in a big way, and which earned him the first of many commendations for life saving, happened while he was still in Alice.

It was late 1962, and Jim was once again on a routine patrol with his partner Willie Stafford just south of Freer in Duval County. They were near the Border Patrol check point and were just about to turn around and proceed back toward Alice when the radio suddenly crackled to life with instructions to proceed to a rural address where a shooting had occurred. Their job was to investigate the incident and escort the ambulance to the hospital.

It didn't take Jim long to drive the twisting road, but he was unfamiliar with the rural addresses. Slowing almost to a crawl, he and Willie looked left and right for the correct mailbox. Jim finally spotted a house with an ambulance in the front yard, and he quickly pulled in the drive. Rushing into the house, he was horrified to discover that Andy Duncan, the three-year-old son of a Border Patrol officer, had shot himself in the stomach while playing with his father's .38 caliber service revolver. Andy's veins had already collapsed from loss of blood, and one of the ambulance attendants was frantically radioing for O-negative-type blood to meet the ambulance at the hospital. The other attendant grimly muttered that the child wouldn't make it that far.

Jim overheard the medical technician's assessment of the situation and reacted instinctively. "I have O-negative-type blood," he said. He rolled up his sleeve, immediately volunteering to give a direct transfusion to the dying child.

On the wild ride to the hospital with sirens screaming in his ears, the transfusion was somehow accomplished. Instead of being the escort for the ambulance as originally planned, Jim became the life line that the medical attendants needed for the critically wounded child. Little Andy Duncan lived, and Jim received a formal commendation from Colonel Homer Garrison, then Director of the Department of Public Safety, for saving the child's life.

A side note to this is that thirty years later, Andy Duncan finally managed to track down his lifesaver. In 1992, in an emotional telephone call, which took Jim completely by surprise, Andy Duncan thanked the big Ranger for saving his life.

Three short years after the Andy Duncan episode, Jim found himself involved in a yet another life-threatening emergency north of Alice. He was again on patrol with a partner, heading in the direction of town, when the car ahead of his cruiser suddenly swerved to the side of the road and screeched to a halt. A young woman jumped out and frantically flagged down the officers. "My baby is not breathing!" she screamed in panic.

Her child, a four-and-a-half-month-old girl, was already contorted and turning blue from choking when Jim snatched her up and ushered everyone into the patrol car. They were eleven miles from the nearest hospital, and with his partner racing at speeds of 130 miles-per-hour or better, Jim gave mouth-to-mouth resuscitation to the baby. Mile after mile, the tiny girl cradled in his big arms, he breathed life into her. He had no idea if his first aid attempts were working or not, as the child did not respond, but he thought a flicker of life still remained in her small body. He just knew there might be a chance if they could only make it to the hospital in time.

Just as the patrol car entered Alice at the edge of town where the first red traffic light is located, Jim felt the baby go completely limp.

"I thought, 'Oh, no! Don't let it happen now,'" Jim said. "We were only blocks from the hospital, and I thought she had just died."

He stared in anguish down at the child---and was startled to see the child staring back. Jim looked closer. Not only did the baby appear to be breathing normally, she also appeared to be highly interested in her surroundings. The obstruction in her throat had cleared. Jim still vividly remembers the relief that he felt. Texas did, too, and he received another commendation for his quick thinking.

It wasn't the last of his life-saving exploits. Several years after he became a Ranger, he was again saving the life of a small child. He was with a deputy sheriff at the time, and they were in Rockport planning to interrogate a witness to a burglary. Suddenly, their car radio reported the news that a child had stopped breathing.

By that time, Jim had babies of his own, and he knew how frantic the mother must be. Since the location was only minutes away from their position, the two men quickly raced to the scene. They found the mother almost completely hysterical and totally unable to do anything. While the deputy tried to calm the distraught mother, Jim administered mouth-to-mouth resuscitation on a tiny baby girl, until the ambulance crew arrived five minutes later. Again thanks to Jim, another little girl survived.

THE GREAT FREER MANHUNT

In February 1962, Jim participated in one of the largest manhunts in Texas history---the largest being the hunt for the notorious Bonnie Parker and Clyde Barrow bank-robbing, murdering duo of the early 1930's in which another famous Texas Ranger, Frank Hamer, finally succeeded in tracking down and killing. "The Great Freer Manhunt," as it is still called, was the first time Jim ever really worked directly with the Texas Rangers on a day-to-day basis for any length of time. As he watched and admired the efficient and authoritative way they handled themselves, he renewed his vow to someday become a Ranger himself. It was a goal that never left his mind during his twelve-year career with the Highway Patrol.

The manhunt began after State Game Wardern, B.G. "Bubba" Reed and Deputy Constable Andres Hassatte surprised two men at a restaurant near downtown Freer. It was shortly after midnight, early on a Wednesday morning, and the two officers were already at the cafe when the two strangers walked in for coffee. Since the pair seemed very nervous to have the lawmen in the same room, Reed and Hassatte decided it would be prudent to check out the pair's vehicle. Bubba suspected the strangers to be poachers, and he planned to search their car for illegal game.

The lawmen walked outside. It was easy to spot the strangers' car at that time of night in the nearly deserted parking lot, and the lawmen quietly peeked inside the vehicle. Lying on the back seat was a 30-30 rifle and a bank bag. Right then, Reed and Hassatte decided to wait and question the two men.

When the two strangers finally walked out of the cafe, Bubba challenged them. "Hey!" he yelled. "Come here!"

At the sound of Bubba's voice, one of the strangers quickly veered around the corner of the cafe, walking so fast that it was almost a trot. Bubba was instantly in pursuit, yelling for the man to stop. The other stranger was partially crippled and couldn't get away. Andres Hassatte grabbed him and just sat on him until he could get handcuffs on the man.

Bubba chased his man through the parking lot and around the building, where the fleeing man suddenly turned and fired a shot. Bubba promptly drew his gun and fired back. Neither one hit anything, and the chase was on. The fugitive fled down the street, between the buildings, and through a residential neighborhood, exchanging gunfire with Bubba Reed a total of four times. The escapee finally reached the northeast edge of town, where he darted into the dense brush.

Meanwhile, Hassatte had called for roadblocks. When Jim arrived in his patrol car, he was instructed to take the captured man to the Freer jail. On the way to the jailhouse however, the prisoner, Hilton Ward Walters, confessed that he was an ex-con with a terrible heart problem. Walters claimed that he had to go to the hospital and get a shot for his condition because he was feeling really sick and desperately needed medication. He moaned and groaned and whined for Jim to remove the handcuffs, acting for all the world like he was in deep pain and would die any minute.

Jim couldn't tell if the man was telling the truth or not, as Walters, although crippled, looked to be really strong. Jim actually took him to be some kind of weight lifter. Walters had a well-developed chest and shoulder muscles accompanied with big hands that looked strong enough to rip phone books in half. Even with his moaning and groaning and his crippled appearance, he looked dangerous.

Jim is no fool, and he does not take chances. Furthermore, it struck him as odd that Walters didn't have his medicine with him if he was, indeed, that bad off. Nevertheless, Jim turned the patrol car around and headed toward the hospital, but he adamantly refused to unlock the handcuffs. The suspect had already admitted to being in prison, and chances were that he was going back. Suppose the complaints were all a ruse to keep from going to jail? Jim did not trust the man.

Once at the hospital, Walters again began to plead. He begged for Jim to remove the handcuffs, complaining that he was feeling really ill, that his chest really hurt, that he really needed his medicine, that, in general, he really wanted his hands free. He was putting on such an act that Jim began to feel a little sorry for the guy.

Looking about the room, Jim decided the only piece of equipment strong enough or cumbersome enough to restrain the suspect was a heavy, steel lamp next to the examination table. It wouldn't keep Walters from trying to escape, if that was what the man had in mind, but it did look awkward enough to slow him down long enough for Jim to recapture him. Jim cuffed one of the suspect's strong arms to the lamp, leaving the other one free to clutch at his chest as he moaned and groaned.

The nurse came in at that point, and Walters told her what he needed to have for his heart problem. She called the doctor, spoke to him briefly, and then turned to Jim and said that the doctor needed to speak to him. When Jim picked up the phone, the doctor said, "That liar. He doesn't have to have that. The medicine is something you take periodically. It's not something you've got to have for a sudden illness. Go ahead and put him in jail."

Jim promptly recuffed Walters and drove him without further incident to the Freer jail, which was not an impressive building as far as jails go. It was a tiny, wooden stockade with wooden floors and wooden sides. It did, however, serve the purpose. The cell had three wooden bunks made from four-by-four lumber, and the bunks were stacked three high against the

47

back wall. Above the top bunk was one tiny window covered in bars.

Jim instructed the prisoner to lay on the bottom bunk, put his hands up over his head and around behind the post. In this position, Walters would be handcuffed to the bunk and unable to escape. And when the rest of the police got back, they could finish the incarceration process.

"No, don't do that," Walters pleaded. "If I vomit or get sick or something, I'll drown in the vomit, and I can't take care of myself..."

"Okay," replied Jim. "Get up on the top bunk and handcuff one arm to that jail window up there."

"Oh, no....I can't climb up there. You help me up."

It was obvious to Jim that Walters was just a big liar. Refusing to be conned, Jim instructed the prisoner to use the chair to climb onto the top bunk. The suspect finally complied and handcuffed himself to the window. Jim then climbed up and checked to make sure. Satisfied that Walters could not escape, Jim left, going back out to the roadblock where the search was still on for the other suspect.

Jim had been at his post only a few minutes when he was asked to return to the jail to interrogate the prisoner in an effort to find out who the other man was. But a big surprise awaited him when he got to the jail. Walters had cut himself loose! Unknown to anyone, the prisoner had a strong pair of snips hidden inside the heel of his shoe. He had already cut the chain on the handcuffs and had the cell window almost out.

"Another fifteen minutes," Jim said, "and he'd have been gone."

The missing fugitive turned out to be Lloyd R. Ranels, a forty-seven-year-old ex-convict. He and Walters were wanted in Columbus, Texas, for two safe burglaries. Bubba Reed signed a complaint against Ranels, charging the fleeing man with assault with intent to murder. With Walters captured and Ranels on the loose, a posse quickly shaped up with practically every law enforcement agency in South Texas represented in the manhunt.

It was still dark when the first of the search teams arrived. For South Texans, Freer is in the heart of hunting country. It has water and plenty of dense brush, most of it full of razor-sharp thorns. All manner of wild game prospers in the area, sometimes growing to immense size. In some places, the brush is so thick, the terrain so rough, that the only practical way to get around is by horse. And that's exactly what happened.

An Old West-type posse complete with Texas Rangers, State Highway Patrol, Border Patrol, Fish and Game officers, Kingsville and Alice police, sheriff's deputies from as far as Laredo---every law enforcement agency in that part of the Lone Star State showed up to help in the manhunt. Even a Special Ranger from the Cattle Raisers Association came. Jim and five of the others donned chaps and cowboy tack, saddled up, and rode horseback into the thickets.

All day Wednesday, the search continued for the missing Ranels. Bloodhounds trailed the fugitive northeast of town into the rangeland, and Jim and the posse followed doggedly in hot pursuit. The dogs, however, appeared to have difficulty in picking up a trail in the dry dust. Bubba Reed, who watched the dogs and the searchers from an airplane, said it appeared they could not pick up a trail. He doubted Ranels was still in the area, as most of the brush was about waist-high and beginning to thin in several places, as the searchers continued northeast in the search pattern. He believed Ranels should have been spotted under those conditions.

But Bubba was wrong. Brush like the thickets surrounding Freer had hidden the fierce Commanche and Kickapoo Indians from the pursuing Texas Rangers for many years during the settlement phase of Texas history. Why not Ranels? The search for the missing man continued with gusto.

At first, none of the searchers bothered to stop and eat or even take time for a little rest. Some officers searched from their automobiles, creeping along the dirt roads which weaved in and out of the ranchland. Occasionally, an officer would reach the top of a hill, stop, climb atop his car and peer out over the range with binoculars. Jim often stood tall in his saddle and scanned the horizon. Ranels was afoot, and the consensus was that he would be caught before nightfall. But Ranels was as elusive as a will-o'-the-wisp, and by dark, he still remained free. Jim's posse continued on into the night.

The first real break in the manhunt came with a report from the Seven Sisters Community, located about ten miles north of Freer, that a house had been burglarized and a light-colored Stetson and a khaki jacket stolen during the night. Also taken was a khaki shirt hanging on a clothes line near there. Jim and the posse swarmed into the area, but by noon, the weary posse had again changed directions to concentrate their search eight miles east around an area of the vast Welder Ranch fronting Highway 59. It was in that area that Texas Ranger Frank Horger fired four times at a man believed to be Ranels.

Ranger Horger spotted the man around mid-morning while looking through binoculars from atop his car. He said the man was wearing a light Stetson and khaki jacket and was standing in the brush about 150 yards from the highway.

It appeared that Ranels was headed in the general direction of the small community of George West, and road blocks were set up on the outskirts of town. Lawmen had discovered where Ranels had burglarized a farm house, taking enough food to last himself several days. Jim's posse had also tracked the fugitive to several windmills in the area, so Ranels had plenty of water. As they had done the day before, the posse planned to take little time to eat or rest during the hunt, so determined were they to catch the fleeing man before sunset.

The temperature was uncomfortably warm in the summerlike weather, and the lack of sleep and food was beginning to show on some of the men. There were sunburns for those who didn't have hats and long-sleeved shirts. Hardly anyone escaped without a few cactus needles and mesquite thorns. From time to time, a hunter would drift in for a drink of cold water.

"This is worse than hunting season," Bubba Reed was overheard to sigh wearily, as he rubbed his reddened, sleep-craved eyes.

"Let's just burn the brush. That'll really smoke him out," one officer hopefully suggested.

On into the second night the hunt continued, and into the third day, as fear mounted in the communities. Many inhabitants dug out rifles they hadn't used in years, and some housewives admitted they didn't know how to shoot them. Some families in the outlying countryside padlocked their doors and moved into Freer, feeling safer in the community than alone at home.

Strung along the highway like some steel necklace were twenty-five or thirty official vehicles, the owners wading through the waist-high weeds and sticky brush on foot. Every officer in the manhunt carried a pistol, a gunbelt full of bullets, and a rifle, but the only sign of Ranels remained footprints in the dust and broken limbs in the brush. Sometimes there were reports that the fugitive had been spotted, and everyone would rush to the spot, but Ranels was always gone.

By Sunday with Ranels still running free, more drastic measures were taken. Freer Constable Reese Hughes asked for more men. Two dogs from Karnes City arrived around sundown, and up to fourteen more dogs arrived around midnight from Houston and Wharton. Still, the suspect remained at large. As the search wore on and Jim's posse failed to turn up Ranels, there was some speculation among some of the officers that the man they were hunting in the brush might not be Ranels at all. A few theorized that the man might be an illegal alien from Mexico.

Lloyd Ranels was finally run to earth upstate. He had found a bicycle in his trek through the range and had ridden over to George West where he managed to secure another form of transportation out of South Texas. He later revealed that while he had been hiding in the brush, a deputy had ridden past him on horseback not more than twenty feet away. He said the deputy was extremely tall and thin. No one knows for sure which deputy it was---there were only six horseback riders, including Jim--- but not seeing the fugitive definitely saved the officer's life. When he was captured, Ranels told authorities that he had his pistol pointing right at the officer's head. "If he had once turned and looked at me. I would have shot him dead."

GIDDINGS

It was in 1966 that Jim received a request to transfer to Giddings, a small community located about fifty miles east of Austin, and it turned out to be fortuitous because it was here that he met Texas Ranger Bill Wilson, who kept him apprised of the status in the Ranger ranks. The transfer came about because the DPS officer assigned to the area had requested a transfer after only six months, and Jim's superiors suspected some kind of personality conflict had occurred with other law enforcement agencies in the area. Since Jim had already established a reputation of being able to get along with everyone, he was considered the best man for the job. Still, his superiors left the final decision to him.

Jim decided the best thing to do was to visit the area and acquaint himself with the local lawmen before agreeing to accept the assignment. If there had been a personality conflict with the previous DPS officer, Jim wanted to know what it was. He's always believed in the old adage that 'to be forewarned is to be forearmed,' and he fully intended to iron out all problems in advance---providing, of course, the difficulties were little ones.

Jim spent two days visiting all the local lawmen in the whole area and came away with the feeling that there wasn't going to be any problems with him taking the assignment. The other authorities only wanted to be involved in the activities that occurred in their areas of jurisdiction, something Jim was more than willing to accommodate. In Jim's own words, "they were elected officials of their own communities and they had an obligation to the people who lived there. It was only right that they got as much credit as possible. I always got along with everyone just fine"

Most of his time in the Giddings area was routine with his duties involving the myriad of things all highway patrol officers have. Eighty percent of the time, it was stopping the usual array of drunk drivers and speeders. Therefore, he thought nothing of it when, one night on patrol, he happened upon two black men out joyriding in a big, maroon Oldsmobile with "Soul Brother" and "Soul Sister" plastered in huge, block letters across the rear window.

The men were from Dallas, and they were barreling down the road at a high rate of speed. It was also obvious from the way they were driving that they were not going to let anything spoil their fun on the blacktop---especially a highway patrol officer with a ticket book. When Jim turned on his red lights, they took off, headed for town.

It's a common misconception that DPS officers have no jurisdiction inside city limits---that city police are the only ones who can make arrests and issue tickets inside the city community. This is totally untrue. The DPS officer has that authority on any highway in the State. So, when the two men in the big Oldsmobile raced into Giddings, Jim followed them right into the heart of town.

The two fugitives were determined not to be caught. They flew around corners on two wheels, raced up and down all the side streets, and zoomed from one side of town to the other with Jim in constant pursuit. The finally located the black section of town and skidded to a halt in front of three beer joints. Jim was right behind them with his siren going and his lights flashing. He knew what part of town he was in, but he refused to be intimidated by the situation, especially since he always got along with everyone just great.

Jim got out of his car and began writing out the ticket, and as he was writing, he noticed that he was carefully being surrounded by about a hundred black men from half a dozen beer joints in the immediate area, who had come outside to see what the ruckus was all about. Some were holding cue sticks, others bottles of beer, and Jim could hear a low rumble rippling through the crowd.

All law officers have a sixth sense about situations. It's what keeps them alive in the face of danger. They can tell when to run and when to stay put. In a situation like the one Jim found himself facing, another officer might have decided it would be more prudent to leave. But not Jim. He is also gifted with a seventh and eighth sense, and he followed his intuition.

"I backed up against my patrol car, trying to remain calm, and kept writing," Jim said, "and pretty soon a spokesman for the spectators came up to me and said, 'Mr. Peters, we're sure glad you're giving them out-of-town folks a ticket. They're not supposed to come in here driving like that in our town!' I just relaxed after that."

The two men from Dallas never did show up in court for the ticket, and about two months later, Jim had arrest warrants for them. As he patrolled the area, he kept a lookout for their Oldsmobile. It was easy to spot because the "Soul Brother" and "Soul Sister" in huge letters across the back window was unlike anything he had ever seen before or since.

Late one night as he was working alone about ten miles north of Giddings on Highway 77, he spotted the "Soul Brother" car going the other way. He turned his patrol car around and gave chase, thinking, "Oh boy, I've got him this time." He finally managed to pull the car over, and when he did, another car pulled over in front of the Oldsmobile. There were three blacks in the front car and four in the "Soul Brother" car, and six of them got out, leaving only one in the right front passenger seat of the "Soul Brother" car.

"What are you stopping us for?" one of the men from the front car demanded to know. "We haven't done nothing." His tone was belligerent, and his movements were threatening.

53

Jim promptly replied, "Wait just a minute, now. I've got a warrant for old [so and so]. They never showed up in court. That's his car, and I think that's him up front."

"That ain't him," snapped the black man from the front car. "That's his brother. He's not in that car."

The black men started pressing in around Jim, and the situation grew tenser, if that was possible. The one that had been doing all the talking continued with, "I pay your salary, and here you are out stopping us. I pay your salary!" The black man was angry, ready to fight.

Realizing that things were getting out of hand and that he'd better do something quick to assuage the situation, Jim reached into his pocket and brought out a penny. "Here," he said. "There's your part of my salary. Now, go sit in that car and be quiet."

It broke the ice. Everybody backed up, grinning, and began to laugh. Jim then walked up to the passenger side of the "Soul Brother" car. Sure enough, it was the brother and not the man on the warrant.

It was in Giddings that Jim again demonstrated just how compassionate and understanding he is of human nature. It was early in the morning, around two a.m., when he came upon a Pontiac travelling west at a high rate of speed. Turning his cruiser around, he gave chase and finally managed to overtake the speeding car and force it to the side of the road. In the driver's seat sat a pretty young woman in her mid-twenties. She told Jim that she was from Pensacola, Florida, and that she was on her way to meet her husband who was flying into a military base in El Paso.

The time frame was during the middle of the Vietnam War, and the woman told Jim that her husband was a pilot flying missions in Southeast Asia. He had been gone a long time, and she tearfully confessed how much she had missed him and had worried about him and was so scared for him all the time.

The two strangers talked for a little while there in the dark by the side of the road, and Jim listened sympathetically as the woman told of her fears and loneliness and anxieties. She confessed to being afraid of driving by herself on the lonely road and of wanting to hurry and get to El Paso, of being afraid of what her husband might be, both mentally and physically, when she saw him. She expressed fears of being afraid for the success of their marriage after the terrible realities her husband had seen in the war. As she poured her heart out to Jim, she dabbed tears from her eyes.

When she was through and was sitting silently, Jim quietly spoke. "Young lady, you know how you have worried about something happening to him all this time? Wouldn't it be terrible for you to have a wreck between here and there and injure or kill yourself when he is expecting you to be there waiting for him? He's just as worried about you as you are about him.

It won't take you but an hour longer to get there if you cut your speed down and drive safely at the speed limit. If some cow steps out in front of you, or you come upon somebody with no tail lights on the road, you're going to have a wreck. Slow down, take it easy, and you'll get there safely. Both of you can then enjoy seeing each other again. Go on, now, and take it easy for the rest of your trip."

Jim never did ticket the woman, and a few months later he received a letter from her explaining how joyful her reunion was with her husband. She gratefully thanked Jim for his advice.

"Things like that really make you feel good," Jim said quietly.

All highway patrolmen know that feeling. The really good officers would sooner caution a person as to ticket him, provided the situation called for it. In this manner, the lawbreaker learns a valuable lesson on safe driving and becomes a better driver, and the lawman avoids an accident. There is nothing that can turn an officer's day into a nightmare faster than being summoned to investigate an accident scene.

One of the worst accidents Jim ever investigated happened in Giddings. It was 1968, and since Jim's patrol headquarters was in the larger town of College Station, home of Texas A & M University, the "Texas Aggies," it was common practice for the nearby highway patrol officers to go to the Aggie home games and then direct traffic at the edge of town afterwards to help the city officers.

On the night of the accident, it was raining so terribly hard that Jim huddled up under one of the concrete bleachers while waiting for the game to end. His patrol sergeant finally found him and said, "James, you'd better go to the house. You've got a bad wreck over there." Jim asked, "Where?" and the sergeant said, "On Highway 21."

At that time, Highway 21 was a two-lane, up- and downhill highway most of the way, and Jim had to exercise extreme caution in the pouring rain. Visibility was so badly hampered that it was hard for him to see the road in front of his car, and he drove mile after mile at a near crawl, never knowing what he would find cresting each hill. He fully expected road washouts in the valleys or cars off the sides in the ditches along the way, but he made the trip without incident. Nearing Giddings, the rain slackened and then ceased. The road was still wet and dangerous, but at least he could see clearly.

Topping one of the hills a few miles outside town, an appalling sight met his eyes. He saw cars everywhere. They were lined up on both sides of the highway for what looked like miles, and right in the middle of the tangle, strung out all over the highway, were pieces of wrecked vehicles, bodies, and all manner of debris with blood still mixing with the rain water and running crazily in all directions in the tiny cracks of pavement. The scene was a nightmare, and Jim hardly knew where to start.

He learned that it had all begun when three college students, driving at a speed later estimated to be approaching 100 miles per hour, lost control of their Chevrolet in the downpour while crossing the top of the hill. Their car turned sideways and skidded on all four wheels down the hill just as a Mustang approached from the other direction. The Chevrolet, going sideways, hit the Mustang, and the Mustang cut the Chevrolet in half. Half of the Chevrolet then spun onto its side and lay in the middle of the road. The other half skidded off into the bar ditch. The three boys in the Chevrolet were thrown out and dumped everywhere in the road, killed instantly.

The Mustang carried five people, and when it hit the Chevrolet, it careened crazily off to one side of the road. It came to rest in a crumpled mass with all the doors jammed. All five people inside were killed.

Before any warning could be given to other drivers, an old man and woman in a Cadillac pulling a travel trailer crossed over the top of the hill and slammed into one piece of the wrecked Chevrolet. A piece of the Chevrolet's body frame went through the Cadillac and hit the old woman, seriously injuring her. After that, a banker with his wife and child topped the rise, skidded over gas tanks and debris and such, and managed to run up the side of a hill with no injuries.

"When I got there," Jim said, "there were eight dead, one injured, four cars wrecked, and I was all by myself. I felt so small. Then, a game warden buddy of mine, who used to be a police officer up near Dallas, arrived at the scene, and he helped me. It took us all night to straighten things out. Things like that stick in your mind forever. You just can't forget them."

Jim met Texas Ranger Sergeant Bill Wilson in the DPS office in Giddings Immensely interested in the Ranger organization, it didn't take long for Jim to strike up a conversation with the big Ranger, turning an informal meeting into a lasting friendship. A few weeks later, he began working closely with Ranger Wilson in criminal investigations, studying the Ranger's methods and admiring the Ranger's expertise and knowledge. But Ranger Wilson didn't stop with investigative instructions. He knew Jim wanted to become a Ranger, and he took every opportunity to school Jim in the Ranger organization as a whole. On the day that he said that the Ranger force was expanding, Jim made his historic trip to Austin to sign up.

PART THREE
TEXAS RANGER

When Jim learned in March 1968 from his Ranger friend Bill Wilson, who later went on to become the Senior Ranger Captain supervising all the Rangers in the whole State, that the Ranger force was about to be expanded from sixty-four to eighty-two men, he immediately drove over to Austin to sign up, realizing that there might never be a better opportunity to fulfill his dream of becoming part of the elite organization. He knew that Rangers didn't just get appointed to the position or walk up and enlist as they did in the past. Each candidate had to be tough, full of spirit, and have the patience of Noah waiting for the deluge to subside. He also knew that it sometimes took years to join the organization. However, with so many vacancies now in the ranks, he felt he had a better than even chance of making it. He wasn't going to let the opportunity slip away.

Ranger qualifications are strictly enforced. They are also overwhelmingly stringent. Each applicant must be between the ages of thirty and fifty and has to undergo careful scrutiny, which includes educational and physical requirements that would make Superman proud. Each has to also meet a minimum requirement of eight years of law enforcement experience, which must include a record of investigative excellence. In fact, the requirements are almost superhuman and nearly impossible to attain, but they ensure that the Rangers are, without a doubt, the most elite law enforcement agency in America.

Jim knew he had the education and rudimentary law enforcement requirements for the job---after all, he had practically been in law enforcement since he was eighteen---and he fully expected he could handle whatever other requirements might also be required. He was forty-one years old, an age he considered the prime of his life. He didn't think he would have much trouble in the application process, but he was wrong. The problem, as he found out when he arrived in Austin, was that signing up wasn't all that easy. He was not prepared for what awaited him at Ranger Headquarters. After discoverering that the moral and physical standards for applicants was next to impossible, he was astounded to discover that practically every law enforcement officer in the State of Texas, not to mention several from outside the State, wanted to be Texas Rangers, too.

"We have eighteen openings," Colonel Wilson "Pat" Speir told him when he arrived, "and I have 400 applications on my desk this morning. But go ahead and try it, son. If you don't make it the first time, try again. Some men wait years to join us."

Although discouraged by the sheer numbers of applicants, Jim was not really surprised. He fully expected the competition to be tough. How else could the organization sustain its awesome reputation? He certainly had never heard of any Ranger wanting to be the local sheriff or policeman or highway patrol officer, and he was sure that no one else had, either. It only stood to reason that every lawman in the State wanted the coveted job. He did figure, though, that the odds had to be stacked in his favor because he was sure no one else wanted it more than he did. He'd been dreaming of it since he was a kid. He looked at Colonel Speir, nodded his head, and forged onward.

After wading through the four hundred applications that arrived for the Ranger vacancies in 1968, officials chose 150 to take the written examination. The high-scoring, top ninety were then selected to take the grueling oral examination. Jim made all the cuts.

The oral examination was in front of a five-man review board, and they questioned Jim for what seemed like hours on search and seizure, code of criminal arrest procedure, and investigative techniques. After the oral examination, the review board cast a secret ballot based on Jim's answers to their questions, totalled the scores, and divided the sum by five, thereby providing a final score. Jim knew he had about a "one in a hundred" chance of making it. But so did everyone else. And with his chances equal, he began the wait. After what seemed like an eternity, but which was in reality only a few days, Jim was one of the eighteen men sworn in as a Texas Ranger. His dream was finally a reality!

There really is no such thing as a Texas Ranger Academy like the Department of Public Safety Academy that Jim attended when he first became a law enforcement officer. Since the Texas Rangers are all part of the Department of Public Safety, each Ranger just attends in-service training in specialized areas such as fingerprinting, photo identification, new rules and regulations, and so on. When Jim became a member of the elite force, he spent several weeks in different schools in Austin, as well as one week of homicide school at the University of Oklahoma in Norman, before reporting for duty. Later, as new and better techniques needed to be acquired, he went back to school to learn about them.

Jim became a Texas Ranger on October 8, 1968, and it was the best birthday present he could ever have hoped to get. He was issued the tools of his trade: a .357 Magnum revolver, a 30-06 automatic rifle, and a 12-gauge shotgun. The prestigious and distinctive badge was pinned to his shirt. When Ranger superiors asked him where he would like to be assigned, rightly reasoning that he would do a better job for the State if he were in familiar and desired territory, he promptly answered "anywhere." And he meant it. He would have gone anywhere and loved it.

As luck would have it, the great Captain Alfred Young Allee, Sr., of Company "D" was preparing to retire, and one of the Rangers in his

Company, John Wood, was being groomed to take his place. That meant there would be an opening in the Company, which had South Texas as their district. Jim became assigned to Company "D" under Captain Allee and worked alongside John Wood in Corpus Christi for two years. John Wood became his mentor and friend.

When Jim became a South Texas Ranger, he found himself suddenly responsible for the three coastal counties of Nueces, San Patricio, and Aransas, which completely encompass the Corpus Christi Bay and beach areas. Not only did he already know most of the area from his days with the highway patrol, not to mention his hunting and fishing excursions and his Marine duty at the Naval Air Station in Corpus Christi, but he also knew most of the law enforcement officers in the territory. It was like coming home after a two year absence. Jim was elated!

One of the first things he did was to settle himself in the Texas Ranger office located in the Department of Public Safety building on Port Avenue---DPS would later move to a new building on South Padre Island Drive---in the largest city in the three county area, the sprawling metropolis of Corpus Christi. And the city really does sprawl. It lies in a half-moon curl that is most confusing to the uninitiated, who tend to drive relative to the position of the sun in the sky.

At the time Jim first moved into the city, the population barely topped 100,000 people. Today, it is over 250,000 and still climbing. The city limits begin at the Nueces River bridge about a mile north of where Interstate Highway 37 and U.S. Highway 77 split. It then runs around the west and south sides of Corpus Christi Bay all the way to Padre Island. If the streets run west one minute, they are just as apt to turn south in the next block, sometimes changing names in the process. But it's a beautiful city with a beautiful climate, and Jim couldn't have asked for a better place to begin his new job.

His duties became the normal activities associated with investigations requested from the local law enforcement agencies, and it didn't take long to make his presence felt. In a typical week, he helped solve an embezzlement case for the local power company, assisted security officers in smashing a copper wire burglary ring, investigated a land swindle that involved innocent speculators in Mexico. He became involved in a Green River, Wyoming, murder investigation, located $3,000 in property taken from a furniture store, and assisted Ranger Milton Wright in surveillance of oil field thieves traveling through the area. As a Ranger, his case load encompassed a myriad of investigations and judicial proceedings from escorting the Governor to assisting the Federal Bureau of Investigation. Even the unusual occasionally cropped up in his everyday routine, like the day he assisted Texas Parks and Wildlife officers in searching for illegal gill nets and stolen property. Almost overnight, all the lawmen, the lawyers, judges, jailers, private investigators, security personnel, and even the criminals in the whole area knew who "Ranger Peters" was.

Jim always maintained an unique style of dress as a Ranger. When he first became part of the force, the dress code was tan---tan pants, tan leather vest, tan jacket, white long-sleeved shirt, white hat, dark boots, dark tie. The distinctive badge was pinned to the vest. It's a dress code many of the Rangers still prefer. But take away the faces, and everyone looked alike. Jim decided to personalize his Ranger rig with a tie tack that was a miniature automatic revolver. Another tie tack was a miniature Bowie knife, and later, he also added a miniature Ranger badge to the repertoire. It fit the tradition as no other accessory ever could. The early Rangers always carried a brace of pistols and a gigantic Bowie knife, as well as the ever ready rifle. Their badge, made from a single Mexican cinco peso, was always pinned to the shirts.

After the dress code was abolished and the Rangers were allowed to wear whatever they wanted, Jim opted for grey slacks, white long-sleeved shirt, and black leather vest with the badge pinned on the left breast. His boots became black ostrich leather with two inch heels. In the summer, he had his white straw Stetson and in the winter, a dark grey felt. He often wore his Ranger holster over his belt in the fashion of the Wild West. Commander Lou Villagomez of the Corpus Christi Police Department said that Jim was such a formidable sight walking through a doorway that everyone in the room, criminal and lawman alike, just stood in complete awe of him. And if he came in with his hat still on, he looked well over seven feet tall...had to stoop to clear the doorframe.

Jim also normally operated alone. That is, he's usually the only Ranger in a sea of investigators. And since he didn't wear a uniform, he could pass as one of the crowd. Although it's true that he stood head and shoulders above everyone, he only assumed an air of authority when the occasion called for it.

A case in point happened right after he made Ranger. He went back to Giddings for a court case, and since he drove up on a Sunday afternoon and didn't have a whole lot to do, he decided to drive around the town. As he drove through the same neighborhood where he had stopped the two men in the "Soul Brother" car, he noticed six black men clustered around the front of a store. The men were on their hands and knees and appeared to be wildly engaged in a game of craps on the sidewalk. They didn't even see him, or if they did, they totally ignored him.

Jim stopped his car, got out, and strolled over to the men. One or two heads turned briefly in his direction, but no one really took notice. He stood there, blending in with the men---although he was the only white man in the sea of black and dressed in his "informal" Ranger attire---intending to make an arrest if they were, indeed, breaking the law. Sure enough, the men had the dice rolling everywhere.

"Texas Ranger," Jim quietly said. All six heads turned in his direction at the same time, and he could read the signs of total disbelief and astonishment on their faces as their mouths dropped open. "You're under arrest. Get in the car."

Jim said he never will forget how bug-eyed the sheriff was when he drove up with four black men crammed into the back seat and two black men stuffed in the front of his Ranger car.

In was in 1956 that Ranger Red Burton said, "the Ranger is always in the minority where he is. You're never wanted where you go because if you're wanted there, you're not needed." Those words are closer to the truth than most Rangers care to admit. Because of the mystique that surrounds the Ranger organization and the legend that made them a tradition, Jim's presence anywhere always commanded an atmosphere likened to meeting a god. There's even an old saying running around Texas: AND ON THE EIGHTH DAY, GOD CREATED THE TEXAS RANGERS. Many claim that it was popular long before the baseball team of the same name.

Jim had to learn to guard against this type of adoration if he wanted to get along with the local law enforcement agencies he was supposed to assist. He decided he was going to do it in an unique way---by emulating his friend, Sergeant John Wood.

John Wood had already been a Ranger for twenty years when Jim became part of the elite organization, and he is probably the only Ranger sergeant ever promoted to that rank twice through competitive examinations. He was first promoted in 1955, but it meant that he would have to transfer from Midland, where he had been stationed since he joined the force in 1949. Deciding he would rather remain in Midland, John accepted a demotion back to Ranger status, and it turned out to be a lucky break. In 1957, the Rangers reorganized their districts, and the headquarters for Company "E" became Midland. John was again promoted to Sergeant.

"Midland was my first station. In fact, I opened the Ranger station there in 1949, and I stayed until 1967," John once told Jim. He transferred to Company "D" in Corpus Christi in 1967.

While in Midland, John had about three-fourths of the Rio Grande boundary in his district, and a lot of his time was spent stopping smugglers. The smugglers brought wax and marijuana across the border to exchange for guns, which were extremely valuable in Mexico. Today, most of the guns stolen in Texas still wind up in Mexico.

Once, the Rangers asked the Mexican authorities for help in recovering eighteen stolen guns. "They sent us nineteen," John said. "It took us a while, but we finally found the owner of that nineteenth gun."

During John's career, he investigated murders, burglaries, smuggling, and a long list of other crimes. He once pursued a suspect into New Mexico and made an arrest there. "But he had to be jailed there and extradited to Texas." On another case he was asked by Indiana authorities to assist in an investigation of the theft of $75,000 in platinum gauze which was used as a catalyst in making sulfuric acid. "One of the suspects had moved to Texas, and the Indiana authorities asked me to keep an eye on him."

It was John Wood's rule that ultimately became Jim's motto: "TREAT EVERY INDIVIDUAL WITH RESPECT THE WAY YOU WOULD WANT TO BE TREATED IF YOU WERE IN THEIR PLACE, AND YOU'LL GET ALONG FINE." It's the credo which has governed Jim's life and has made him so well-respected among investigators and criminals alike.

As a modern Ranger, Jim knows he is practically omnipotent in his powers and that he can make arrests on planes, trains, boats, or highways anywhere in Texas. He knows that he's only there to assist as a highly specialized criminal investigator, giving every municipality, regardless of size, access to the DPS Crime Lab in the State Capital. But he also knows that when he leaves, when the investigation is over, the local lawman still has to live in the community.

"I don't like to talk to the press or TV. That's something I don't do is give out news releases on cases," Jim explained. "While I was a highway patrolman, if I worked a major wreck or something like that, as soon as I got time, I'd pick up a telephone and call a reporter that I always talked to with the details. I'd say, 'Hey, this is what happened,' and I'd give him the story because he wanted it, he needed it, and I needed my sleep.

"But then I came to work as a Ranger, and I had a bad experience once with news reporters. One day, a deputy sheriff friend of mine called and said, 'Hey, Jim. I'm fixing to run a search warrant out here on a house. I've been working on this "ole boy" for quite some time, and I think I finally got the goods on him. I'm going to go out and search for some stolen property. You want to come along?'

"Well, sure, I wanted to go along. I went with him. We arrested the "ole boy" and found the stolen property. When a newspaper reporter heard about it, he called me and said, 'I understand y'all raided such and such.' I told him, 'Yeah, sure did. Deputy Jones and myself went out there and arrested ole so and so.' I told him what we seized, and he said, 'Fine.'

"The next day, the newspaper had this headline in big print: 'TEXAS RANGER ARRESTS, RECOVERS...' and somewhere way down in the small print, it mentioned this deputy who had done all the work. It made me feel about this big. [Jim held his fingers an inch apart.] I went to my friend and apologized. I told him it wouldn't ever happen again. And it hasn't. I tell every partner I have here, 'Look, if they call you, just tell them to talk to police officer so and so. It's his case.'"

It's been Jim's number one rule ever since, and it has made him highly popular with the community lawman who needs all the credit he can get for his livelihood. But although Jim makes it a point to be non-threatening to the local law, the Ranger legend still tends to get in the way. Sometimes, the news media does come to him for informational releases, and when that happens, he just gives a broad smile and automatically points to the local authorities.

"Besides," he once said with a big grin, "it's their case. They file it. And it keeps me out of the court room."

THE GREAT SLOT MACHINE CAPER

Jim had been a Texas Ranger just over a month when he and John Wood pulled a slot machine raid in Port Lavaca. Port Lavaca is a small fishing village located twenty-five miles south of Victoria on the Gulf of Mexico, and Victoria is about 100 miles northeast up the coast from Corpus Christi. Like most small towns, there isn't a whole lot to do, and boredom quickly becomes the number one pastime. To compensate for this boredom, the local VFW Hall had located eight slot machines in their back room.

Actually, it wasn't really much of a back room---just a long, narrow closet-type enclosure having the machines around the walls. How they managed to squeeze the machines in that tiny area and still have enough room to do business is anybody's guess.

Gambling is against the law in Texas, and possession of any part of a slot machine is a felony. When John Wood learned of the machines in Port Lavaca, he called the Sheriff of Calhoun County and told him about the VFW Hall and the slot machines, advising the sheriff to close the operation down. The sheriff agreed.

A month or so later, the machines were still going strong. This time, instead of calling the sheriff, John Wood devised his own plan. He got a DPS intelligence agent to go into the VFW Hall and verify that the machines were still in the room and were still being used. Armed with this confirmation, John and Jim decided to raid the place that night. With the intelligence agent on the inside, they didn't need a search warrant. All the agent had to do was to open the door at a certain time and let the Rangers inside.

About five minutes before the two Rangers were to make their raid on the VFW Hall, they called for a sheriff's representative to go with them. When the sheriff's deputy drove up, John Wood informed him that they were going into the VFW Hall to raid the slot machines and that they wanted the sheriff's department to go along with them and to be aware of it. John and Jim then headed toward the door.

John Wood is also six feet, five inches tall and seeing the tall, broad backs of the two Rangers marching determinedly toward the VFW Hall panicked the sheriff's deputy. "No, no. Wait, wait, wait," he cried, frantically trying to deter the Rangers. "I need to talk to the sheriff. Let me get the sheriff first."

"Well, we don't have time," drawled John Wood in a conversational tone of voice. "We're going in there now. If you want to go along with us, come on."

When they got inside, the Rangers headed straight to the closet which contained the eight slot machines. When patrons saw the Rangers coming, they scattered. All, that is, except a very pregnant lady who insisted on playing the machine closest to the door on the right side of the closet. John Wood stared at her for a moment, shook his head at Jim, and then started listing the machines, beginning with the one closest to the door on the left side. John turned each machine over and read the serial numbers aloud, and Jim stood by with pad and pencil, ready to write down each number as John called it out.

Meanwhile, the pregnant lady completely ignored the two Rangers and their repeated requests for her to leave. She kept feeding the machine her dimes as fast as she could, making all sorts of contortions and twists to keep up a steady rhythm with her tummy out of her way. And it worked just fine for her. Her belly was out of HER way, as she played the one-arm bandit in front of her, but it was not out of JIM's way, as he worked alongside John Wood. She was so huge that Jim judged her dangerously close to giving birth at any moment. In that cramped closet, her huge tummy jutted and protruded into Jim's back and ribs at each pull on her machine's handle.

At first, Jim was the perfect gentleman as he tried to keep out of her way. Each time she whacked him with her belly, he'd turn and apologize. But, as the Rangers drew closer to the woman's machine, she increased her pace, feeding it dimes in a frenzy, until her jutting tummy just interfered with everything Jim tried to do. He tried every way he could to get her to leave, but she was determined to play. Her tummy bumped and thumped with every pull of the handle.

"Lady," Jim said, "you have to go."

Chink, thump, whrrrr...another dime disappeared.

"Lady, pleeeease. You must stop."

Chink, bump, whrrrr...chink, thud, whrrrr...chink, whrrrr.

"Lady. I'm not going to ask you again. Go on, now."

Chink, thump, whrrrr.

Finally, Jim had had enough. He put his pad and pencil in his shirt pocket, set his teeth, and with John Wood looking on, a grin plastered across his face, Jim turned and resorted to drastic measures. Reaching both hands out, Jim forcibly pried the woman's hand from the handle of the machine and instructed, "Lady, if you don't quit, I'm going to arrest you, too. Now, go on. Get out of here."

The Rangers took all eight machines to the Port Lavaca Police Department, instead of to the Sheriff's Department, and stored them in the vault. Later, after the judge ordered them destroyed, all the money was removed and donated to charity. The machines were then taken to the city dump and beat into smithereens with a sledge hammer.

THE CAPTAIN ALLEE ASSASSINATION ATTEMPT

Jim had been a Ranger about one year when word got around that his Captain, Alfred Young Allee, Sr., was about to be assassinated. Things like that cropped up every few years or so in the Ranger ranks, and usually nothing much ever came of it, but the threats were never ignored. In Captain Allee's case, his Company had good reason to believe in the threats because their Captain was from the old school of SOUTH TEXAS RANGERHOOD---the one that claimed ANYTHING the Rangers did was an extension of Texas law, whether it was right or not. Captain Allee took guff from no one, and in the process, made any number of enemies.

Captain Allee was Jim's first captain, a character so tough that his enemies claimed he had ice water for blood. He once told a critic, "Mister I never ATTEMPTED to arrest anyone. I either arrested him or I didn't arrest him." Even the crooks seem to recognize the wisdom in that. "Mess with anyone you want, but don't mess with a Ranger," muttered one suspect as he headed for the Nueces County jail.

It seemed that the South Texas area that Captain Allee commanded was a breeding ground for the accumulation of a century's worth of animosity and hostility. To many of the Mexican-Americans in the area, who are only a few generations removed from the original Mexican families who settled South Texas, the Rangers were "*Los Diablos Tejanos*," or Texan devils---oppressors of the poor and flunkies of the wealthy Anglo ranchers. It was certainly true at the turn of the century when cattle rustling was the name of the game with most of the rustlers coming from Mexico. Cattle was being stolen at the rate of 30,000 head or more per month with most of them being herded across the border at the lower Rio Grande. At that time, cowhide itself was more valuable than beef as a commodity. When the ranchers screamed for protection, Texas responded with Rangers who hated the Mexican bandits and did everything they could to keep the big herds in Texas.

But it's also true that many of the big South Texas ranchers, like Richard King of the King Ranch, and John Armstrong of the Armstrong Ranch, who was himself a Ranger under the legendary Leander McNelly, earning the nickname "McNelly's Bulldog," did much for the Rangers by outfitting the Companies with as many supplies and horseflesh as they needed, often at no cost to the State. Rangers never forget little things like that. And certainly not Captain Allee. He never let anyone criticize the Rangers and get away with it. His belief was that if it weren't for the Rangers, South Texas would still be a "no man's land."

Captain Alfred Young Allee, Sr., was born September 14, 1905, in Encinal, Texas, one of four generations of his family who have been Texas

66

Rangers. His grandfather, Alfred Young Allee, and his father, Alonzo W. Allee, were early-day Texas Rangers. In fact, his grandfather was something of a Texan legend with a lightning temper and quick draw. The old man once trailed a wild, vicious train- and bank-robber named Brack Cornett across the prairie before finally shooting him out of the saddle in a pitched gun battle that had both men racing their horses toward each other with two guns blazing away.

Although his grandfather died before he was born---the explosive peace officer died in Laredo, Texas, on August 19, 1896, when he was stabbed in a barroom brawl---Captain Allee took after his namesake. He learned a lot about the tradition of the force from his father, a tradition he faithfully adhered to all his life, but he thrived on the stories told about his grandfather. He was more like the old man with his daredevil attitude and quick temper than anyone in his family cared to admit. The Captain's son, Alfred Young Allee, Jr., also became a Texas Ranger.

Captain Allee's career reads like a wild west adventure, which if all the truth be known, it really was. He worked as a deputy sheriff in Zavala County before joining the Rangers in 1931. When Governor Miriam "Ma" Ferguson came to power in 1933, he resigned to become a deputy sheriff in Bee County, working out of Beeville until he rejoined the Rangers in 1935, after the despised Ferguson had been defeated at the polls. He inherited Company "D" in 1947, and by the time he was forced into mandatory retirement at age sixty-five in 1970, he had amassed an indignant element of enemies that would have paid anything to see him assassinated.

In the early 1950's and 1960's, he gained national attention fighting political bosses and breaking up farm hand strikes in South Texas. One politically corrupt County was Duval, run by George Parr, the "Duke of Duval." During the Duke's reign, enough votes were manipulated in the 1948 elections in the infamous "Box 13 scandal" to dictate the outcome of the razor-close election of a U.S. senator from Texas, a senator who later became Minority Leader, Majority Leader, Vice President and then President of the United States: Lyndon Baines Johnson. Ever after, Johnson counted Parr a bosom friend, and George Parr counted himself above the law.

George Parr had Duval County sitting in his lap, but Captain Allee played no such favorites. One particularly audacious confrontation between the two happened in the Jim Wells County Courthouse. George Parr had gone to the courthouse to answer charges of pulling a gun on a businessman, and while there, he grabbed the gun of another Ranger---a definite no-no in any Ranger book, especially Captain Allee's.

Captain Allee was on Parr like a tick on a dog. "I caught the gun and twisted it out of his hand," Allee told a reporter covering the incident, "and pulled my gun. I told him, 'Loose your hand up and let me have that gun, or I'll kill you right here.'"

When the United Farm Workers organized a strike in Starr County in 1967, Captain Allee waded in with characteristic vigor. The Valley, along with California and Florida, is the Nation's major producer of fruits and vegetables. Any strike there cripples the economy throughout the land. The Captain arrested a minister and his wife, who were not carrying pickets, delivered a concussion to an organizer, and informed demonstrators that the Rangers would do whatever it took to break the strike. He broke the strike, all right, but his rough exterior and stern measures promptly resulted in charges of brutality against the mostly Mexican-American farm hands, charges he adamantly denied. Although he remained unrepentant, his behavior was vilified clear to the United States Supreme Court. Eight years later, with his antics still a sore spot throughout Texas, his son, Ranger Alfred Allee, Jr., was denied permission to go to Presidio to assist in a strike organized by Cesar Chavez. "We saw what mess your dad got us into before," young Allee was told.

In the wake of the farm worker strikes, critics began to ask DPS officials why there hadn't been a Mexican-American Ranger present. The implications didn't faze Captain Allee one bit. "I don't see any Japanese here," he snapped at the critics. "I don't see any Chinamen. We can't hire every doggone breed there is in the United States."

About a year before he retired, the Captain helped thwart a breakout in the Dimmit County Jail in Carizzo Springs. The inmates, led by a prisoner sentenced to life in the State Penitentiary, had broken into the deputy's apartment downstairs and captured his guns. By the time the Captain arrived with Ranger Joaquin Jackson, tear gas poured out the windows, and the prisoners wanted to talk terms.

"You want to talk," Captain Allee hollered, "I'll give you till the count of ten to come out of there." He then counted off in a loud voice, reached the number ten, and proceeded up the stairs of the jail, clearing the way with a scattergun. When the two Rangers got inside, they found four men in the drunk tank huddling under two, low metal bunks.

"Until this day, none of those men have been back in jail," said Joaquin Jackson with a laugh. "I figured it was a good cure for alcoholism."

The Captain also had a heart as big as a washtub when the occasion called for it. Ranger Jackson remembers the Captain reaching into his pocket, withdrawing his wallet, and buying many a meal for many a derelict. "On the other hand," said Jackson, "if you were in the wrong, he'd likely shoot you dead."

Captain Allee was the focus of much fear and contempt. Many people hated his guts. Sued and investigated several times for his conduct

68

in South Texas, he readily admitted to assaulting attorneys, smacking a Mexican labor organizer over the head with a rifle butt, and pistol-whipping George Parr. Still, it was sheer folly to think anyone could bring him down---he lived with a machine gun and knew well how to use it.

The height of the assassination scare occurred over the Christmas holidays of 1969. At that time, the headquarters of Company "D" was at Carizzo Springs because that was where the Captain had his ranch. Carizzo Springs is also only a rock's throw from the Mexican border. Fearing their Captain might be wounded or killed, with the assassin escaping into Mexico and out of their clutches, several Rangers, including Jim Peters, John Wood, Joaquin Jackson, Glenn Krueger, and Dudley White, thought it prudent to camp at the ranch for a few days.

Jim had never known anyone quite like the Captain. The man was as mean as a snake and absolutely fearless, yet totally protective of his family and men. Even on the verge of retirement, Jim didn't think the Captain appeared old. The tough Ranger still carried authority like a bullwhip.

Captain Allee and his wife Pearl lived in a nice, spacious ranch house on the ranch right outside town. That part of the country is fairly flat and desert-like, but it does harbor enough low mesquite and scrub brush to offer cover for illegal Mexicans stealing northward---or for anyone seeking a retaliation ambush.

The house itself sprawled in a clearing well back from the main road, and the clearing extended for a hundred or so yards in all directions surrounding the house. Also living on the property in a house trailer near the main house was Pearl Allee's sister, and the sister graciously volunteered the use of her trailer to the Rangers as a bunkhouse for the duration of their stay. She moved into the main house where she said she felt safer because of the Captain's machine gun.

Since the house and trailer would obviously be the main targets for any assassination attempt, the Rangers discussed the best method of securing the perimeter around the clearing surrounding the two buildings. One suggestion was to post a guard all night, but that was quickly squelched when someone pointed out that they weren't guarding a campfire on the trail. It would take an army to adequately cover the large area around the house.

Another suggestion was to booby trap the doors and windows of the house, but that plan was discarded as being too flimsy. Finally, they settled on booby trapping the entire area. Using all their ingenuity, the Rangers "wired" the house, the trailer, and surrounding brush with all sorts of apparatus strung out on fishing line. There was absolutely no way anything or anyone could have ever penetrated the perimeter without them knowing it.

Along about midnight, the Rangers all retired---the Captain to his ranch house, and the others to the house trailer. Jim's friend, Dr. H. A. "Cap" Hodges, describes best what happened next:

"They were all sound asleep in the trailer, secure in the knowledge that NOTHING could get by their booby traps, when out of the blue, that machine gun went off with a burst of bullets that must have stampeded cattle in all directions. No one had heard any of the booby traps sounding the alarm, so the machine gun chatter spooked the entire camp. "The men raced from the trailer pulling on their trousers, their adrenalin pumping at an all time high, pointing their guns into the darkness, trying to see everywhere at once. When that machine gun went off with a second blast, they all hit the dust. It was so dark no one could even see the Captain. All they could see was the fire from the muzzle of the gun as the Captain blasted the bushes.

Racing up to the Captain, Jim yelled, 'Where are they? How many did you get?' "Captain Allee stood in a crouched stance scanning the dark, the machine gun primed and ready for another blast. It was so quiet that not even the breeze stirred. 'Well, if it's a man, we'll find him in the morning,' the Captain finally drawled, 'and if it's one of the cows, we'll have barbecue tomorrow.'"

When Captain Allee retired in 1970, John Wood became the new Captain of Company "D." Headquarters for the Company then moved to San Antonio and John Wood along with it, leaving Jim to work the three counties alone with occasional help from fellow Rangers Glenn Krueger of Beeville and Steve Black. John Wood remained Captain of Company "D" until he retired in 1978. Jack Dean then became Captain of Company "D," and Jim worked under him until Jim retired in 1987. Captain Jack Dean is now retired from the Rangers, but he remains in law enforcement as the United States Marshal for the Southern District, a position he attained March 1, 1994.

Captain Allee died at age eighty-one after a bout with cancer. "He was hard, and he was stern, but he helped a lot of kids out of his own pocket," said Jack Dean.

DOYLE SKILLERN

It was the beginning of June, and South Texas was already becoming uncomfortably warm with temperatures soaring into the 90's every day. Temperature changes never really bothered Jim all that much, as he liked the outdoors in good weather or bad, but early that June, for days on end, the normal 15-knot offshore winds were unusually still. With the ever-present high humidity and no cooling breezes, sweat just rolled down his body each time he stepped outside. It got to where he welcomed every opportunity to enjoy the air-conditioned confines of his office or car, only that kind of activity seemed to dull his senses. He was a tracker, a physical hunter. He thrived on knocked-down, dragged-out investigations of the worst sort.

The locals have a saying: "If you don't like the weather, stick around for a day or so, and it will change." And it always does, only that June, it was later than usual in coming. After nearly a week of no wind, high humidity, and temperatures close to 100 degrees, the heat index felt like 120 degrees in the shade. Everybody's nerves were raw, and it was all the authorities could do the keep up with the complaints. When the cooling offshore breezes did return, they brought with them an investigation that used all of Jim's intuitive powers to crack. He relished every minute of it.

It began with a phone call from a local attorney, who was deeply concerned about a missing client of his. The missing man, Milton Skillern, was the wealthy heir to the Texas chain of Skillern's Pharmacies. He was also notorious for his business acumen and work ethics, and everyone in the business community knew it. In fact, he positively glowed with punctuality. He visited all his pharmacies every week, and knew all his employees personally. When he failed to show up that week, and no one knew why, one of his Corpus Christi store managers became concerned.

Milton's sister Louise* lived in Houston, and after checking with several of the other pharmacies in the chain, the Corpus Christi manager contacted her about the missing millionaire. "I'm sure everything's all right," Louise replied to the store manager's questions, "because I received a post card from him. He's on vacation in New Orleans."

After hanging up the phone, Louise retrieved the post card and studied the type-written message. It had the usual "wish you were here" greetings on the back in the fashion someone on vacation would write, and the picture side was of a French Quarter tourist scene. Yet, when she had first received it, Louise had had misgivings about it. For one thing, she had never received a TYPED post card from anyone, let alone Milton. She actually doubted that anyone would take the time to type---postcards were deliberately designed for quick correspondence when one didn't want to sit down and write a letter.

The postcard had also been carelessly signed "Skip." It was Milton's childhood nickname, and although many people knew it and called him by it, HE never used it on correspondence. He was a professional businessman right down to the last tiny detail.

The store manager's phone call bothered Louise. Although the post card held nothing that would indicate anything amiss, something just didn't appear right. It kept nagging at her. It just wasn't like Milton to go off by himself without telling her where he was going or when he would return. She had initially shrugged that discrepancy aside by chalking it up to creeping old age. After all, Milton wasn't a young man any more, and some of his habits were changing. It hadn't seemed plausible, but maybe he really had gone on vacation without telling anyone, thinking that he had. Only, how to explain that signature?

Several days earlier when she had first received the card, she had laid it aside and debated whether or not to call her brother's home in Corpus Christi. It had taken her all day to talk herself into it, only when she had finally picked up the phone and dialed, she had received no answer. Unsure of what to do next, she had finally shrugged her suspicions aside, deciding to wait and see what happened. Well, things finally happened. A store manager was concerned enough to call her about her brother's disappearance. Apparently Milton had left home without telling ANYONE what he had planned.

Louise picked up the phone and tried his residence again. Still no answer. She then began calling friends and associates, but it was already mid-day and most were at work. The ones she did reach hadn't heard from him, and the family lawyer was busy on another phone. She made a mental note to call the lawyer again in twenty minutes, and went to the mailbox.

In the mailbox was a letter from Milton. It bore a postmark from Mexico, contained newsy notes of tourism, and was neatly type-written, but the uncharacteristic "Skip" scrawled at the bottom demanded action. With a feeling of dread, she called the family lawyer and asked for advice.

The missing man's lawyer had acted immediately. He contacted the Texas Ranger office, and Jim agreed to enter the case because of the wealth of the missing man. Milton Skillern was a millionaire several times over, and if he was also the victim of a crime, the motive could be for financial gain, even if no ransom note was ever received. The usual people to profit financially in crimes of that nature were members of the immediate family.

Jim made arrangements to obtain the two pieces of questionable mail from Louise, and he sent these two documents to the Department of Public Safety's ultra-modern Crime Lab in Austin, accompanied by samples of Milton Skillern's handwriting. The report from the graphology section wasn't long in coming. The comparison signatures weren't even close; they were bad forgeries. Also, both the post card and the letter had been typed on the same machine. Jim thought it inconceivable that Milton Skillern would go on vacation carrying a typewriter with him to New Orleans and then taking the same machine to Mexico. The whole idea was ludicrous. When Jim also learned that Skillern's younger brother, Doyle, had been seen driving around town in Milton's shiny new Cadillac, Jim's Ranger senses went into overdrive.

Milton Skillern had not been seen for at least a week, maybe longer, and Jim suspected foul play. Deciding that the most obvious suspect in the disappearance of the missing millionaire was Doyle Skillern, he concentrated his investigative efforts on the younger brother. Almost immediately, he struck pay dirt. Doyle was a leech. There's no other word to describe him. He was a no-good, unemployed, whiner---a regular bum. He was always wheedling and needling Milton for money, which Milton usually supplied after a short lecture that always seemed to fall on deaf ears. Doyle was also rumored to be a narcotics addict, and his good friend, Charles Sanne, was none other than a well-known Houston police character.

Doyle had told his sister that Milton had sold the Cadillac to Charles Sanne, but Louise remained doubtful. Milton had just bought the car. He had less than five thousand miles on it, and he had voiced no complaints about the car's performance. Since he was so proud of it, it made no sense to her that he would sell it to a virtual stranger.

It made no sense to Jim, either, and he promptly obtained the new title transaction to the car from the Texas Bureau of Motor Vehicle Registration. He sent that document to the Crime Lab, and it proved to be another forgery. Jim then decided to investigate Milton Skillern's bank account. Just as he suspected, it was cleaned out. Checks and drafts had been cashed all over Corpus Christi, and most of them were marked with the notation, "Irregular Signature."

A check of Milton Skillern's post office box in Flour Bluff on the south side of Corpus Christi revealed another piece of interesting evidence. Doyle had sold his brother's furniture to a clerk in the post office. The check had been made out to Milton, but it had been endorsed on the back and cashed. Jim sent it to the Crime Lab, and it, too, proved to be another forged signature.

Jim now knew Milton Skillern was dead, but knowing it and proving it were two different things. What he needed was the body, and he had no earthly idea where to look. Deciding that the best place to start would be at Milton's residence, he drove to the exclusive waterfront home on Gallion Bay in Flour Bluff. To his surprise, he found a family living in the house!

Flour Bluff lies on the south side of Corpus Christi near the tip of Corpus Christi Bay. It is also the gateway to Padre Island National Seashore. Now incorporated as part of the city, it has a most unique history. It was once the portal for smugglers in 1838 when France blockaded the coast of Mexico during the so-called Pastry War. Unable to receive supplies in the normal manner, Mexico declared Corpus Christi a port of entry, and the badly needed supplies were then carried overland across the Rio Grande. Although only a Republic for two years and President Sam Houston didn't want to antagonize Mexico, he rallied Texans to drive the invaders from the Republic's boundaries. When the volunteers reached the area, they found the Mexicans scattered in all directions, leaving about 100 barrels of flour and parts of a steam engine. The area has been known as Flour Bluff ever since.

Flour Bluff is also home to Corpus Christi's Naval Air Station, where Jim once pulled duty as a U. S. Marine. The Station is on the Bay while the remainder of the tiny community entwines around the Laguna Madre. The area is dotted with waterways and canals lined with beautiful homes and condominiums. With boats tied at the docks and palm trees swaying in the breezes in the yards, it's a virtual paradise.

When Jim approached the new owners at Milton Skillern's house, they told him that they had bought the property just the week before and had only moved in the previous day. They knew absolutely nothing about the previous owner. In fact, they had never met the seller. All the transactions had been handled by the Realtor, and he had told them that the seller was on vacation in California. Everything had to be done through the mail and over the telephone.

A visit with the Realtor confirmed Jim's suspicions on the sale of the house. Doyle Skillern had sold his brother's property on a claim of power of attorney. Jim obtained that document and sent it to the Crime Lab. He wasn't surprised when it, too, proved to be forged.

It was now time to obtain a search warrant, and with the full cooperation from the new owners of the house, Jim went over the dwelling like Sherlock Holmes with a magnifying glass. He found a syringe and other narcotics paraphernalia hidden in a closet in the guest room, and a box of stationery identical to that of the questionable letter which had been sent from Mexico to Milton's sister, Louise. The most intriguing discoveries, however, were the new patch to the carpet in the living room and the obviously newly poured patio at the back of the house.

Jim now thought he knew where the murder had been committed and exactly where to find the missing body, but without some kind of corroborating evidence, he had no authority to just dig up the patio.

Deciding to test his theory, he again visited Skillern's bank, hoping to find a cashed check from a concrete contractor showing exactly when the new patio had been poured. He also hoped to find a cashed check from a carpet repairman for a similar date. Sure enough, both jobs had been done only days after the letter from Mexico had arrived at the sister's house in Houston. Not surprisingly, the signature on both checks also proved to be forgeries.

There was now enough probable cause for Jim to present his evidence to a magistrate and request warrants for the arrest of both Doyle Skillern and Charles Sanne for forgery. The magistrate duly issued the warrants, and the Nueces County Constable's Department duly went on the alert for the wanted pair, even though the two men were known to be in California at the time. The Realtor had mentioned that the men were on vacation, but they were due back on July 1st to collect a large check, which Doyle expected on that date.

As far as Jim was concerned, it was all over but the waiting, and he has magnificent patience. During the interim, though, he consulted with Milton's attorney and learned that the missing man was due to receive a check for $3,000 on July 1st. Reasoning that it was the check which Doyle had mentioned to the Realtor, Jim ordered the Flour Bluff post office put under surveillance. As an added precaution, he also put Milton Skillern's house under watch.

On the last day of June, around midnight, the stakeout officer at the Skillern house radioed that the suspects had just driven past in the Cadillac. Charles Sanne was behind the wheel, and Doyle Skillern sat next to him. The constable followed the pair at a discreet distance, but Sanne appeared to have no particular destination in mind. He drove aimlessly around Flour Bluff, then turned onto Padre Island Drive and headed out toward Padre and Mustang Islands. Sanne finally turned the car around and headed back toward town. He parked in front of the Flour Bluff post office. The constable joined the surveillance team at the building.

Meanwhile, Jim and officers from the Corpus Christi Police Department, the Nueces County Sheriff's Department, and the Department of Public Safety Highway Patrol converged on the scene. Greatly outnumbered, the suspects meekly surrendered. A careful search conducted on the Cadillac turned up a large amount of heroin, and the illegal possession of a controlled substance was then added to the forgery charges against them.

When Jim questioned the suspects about the missing man's whereabouts, Sanne refused to make any type of statement altogether, and Doyle arrogantly denied knowing anything. In fact, Doyle took every opportunity to impugn his brother's personal ethics. In a character assassination, Doyle claimed that Milton had been acting erratically since a recent divorce, had been drinking heavily, and had also been harassing him unceasingly about personal matters. It was only after Jim confronted Doyle with the forgeries that the suspect fell silent.

Doyle's statements still had to be investigated, although Jim already knew that Milton was beyond reproach in his business life. The millionaire was liked and admired by associates all over the State. Jim conferred with Milton's attorney and learned from the lawyer that Milton Skillern was also beyond reproach in his personal life, which didn't surprise Jim all that much. Knowing what kind of leech the younger Skillern was, it only stood to reason that Doyle would turn out to be a barefaced liar.

Although Jim had Doyle Skillern made on forgery charges, he still had to prove the younger brother guilty of murder. Up to now, all he had was circumstantial evidence---the poured patio, the patched carpet, and the forged documents---but no concrete proof that Milton Skillern was dead. It was unlikely, but the missing man really could be in Mexico. Jim had authorities on both sides of the Border searching for the millionaire. When the final break came in the case, it was a surprise straight from left field.

Shortly after Jim had conferred with Milton's lawyer, Doyle had asked to speak to the attorney. The astounded lawyer listened as the younger Skillern confessed to killing his older brother. Doyle said that he and Milton had gotten into an argument, which had led to a shouting match and then a shooting. He had asked his older brother for more money, which he always did when he was low on funds and needed to feed his narcotics addiction, only this time Milton had become extremely angry about his use of narcotics. Not only had he refused to give the money, Milton had also pulled a gun and threatened to shoot Doyle if the younger brother didn't seek help and kick the habit. When Milton cooled off enough to lay the gun down, Doyle had picked it up and shot his brother once in the head, killing him instantly. "It was an accident," Doyle claimed. "I buried his body under the new patio."

With the attorney's information, Jim obtained a court order to break up the patio and search underneath it for the missing body. Nueces County Deputy Sheriff James Duke began work on the patio with a jack hammer, as Jim stood by with a camera. When the concrete was finally broken into pieces and removed, the officers shoveled away the dirt. They found Milton Skillern's body wrapped in a bedspread. They also found a piece of carpet, a towel, and a blanket. Strangely enough, a pillow lay beneath the dead man's head.

An autopsy performed by Doctor Joseph Rupp, the Nueces County Medical Examiner, legally identified the badly decomposed corpse as that of Milton Skillern. The autopsy also revealed that the deceased had died as the result of a single gunshot wound to the head, just as Doyle had claimed. Capital murder charges were then filed against Doyle Skillern and Charles Sanne.

What followed next is another one of those strange quirks of justice which so frustrate police and prosecutors everywhere. A series of legal and technical problems resulted when Charles Sanne turned State's evidence. All charges against him were dropped, except for one count of forgery. Doyle's attorney then raised the question of whether or not Doyle's confession to Milton's attorney had any legal standing at the trial. He claimed the statement could not be used as evidence, and he demanded--- and was almost granted---a mistrial on those grounds.

When the trial finally did proceed, a juror fell ill. After another delay, the judge ordered it continued with just eleven jurors. Doyle Skillern was finally sentenced to five years in jail for murder without malice, and Charles Sanne received three years for his one count of forgery.

Considering the scope of the crime and the characters of both Doyle Skillern and Charles Sanne, Jim was disappointed. Justice had been served, but his instincts told him he would see the unsavory menaces again. He was so right.

A mere three years later, both Skillern and Sanne were released from prison, and they promptly returned to their old habits involving narcotics and crime. This brought them to the attention of the State's narcotics investigators. Although Jim wasn't officially involved in the sleuthing, he kept his Ranger eye glued to the proceedings.

On October 23, 1974, Patrick Randel, a narcotics agent working undercover for the State, arranged to buy a quantity of heroin from Doyle Skillern and Charles Sanne. He had in his possession, a large sum of marked money for the buy. Around 8:00 p.m. that evening, a state game warden stumbled across Randel's parked car about four miles east of the small town of George West. Inside lay Randel's dead body. The murdered agent's gun and the marked money were both missing.

An all points bulletin was immediately issued for Skillern and Sanne, and they were quickly apprehended a few hours later in the Rio Grande Valley. In their possession was the heroin, the marked money, and Agent Randel's service revolver.

Two days later, a sanitation worker called the Ranger headquarters in Corpus Christi and told Jim that he had found a pistol. Jim immediately drove to the scene and took possession of a .38 caliber revolver. The weapon turned out to also belong to Agent Randel, and ballistics tests revealed that it was the murder weapon.

The .38 caliber weapon was the key evidence in the trial of Skillern and Sanne. Upon conviction, Skillern was sentenced to death and Sanne to life in prison. This time, the sentences satisfied Jim. The murdering duo had finally been permanently removed from society.

THE EDNA MOATS MURDER CASE

The psychological aspect of the Ranger badge also worked in solving an Aransas Pass murder case which Jim got called to investigate. Although he was busy on another case when the Ranger Office was first contacted, and his good friend, Ranger Glenn Krueger from Beeville, made the preliminary investigation, Jim finally entered the case with his customary tenacious determination, which eventually brought the culprit to justice.

It was often the smaller communities who needed Jim's help the most because, as Commander Lou Villagomez of the Corpus Christi Police Department once explained it, "They don't have fifty detectives sitting on the force like Corpus Christi has. Their manpower has to do everything, not specialize in areas of homicide, burglary, and so on. And being small communities next to a big metropolis, suspects often cross jurisdictional lines. They need a Ranger's help. But, we use him a lot, too, and we're mighty glad to have him."

The convenience store case began right after Christmas, December 29, 1972, in the sleepy little community of Aransas Pass, located about twenty miles northeast from Corpus Christi. Aransas Pass and her sister city, Port Aransas, are year-round meccas for fishing enthusiasts. On that day in December, the temperature was a balmy seventy degrees at 11:00 a.m., and sports fishermen from all over the United States were busily pulling in record catches of mackerel, red snapper, and trout. Even the shrimp boats were disgorging huge cargoes of the pink crustaceans destined for thousands of dinner tables across the nation. The city's entire economy revolved around the shrimping, crabbing, and fishing industry, and nearly everyone living in the area had someone in the family working in the industry.

At 11:40 a.m., sixteen-year-old Sharon Burnett* rode her bicycle to a convenience store on East Commercial Way for a loaf of bread. She parked her bike outside, walked inside, and was surprised to discover the store wide open with no one in sight.

The small store was owned by Bill and Ruth Martin*, a couple who always opened it at 7:00 a.m. every day. Their clerk, Edna Moats, always arrived at 8:00 a.m, and throughout the day, there was usually two people at all times working in the store. That Friday morning, however, Ruth Martin had gone home at 11:00 a.m. to prepare lunch for her husband, and Bill Martin had left to take the previous day's receipts to the bank. He left $200 in cash in the register, plus the morning's receipts, which didn't amount to a whole lot. After making his bank deposit, he then drove home for lunch. Edna Moats was left all alone in the store.

When Sharon walked into the store for the loaf of bread, she thought Edna was busy in the back room. Seizing the bread from the shelf, Sharon walked to the counter, intending to call out for Edna's attention. It was then that the teenager noticed the cash register standing open. Looking down behind the counter toward the floor, Sharon recoiled in horror.

Edna Moats lay sprawled on the floor, her head pooled in blood. Her left eye was blackened and swollen shut. There was a tiny puckered hole in her forehead over the eyebrow, and her chin lay gashed open. A fistful of one dollar bills and loose coins was scattered all over the place. As Sharon stared in shock, her heart pounding wildly, Edna moaned and gasped for air.

The girl dropped the loaf of bread, ran to the pay phone at front of the store, dialed the operator, and in an hysterical voice, cried that she needed the police and an ambulance.

At that time, the Aransas Pass Police Department had only eight men for the small community, and even with the usual hectic events of the holidays, their case load was light. There had been a total of fifteen arrests in the past seven days. Eight of them were for traffic violations, and seven were for criminal charges. Of the criminal offenses, five were for public drunkenness and two for disorderly conduct. Crimes of violence just didn't happen in Aransas Pass.

Assistant Chief of Police Virgil Patterson and Sergeant Leo Hudgins were on patrol on the east side of town, engaged in a good-natured argument over the best place to eat lunch, when the radio mounted under the dashboard sputtered and to life. "What's your Ten-Twenty?" the dispatcher's voice demanded to know, which is police jargon for "where are you located at this very instant?"

Patterson looked over at Hudgins and shrugged his shoulders. Both knew instinctively that there would be no lunch that day. He depressed the transmitter button, gave the location of the police car, and asked what the problem was. What followed caused him and his sergeant to listen in shocked silence. "Investigate possible homicide and robbery at the grocery on Commercial Way."

The news sent the cruiser fishtailing into a screeching U-turn, as Patterson gunned the motor in his hurry to reach the grocery store. Hudgins automatically switched on the flashing overhead lights and activated the siren. In a matter of seconds they were skidding to a halt amid a cloud of dust and loose gravel in the grocery store's parking lot.

The two lawmen raced inside the store and were horrified to discover their worst fears had come true. A woman they both knew from the community lay in a pool of blood behind the counter, her chest heaving desperately, as her severely damaged brain struggled for life-giving oxygen.

Gray matter and tissue from her damaged cranium protruded from the rapidly swelling hole in her forehead.

Sergeant Hudgins leaned down behind the counter to examine Edna's wounds, trying to determine the severity of her injuries, while Assistant Chief Patterson tried to calm the now crying teenager. It took only seconds for Hudgins to realize that he could do nothing to help his wounded friend. He called over his shoulder to his superior that she had been shot in the head, and he didn't think she had a chance.

Patterson turned the crying girl over to Hudgins and raced to the patrol car. He summoned the Aransas Pass Chief of Police, Felix Turnbough. Turnbough was a veteran lawman with more than thirty years of experience. He listened quietly while Patterson described the scene, and when Patterson was through, Turnbough calmly dialed the Aransas County Sheriff's Department in nearby Rockport. The convenience story lay about 150 feet outside the Aransas Pass city limits, and jurisdiction actually lay with the county authorities, but it was only a formality. Both agencies would do everything possible to solve this crime. Chief Turnbough hightailed it to the store.

Chief Turnbough arrived just as the ambulance pulled away bearing Edna Moats to the community hospital. The chief slowly surveyed the scene. Sharon was sitting quietly off to one side sipping a Coke and answering Virgil Patterson's questions. Leo Hudgins had made a chalk outline of where Edna Moats had fallen, and had also circled a spent .25 caliber shell, which he had found lying on the floor in front of the counter. He was now in the process of searching for the bullet which he was sure had gone completely through Edna's body. The store owners had been notified and were on the way. Turnbough was satisfied that everything had been done that could be done for the moment.

At about the same time as the store owners arrived, Aransas County Sheriff Bob Hewes and Deputy Jim Russell drove up. Another Aransas Pass police car driven by Sergeant Rudy Ramirez also arrived, and with the gathering of official cars in the parking lot, spectators by the dozens began to flock to the store. Sergeant Ramirez was soon very busy handling the traffic and keeping the curiosity seekers away from the crime scene.

When Ruth Martin finally learned the details, she tearfully went to the telephone and called Edna's husband. She told him that his wife had been shot and was not expected to live, that he needed to get to the Aransas Pass Community Hospital immediately if he wanted to see his wife of twenty-five years while she was still alive.

Chief Turnbough dispatched a police officer to provide an escort, but when the distraught husband arrived at the hospital, he learned that the emergency room technicians were not prepared to handle such grave injuries as Edna's severe head wound. The injured woman had gone straight to Memorial Medical Center's trauma unit in Corpus Christi.

While the Aransas County Sheriff's Department personnel examined the crime scene for latent fingerprints and other incriminating evidence, Sheriff Hewes and Sergeant Ramirez rushed to the hospital in Corpus Christi. If Edna Moats regained consciousness, they wanted to be there to take down whatever testimony she might provide. When they arrived, however, a tense drama was already underway in the operating room. Edna Moats had sustained a bullet wound two inches above the bridge of her nose and slightly to the left of center. The .25 caliber shell had traversed through the frontal lobe of her brain and the upper cranium and had come to rest against the cranial vertebrae. The bullet's course had also created a massive brain hemorrhage, shutting off the vital supply of oxygen to the brain. If Edna lived, there was a good possibility she would remain in a vegetable state for the remainder of her life.

The woman's condition, however, rapidly deteriorated. During the operation to remove the bullet fragments, she stopped breathing. Expert hands once again restored vital signs, but she remained precariously close to death. When she was finally wheeled to a recovery room, a doctor waited tensely by her bedside. The two lawmen also waited, but Edna's wounds proved to be worse than imagined. She wasn't expected to live. The officers stood by, anyway, just in case she regained consciousness long enough to speak of her attack. The consensus was that she had known the robber or else she would not have been shot. She was far too intelligent a person to resist a holdup man.

As the two lawmen waited impatiently at the hospital, others at the crime scene were deeply involved in gathering evidence and questioning neighbors. The sheriff's men worked inside the now padlocked store where the only tangible evidence turned out to be the spent .25 caliber shell. All fingerprints from such a public place were unusable. It was a clear cut case of robbery with no leads and no suspects.

With the sheriff's men inside, Chief Turnbough instructed his men to canvass the neighborhood. They had a little better luck. A woman living nearby said she heard what sounded like a single shot coming from the store around 11:30 a.m. Another woman living across the street claimed she saw a white or light gray Ford Mustang leaving the store area at around the same time. It was driven by a dark complexioned man, who sped off at a high rate of speed.

From a lawman's point of view, one of the most frustrating aspects of living along the Gulf Coast is the myriad of small communities and large number of counties surrounding the Gulf of Mexico. "All roads lead to the water" aptly describes the situation. With the possibility of the robber fleeing practically anywhere, and the probability that he headed toward Corpus Christi, the authorities of Nueces and San Patricio counties were notified to be on the lookout for a lone male, possibly Negro, driving a white or grey Mustang.

Edna Moats died at 4:55 p.m. without ever regaining consciousness. Sheriff Hewes telephoned Chief Turnbough with the news. Robbery and assault with the intent to kill had just escalated to become "Murder One."

Realizing his small police department simply wasn't equipped to cope with a crime of this nature and magnitude, Chief Turnbough made a decision that would ultimately lead to Jim's presence, which would result in eliciting a confession from a suspect. The Chief placed a telephone call to the Texas Ranger office in Corpus Christi. Jim was out of town on another case, so Ranger Glenn Krueger from Beeville was temporarily assigned. He arrived in Aransas Pass that same evening.

Glenn Krueger immediately demonstrated his expertise in the field of criminology. He and Chief Turnbough went to the scene of the crime, and the Ranger examined the blood-spattered cash register, removing some tiny shreds of skin from the money drawer. He then telephoned Nueces County Coroner Joseph Rupp in Corpus Christi and requested an autopsy on the victim as soon as possible. He wanted particular attention paid to Edna's fingernails to ascertain if she had possibly struggled with her assailant. Krueger next tagged and filed the small envelope containing the skin that he had found on the cash register left by Edna Moats chin as she fell to the floor.

Meanwhile, over in Corpus Christi, things were progressing at a steady pace. Sheriff Bob Hewes contacted Deputy John Messer, a member of the Corpus Christi-Nueces County Organized Crime Control Unit. He told the Deputy that the driver of a white Mustang was wanted for questioning in the murder of Edna Moats.

Deputy Messer remembered a robbery case from the previous year that might have some bearing in the current investigation. He told of three men being apprehended in Robstown, a Corpus Christi "suburb" a few miles west of town. They had been driving a white Mustang. He also revealed that a white Mustang had been seen at the Methadone Clinic at Memorial Medical Center during the past week. Deputy Messer promised to detail an investigator to stakeout the clinic and apprehend the driver of the vehicle for questioning, if and when he reappeared again.

Sheriff Hewes and Sergeant Ramirez then returned to Aransas Pass and discovered that Chief Turnbough had issued a statement to the news media in which he mentioned that a man driving a white Mustang was wanted for questioning. This information elicited a flurry of phone calls from helpful citizens, and each report had to be checked out. The police station was a veritable beehive of activity.

With Sheriff Hewes, Glenn Krueger drove back to the convenience store on the outskirts of town. Their purpose was to examine the tape from the cash register, suspecting that it might reveal what the last purchase had been before the crime and also, perhaps, determine exactly how much money had been stolen in the robbery. Their examination revealed that approximately $270 was missing, $200 that Bill Martin had left in the till and $70 in the day's receipts. It was now the end of the day, and the investigators decided to call a halt for the night.

The news of Edna Moats' murder spread throughout Aransas Pass. She had been well-liked in the community, and the citizens were shocked that someone had so brutally taken her life. That evening a group of businessmen discussed the crime and decided to offer a reward for the apprehension of Edna's murderer. On Monday, they deposited $1,240 in the bank, as motivation for information leading to the arrest and conviction of Edna's murderer.

The investigators spent the weekend piecing together all the details they had uncovered. Sheriff Hewes and Glenn Krueger obtained the spent bullet that had killed Edna Moats, and sent it, along with the empty cartridge case, the skin tissue from the cash register, and the nineteen one dollar bills that had been scattered around the body, to the State Crime Lab in Austin. The autopsy results were obtained from Doctor Joseph Rupp, as well as a set of fingerprints taken from the body by County Medical Examiner Vernon Moore. The investigation then ground to a halt.

In the days that followed, the investigators checked lead after lead after lead. Nothing. Not one single scrap of new evidence turned up. The authorities knew from the State's crime lab that Edna Moats had been killed by a bullet of Remington-Peters manufacture, a .25 caliber, which had been fired from an automatic pistol, but the grooves were not sufficiently clear to determine what make of gun had fired it. The skin tissue from the cash register drawer was definitely from Edna Moats' chin, and the theory was that she had fallen against the cash register and gashed herself after being shot. There were no fingerprints on the money, and so on, and so on. If anything, all that really happened was the generation of more questions to be answered. One really puzzling clue was the one dollar bills left scattered all over the place. Why hadn't the burglar taken them?

Two weeks after the murder, with no fresh clues in the investigation, Jim entered the case. He began sleuthing where Glenn Krueger had left off. In checking everything which might have bearing on the case, he discovered that one week after Edna Moats died, Deputy Sheriff Carroll Copeland had died in a gun battle with two men in Shamrock,

Texas, in the northern part of the state. Even though he had been mortally wounded in the shoot out, Deputy Copeland had managed to return fire, wounding one of the suspects with three shots. The Deputy had stopped the men for driving a stolen car.

The car was later stopped at a roadblock ten miles inside the Oklahoma state line, and the men were returned to Texas. It turned out that they had been roaming the state stealing cars and gasoline, and they were responsible for several armed robberies. Their favorite targets were convenience stores like the one in Aransas Pass. One of the suspects even had a .25 caliber automatic pistol, but ballistics tests proved that it was not the murder weapon sought in Edna Moats' killing. A dead end.

The stakeout at the Methadone Clinic finally turned up the suspect driving the white Mustang. The man was taken into custody, and he turned out to be an addict with a long police record. Once more, it seemed that the case was solved. The man even had a .25 caliber automatic pistol in his possession when arrested, but once again ballistics tests proved that it was not the murder weapon. The suspect also had an ironclad alibi for the day of the shooting. Another dead end.

Sheriff Hewes and Chief Turnbough were engrossed in the process of checking the records of gun and ammunition sales in their jurisdiction. It seemed like an impossible task, but after ten days, they finally succeeded in checking---and clearing---forty-four .25 caliber automatic handguns. None was the murder weapon.

Everything then came to a screeching halt for the next two weeks while local officials tried to cope with the worst winter storm to hit the Gulf Coast in a century. The day before Edna Moats was killed, meteorologists all over the Western Hemisphere were glued to one of the strangest weather conditions they had ever witnessed. A massive Artic cold front was pushing down from the North just as a warm, moist tropical storm brewed in the Gulf. The two fronts were destined to meet, and weather forecasters were making no predictions about the outcome.

The Artic front finally won out. It pushed the warm, moist tropical storm back into the Gulf, and the entire Gulf Coast seized up in the resulting sub-freezing temperatures. Shrimp boats rocked idly at their moorings, secured by ice covered hawsers. Roads iced over, causing accidents by the thousands. Power lines snapped. Businesses closed. Everyone fought the unaccustomed icy weather. In the surrounding area, livestock died under the murderous front, as did the citrus groves in the Rio Grande Valley. All available police went on a twenty-four hour watch for two weeks, until the front finally loosened its cruel grip on the South Texas paradise.

When things returned to normal, Jim again worked the Edna Moats slaying. The reward money had now climbed to $1,680, and the Aransas

Pass citizens pushed for a solution. The police still received tips, and each one had to be painstakingly check out. One of the tips came from a police informer, who claimed to have seen a local degenerate flashing a large wad of bills in a waterfront bar the night after the killing. Jim immediately checked into it. The man in question had a long police record, which included a conviction for shooting another man with a .25 caliber pistol. He had then been relegated to a five-year sentence in the state penitentiary at Huntsville. The informer said the man carried a .25 Browning automatic in his boot, and he had a reputation of being a bad one to mess with---he'd shoot at the slightest provocation.

This man appeared to be an ideal suspect, but finding him proved to be tougher than first thought. Aransas Pass police discovered that the man worked on a shrimp boat that habitually sailed the Gulf Coast from Mexico to Key West, Florida. When he was home, he stayed with his mother in Aransas Pass.

Unfortunately, Jim discovered that the suspect had sailed a week earlier for the Louisiana coast, and when Jim requested that the Louisiana authorities arrest the man, they discovered that the boat had already sailed from New Orleans to Florida.

Jim immediately notified the Florida Bureau of Criminal Investigation, and investigators there began a check of all ports and harbors for the shrimping boat. The Florida authorities finally located it in Fort Meyers and arrested the suspect. The man also had a .25 caliber automatic pistol in his boot. He was charged with carrying a concealed weapon and held for Texas authorities on a charge of a suspicion of first degree murder. But, again, as with all the others, the lead petered out. The suspect had an alibi for the day of the shooting. He had been thirty miles out in the Gulf of Mexico, and half a dozen shipmates signed a sworn statement to that effect. The money he had flashed the day after Edna Moats had been killed was his share of the profits from the day's catch. Furthermore, ballistics testing on his pistol proved it was not the gun that the police wanted for the murder.

Although Jim worked other cases, he continued to run down the myriad of leads and false trails generated by people seeking to claim the reward money in Edna's murder. The three robbery suspects arrested the year before in Corpus Christi in a white Mustang were questioned about the crime in Aransas Pass. Nothing. A man was arrested in Georgetown, Texas, carrying a .25 caliber pistol stolen in Oklahoma City. Another dead end. Gun after gun was confiscated and checked in the crime lab in Austin with no match to the bullet that had killed Edna Moats. When the break finally came seven months later, it was purely by accident.

All police departments have informers, and without their help, many cases would go unsolved. In Corpus Christi, Detective Sergeant

Richard Hawkins received word that one of his informers, a young troublemaker known as Angel, wanted to see him.

Angel was a small, wiry Mexican-American who just couldn't seem to stay on the right side of the law. Although he was picked up often for various infractions, he always remained affable and friendly, willing to cooperate in any way he could. He was currently in jail on a narcotics charge, and he shared a jail cell with another addict, a handsome young Chicano from Aransas Pass known as Tony Rodriquez.

"Say, Mr. Hawkins," Angel preened, strutting proudly before the detective like a banty rooster on parade. "I'm a pretty good detective, too."

"What do you mean, Angel?"

"I know how to interrogate. I found you a murderer." Angel was positively gloating.

It turned out that Angel and Tony had gotten into a bragging contest in their jail cell with each one trying to "out best" the other in reprehensible activities. Angel had finally conceded the contest when Tony admitted that he had "wasted a woman in a holdup a few months ago."

"Where did the holdup take place?" the sergeant asked.

"Up the coast, man. Some grocery store."

Sergeant Hawkins immediately suspected that Tony Rodriquez might be involved in the Edna Moats slaying. He advised Angel of the reward and asked him to glean as much information as possible from Tony. Since Sergeant Hawkins and Jim were good friends---indeed, they shared an apartment together---he knew Jim was working on the case. He promptly picked up the phone and dialed Jim with the information. The two of them conferred with Chief Turnbough, who assisted in running a background check on Tony Rodriquez.

It turned out that young Tony had a history of delinquency almost from the moment he was born on April 15, 1953. Tony was a twin, but the labor was difficult, and his mother died shortly after giving birth. Since his father was an alcoholic and not up to caring for the boys, they were shuttled between various relatives and a series of foster homes for the first four years of their life. When the father also died, the boys were declared wards of the state and placed in the Catholic Orphanage in Laredo.

While his brother was studious and pleasant, growing up to become a successful businessman, Tony was sullen and rebellious. He was finally sent to Youth City outside Driscoll, a tiny community a few miles west of Corpus Christi. Youth City was a place where troubled boys and girls could receive guidance and counseling, only Tony wasn't having any of that, either. He escaped any number of times. When he was discharged at the age of eighteen, he was a hot-tempered, hard-faced youth already thoroughly schooled in crime and drugs. Over the next year, his rap sheet filled with one arrest after another.

Tony finally ended up in Aransas Pass where he married a girl from a good family. He promptly moved in with his new in-laws, but he refused to work a steady job. Instead, he spent most of his time hanging out with the groups of delinquents he called friends, and tension began to grow between Tony and his wife.

Jim decided to talk to the family, and under his skillful questioning, he gathered more evidence against Tony, who was now the prime suspect in the Edna Moats murder. Jim learned that Tony had bought a pistol the day before the crime, and the family hadn't seen it since. Tony had also disappeared for about a week right about the time of the murder.

Jim then went treasure hunting, trying to locate the store that had sold Tony a gun in the last few days of 1972. Aransas Pass had already been checked and cleared by the city police, so Jim decided the best place to start looking for a gun transaction was in Tony's favorite hangout of Ingleside, a tiny community a stick's throw down the road from Aransas Pass. He struck pay dirt almost immediately. Tony Rodriquez had purchased a .25 caliber Colt automatic pistol and one box of ammunition on Thursday, December 28th.

Armed with this information, Jim returned to the Police Department in Corpus Christi, where he joined Sheriff Bob Hewes from Aransas County and Sergeant Richard Hawkins. They held a conference for a few moments, while Jim advised them of his findings. Sergeant Hawkins then reported that Angel claimed Tony Rodriquez had killed a grocery story clerk in Aransas Pass around the beginning of the New Year. Sergeant Hawkins sent for Tony Rodriquez to be brought to the office.

Tony was an attractive young man, only twenty years old, and full of cocky arrogance from years of running around with a rough crowd. He also wasn't quite yet ready to talk.

"Let him think about it a little while," Sergeant Hawkins said to Jim and the Sheriff, who were waiting in another room. "He'll come around." Hawkins, like his good friend Jim, was an astute judge of character. He advised Jim and Sheriff Hewes to have a cup of coffee with him.

The three lawmen found a quiet spot to drink their coffee, and Jim and Sheriff Hewes sat down in nervous anticipation, practically biting their fingernails at the delay. They wanted to get in the interrogation room and question Rodriguez, and it was killing them to sit idly by and drink coffee. Sergeant Hawkins, on the other hand, remained relaxed and laid back. He was the exact antithesis of the other two men---the situation didn't bother him one bit.

Sensing his cohorts anxiety, Sergeant Hawkins grinned and said,

"Relax. Give him more time."

It was, however, one thing for the good Sergeant to say it, and quite another for his friends to obey. After fifteen minutes, Sergeant Hawkins left the room to check on the prisoner. He returned, still grinning, and said, "Nope, still not ready yet. Give him a few more minutes. Won't be long now." Jim and Bob Hewes groaned in unison and slouched deeper in their seats.

When Sergeant Hawkins finally judged Tony to be ready, Jim and Sheriff Hewes eagerly entered the room. After acknowledging Jim's Ranger introduction, Tony blurted out, "I'll tell you anything you want to know, Ranger."

Sergeant Hawkins tossed Jim a knowing wink, as Tony broke completely down and bawled like a baby.

Tony Rodriquez signed a detailed confession and volunteered to reenact the crime. He explained how he had purchased the gun in Ingleside and had then driven to a swampy area near Aransas Bay to fire two dozen rounds through the weapon at tin cans. Later that evening, he had gone to a waterfront tavern in Corpus Christi and scored some drugs. High on both LSD and marijuana the next morning, he had killed Edna Moats. He said he had gotten into an argument with his wife, walked out of the house, and rather than go back in and face her again, he had driven to the convenience store for a box of matches.

When he got the to grocery store, he had the .25 caliber automatic weapon in his right front pocket. After noticing that there was only one woman, about fifty years old, in the store running the cash register, he got the matches and paid for them. Then, as he was walking out the front door, he remembered the gun in his pocket. "I got the idea to rob the place," he told Jim. He said he had looked around the store, found there were no other customers, and had taken the gun from his pocket, demanding that Edna Moats hand over all the money in the cash register.

"She said OK," Tony confessed, "and she took the $20.00 bills out of the register and handed them to me. It made me kind of mad because I had told the woman 'all the money.' I repeated, 'Lady, give me all the money.' This time, she just took out the $10.00 bills and handed them to me. I got madder and said, 'Lady, ALL THE MONEY.' She reached back to the register and took out the $5.00 bills and handed them to me. So, I just pulled the trigger on the gun and shot the lady in the forehead over the eye. She made a noise like she was gasping for air, then fell on the floor behind the check-out counter. I walked out of the store, got in my car and drove back to my house. I got a total of $230.00 from the robbery."

Tony then told Jim how he had gone into the backyard of his mother-in-law's home and dug a shallow hole, dropped the gun into it, and covered it over with dirt. He had then hopped into his white Ford, driven to Corpus Christi, bar-hopped until midnight, scored some more drugs, checked into a motel, and finally succumbed to the narcotic effects of his drug habit, forgetting all about the day's murder. A week later, he dug up the gun, drove to the swampy area where he had done his target practicing, and tossed the weapon as far as he could out into the waters of Aransas Bay.

Tony Rodriquez took the lawmen to the pond where he had first used the weapon, and the authorities searched for empty shell cases from his target practice. He then showed the lawmen where he had tossed the weapon off the bridge. Scuba divers were promptly assigned to search the bottom of the bay for the murder gun, but in spite of an intensive underwater search, no trace of the weapon was ever found. Jim theorized that the tide had carried it deep into Aransas Bay.

With Tony's confession and reenactment of the crime, a puzzling detail was finally cleared up. No one could understand why nineteen one-dollar bills had been scattered all over the place. It turned out that Tony had simply gotten mad that he had had to ask Edna for each denomination of bills. When she had finally picked up the one-dollar notes, he shot her in a fit of rage. Falling to the floor, she had dropped the bills, scattering them everywhere.

Tony confessed that he had had a sense of shame, a deep feeling of remorse for what he had done. Late on the night of the murder, he had driven to the convenience store's parking lot, sat in his automobile, and cried.

Late that summer, Angel, Sergeant Richard Harkens police informer, quietly claimed the reward money. In November 1973, Tony Rodriquez was sentenced to sixty years in the state penitentiary at Huntsville for the robbery-murder of Edna Moats.

PERSONAL REMINISCES

Although Jim is an experienced lawman and has pulled his gun many times in the course of duty, he has never had to use it on anyone, which is totally amazing considering that the early Texas Rangers were known to shoot first and then tell a suspect to "put up your hands." Thus, it came as quite a shock to his friends when he shot his first and only man---himself. It was a freak accident and one that never should have happened. It nearly cost him his life.

It was mid-summer of 1973, and Jim planned a fishing trip with one of his helicopter pilot friends, who lived in Portland, the small town on the other side of Corpus Christi Bay. Since the sun peeks over the horizon around 5:30 a.m. at that time of year and wanting to get a head start on all the other avid fishermen, who also head out at the crack of dawn, Jim was up a full hour before daylight loading his fishing equipment---the fishing tackle box, the fishing tackle, life vest, sandwiches, and so forth---into his car. One of the items that he wanted to take was a big, heavy, 48-quart ice chest. He planned on being gone all day, and he needed someplace to store the whopping amount of fish he planned to catch.

Jim wasn't married then, and he shared an apartment on Santa Fe Street with Detective Sergeant Richard Hawkins of the Corpus Christi Police Department. It was a modest, two-bedroom, upstairs apartment, having just a little alcove for a hallway which acted like a noise tunnel funnelling every little squeak to the bedrooms adjacent to it. To keep from waking Hawkins, Jim stole around like a cat burglar on tippy-toes, while he lugged the miscellaneous equipment out the door, down the stairs, and over to his car.

Outside, it was as dark as molasses in a syrup barrel, the moon and stars being obscured by the customary cloud cover which usually hangs over the city each summer night like a pall when the fog rolls in. There were also only a few mercury vapor street lamps strategically placed at each end of the long parking lot, and they provided practically no illumination for the middle of the lot where Jim parked his car. He had to carefully pick his way around the bushes, palm trees, and children's toys, as he stumbled over the dew-drenched grass. His gear clattered and clicked, banging against his body as he walked.

He made several trips down to the car with the fishing gear, which he neatly stacked in a pile near the left real wheel, before deciding to tackled the big, cumbersome ice chest. It wasn't one of the lightweight, Styrofoam models of today. It was heavy and awkward, and not wanting to drag it, he struggled out the door and down the stairs, stopping to pause for breath at the bottom before staggering on with it to the car.

91

Like all Rangers, Jim never leaves home without a gun. "Once a Ranger, always a Ranger" seems to be the credo of the force. Since Jim is always ranging no matter where he goes or what he does, he has to be prepared for every situation, good or bad. Also like all Rangers, he keeps the hammer half-cocked.

One of his favorite pistols is a over-and-under .38 caliber derringer. It's small enough to tuck anywhere he might want to carry it without being in the way, and it's just as intimidating to the lawbreaker as any other pistol.

On his last trip to the car, he carefully tucked the derringer into his right front pants pocket, intending to put it under the front seat when he reached the vehicle. At the car, however, he made his first order of business to load the awkward ice chest into the back seat. And it was no easy feat. The big monster was totally unyielding.

Jim squirmed, and he tugged, and then he gave it a mighty shove. He finally maneuvered it to where he wanted it in the back seat, leaving enough room for the fishing tackle. In the contortions of straining across the seat with the heavy ice chest, however, his pistol worked its way to the edge of the pocket. When he backed out of the car, the gun fell to the ground in such a fashion that it landed on the hammer. The half-cocked safety broke, and the gun fired.

The bullet tore into Jim's right eye, catching it at the outer corner and exiting to lodge at the inside corner at the nose. The force of the impact knocked him over backwards, and he lay like a dead man on the ground. "I don't know how long I lay on my back until my senses returned," he said. "It could have been a few short seconds or several long minutes. Time just stood still. The only thought I had was, 'What happened?'"

When Jim was finally able to think straight, he instantly knew he had been shot in the head. He didn't know how badly hurt he was, but he suspected he would die if he didn't get immediate help. Still, he did not panic.

Jim's always been a tough, logical Ranger, the kind of man who can put pain and suffering aside if the situation called for it. He forced himself to take stock of his situation. It was so early in the morning that no one was up. In his travels back and forth between the apartment and the car, he had seen no lights of any kind in any of the neighboring apartments. He hadn't even made enough noise to awaken Richard Hawkins, so he knew the detective wasn't running to his rescue upon hearing the sound of gunfire. He also couldn't hear any traffic sounds out on Santa Fe Street, which can sometimes be compared to the Indianapolis Speedway during daylight hours, but that didn't really mean anything, either, because he didn't think he could move in order to drag himself to the street.

Not knowing how long he would have to lie on the ground before help arrived, he concentrated on finding his gun. " I thought that if I could find my gun, I could shoot into one of the nearby apartment windows. The breaking glass would awaken someone, thus calling attention to my plight and summoning help."

With his long, sensitive fingers searching through the blades of wet grass, he lay on his back and carefully groped about in the darkness until he located the weapon. He knew it had to be nearby, just inches away. It was also then that he realized that he really could move. In excruciating pain, he forced himself to get up and stagger back upstairs to the apartment. He told a shocked Richard Hawkins to "take me to the hospital. I shot myself."

Sergeant Hawkins broke all speed records getting Jim to the emergency room of Memorial Medical Center, where a well-known eye specialist, Doctor John Sohocki, was immediately called to ascertain the damage. Although bad, Jim was extremely lucky. He lost only the right eye. There was no damage to his other eye or to any other part of his head. When he left the hospital, he wore a black eye patch which gave him a rakish, pirate appearance for several months---until Doctor Sohocki made a false eye and attached it to the proper places in the back of the socket. Jim was off work only two weeks after the accident.

There did occur a few minor inconveniences, though. Jim is right-handed, and since he no longer had a right eye, he had to learn to shoot a rifle and shotgun left-handed, which was a BIG bother on his first bird hunting trip after the incident. Although he took up target practice every day with his pistols and long guns, he had some really dramatic depth-perception problems. The shots were not wide to the left and right of the target. They were usually far too short or way too long from the target. It took weeks before he could shoot as well with his left hand as with his right.

He still has this depth-perception problem, but it is no longer pronounced. For instance, he can now go into restaurants and not knock over his iced tea. He can also pick up pencils and larger items from the floor. But if reaching for small objects, like loose coins or candy, it is another matter. It takes total concentration if he doesn't want to miss.

Another inconvenience is driving. Jim has always been an expert behind the wheel, thanks to his many years on the stock car circuit around Austin prior to becoming a lawman. And because he enjoys driving almost to the point of calling it a hobby, the sudden lack of eyesight on his right side is a true nuisance. No matter what he ever wants to see on that side, he has to always turn his head completely to the right---or drive around the block to take another look.

If Jim calls driving a minor inconvenience., he calls backing the car a downright challenge. He cannot look over his right shoulder and see where he is going when he is backing his car. And no amount of walking around the vehicle prior to moving it---a rule he always practiced long before it was a recommended safety precaution endorsed by the Texas Department of Public Safety---could prevent the unexpected from popping into the picture on his blind side, such as a car turning the corner or a child whizzing down the street on a bicycle. He always has to turn almost completely around in the seat to ascertain that the way is clear. When he got married a year later and started his own family, he established a rule for his children's protection: NO PLAYING BEHIND PARKED CARS, EVER.

Jim met his wife through his good friend Richard Hawkins. The two men used to spend some of their free time together at the various country and western dance halls, where they enjoyed the singing, shared a few beers, and had a lot of laughs. Richard eventually struck up a relationship with the lead singer in one of the bands, and he began dragging Jim all over South Texas following the band's engagements. His girlfriend also had a best friend who was a singer. Her name was Lydia.

Lydia is a tiny brunette having a warm, friendly smile and big, brown eyes that can easily swallow a man whole. At the time Jim met her, she was a very popular country and western singer, having a promising career singing with such top western bands as George Jones and Willie Nelson. In fact, she was under contract to Willie Nelson at the time. But from the beginning, she absolutely captivated Jim. They were married in July 1974. (Lydia still teases that he only wears his eye patch to attract the ladies.)

Jim and Lydia have two daughters, Shelly and Janna, and like any proud father, Jim spent a lot of time with his girls, particularly as they got old enough for him to take to the store, to school, or just around the block. He doted on his daughters, spoiling them rotten with anything they wanted. But Jim was an officer of the law, and it meant that he had special considerations to think about around the house. For instance, what to do with his Ranger life when he wasn't using it? He could no longer leave files out because some of the photographs and other materials were too disturbing. Likewise with his weapons and other paraphernalia.

He solved the problem by locking everything in the trunk of his car, except his weapons, which he either wore or had under his control at all times.

There was one item, however, which he felt comfortable leaving lying around. It was his Ranger hat. If his daughters latched onto it, they couldn't hurt themselves, and it wasn't too unusual to find one prancing around the house with it on her head. In the car, since he was too tall to wear it while sitting in the driver's seat, he'd normally just shuck it into the back seat with the girls, whenever he took them anywhere. All that changed the day Janna went along for a ride to the store.

Janna was about four or five years old at the time, and she squealed in delight when her daddy asked if she'd like a trip to the grocery store. It was before the seat belt rule went into effect, and the little girl stood proudly at her daddy's right ear, leaning over the front seat, looking out the window, and in general, paying little attention to anything happening around her. When her daddy came to the first of several stop signs, he carefully made sure the little girl knew he was slowing the car by telling her to, "Hang on, now." But when he took off, he issued no such warning. Janna tumbled into the back seat.

"Uh-oh," the little girl said, and Jim turned around in the front seat to take a look. Janna wasn't hurt, but his straw hat was destroyed. The crown was smashed flat, there was a rip on one side, and a large crease graced the back where the straw had distressed. Jim ruefully assessed the damaged and decided there was no way of getting around it---he needed to get another hat. He made a detour to the department store, bought another Stetson for fifty dollars, tossed it onto the back seat, and proceeded on to the grocery store.

On his way home, he stopped at another stop sign. When he took off, Janna again tumbled into the back seat. "Uh-oh..." Another hat destroyed.

After buying the second fifty dollar Stetson straw hat in the space of one hour, Jim decided to install a hat holder to the roof of the car. And ever since that day, when he climbs behind the wheel, he slips his hat into the rack and doesn't worry about it any longer.

Jim has always had a strong belief in the importance of the continuity of the family, having learned from his parents that love and affection are handed down generation to generation. And he has always taken advantage of every opportunity to show his family that they were first and foremost in his life. As a highway patrol officer, his father was often a ride-along passenger in his patrol car. When he got married, he devoted his time to Lydia and the girls. Because of his tremendous loyalty to his family, it would be easy to pigeonhole him as "too good to be true." But make no mistake; Jim is as tough a Texas Ranger as they come.

Jim does have a melancholy side, though, and it's one that the public never sees. When his parents died of old age, it left a hole in his life that still aches. Pioneers to the last, his parents left in their wills that their bodies were to be donated to medical science. "I don't have a grave, a physical place to mourn, but it was their wish," he says quietly.

At about the same time that Jim became a Highway Patrol Officer, his brother Bud was also a member of the Department of Public Safety.

Bud's duty assignment was the area around Harlingen in the Rio Grande Valley, and both brothers were ecstatic to be working in law enforcement agencies stationed so close to each other. Bud had been only eight years old when Jim had left home, and although both brothers had become fast friends while working the stock car circuit around Austin, Jim knew they would grow much, much closer now. And he was right.

In 1980, Governor Bill Clements decided to visit selected sites around the State. Since it is the policy for Texas Rangers to provide security and transportation for the State's Chief Executive on such occasions, Jim hopped in his Ranger car and whizzed down the highway to Harlingen to meet the plane for the Valley segment of the Governor's tour. He also promptly called Bud and asked if Bud would like to help, which Bud was more than delighted to do. While the Governor was busy at ceremonies doing his thing, the two brothers could then visit and do theirs.

On the appointed date, Jim and Bud waited patiently on the tarmac at the Harlingen airport for the Governor's plane to land. They leaned up against Jim's Ranger car, engaged in idle chatter, with one ear tuned to the car radio, trying to determine how much longer the Governor's plane would be. Suddenly, Jim remembered to clean out the back seat of his car. He didn't have a whole lot in the back seat, just an overnight bag carrying his shaving kit and toiletries, a first aid kit, a few blank forms, notebooks, papers, and things like that. He gathered it all together in his arms, walked to the back of the car, bent over, and neatly laid the armload in the trunk next to his shot gun, bullet-proof vest, bedroll, tear gas grenades, tear gas gun, gas mask, riot mask, tool kit, and C-rations. Rrriippp! The whole back seam of his pants ripped completely out from the crotch to the waistband.

Jim was positively horrified. Here he was, one of Texas' finest, standing on the tarmac with his pants ripped out and the Governor's plane already in view on its landing approach! There was absolutely no time to hunt up another pair of pants.

He leaned back into the trunk and frantically searched for a stapler, but the only one he could find was the kind that he used to tack notices on trees or bulletin boards. It did not pinch together like most paper staplers and was worthless for what he had in mind.

"Bud," Jim yelled to his brother, who was still leaning idly against the car watching the plane land, totally unaware of what had happened. "Run back inside and borrow a stapler. Quick!"

Bud turned around, grinned at the damage, and ran into the airport terminal. He was back in seconds.

The men's rest room was just inside the building. With the Governor's plane taxiing to the car, Jim raced into the room, shucked his pants, and quickly sealed the seam with a row of staples all along the fold of fabric. He got back to the car just as Governor Clements deplaned. The Governor's itinerary was such that all day long Jim had no opportunity to acquire another pair of pants. And all day long those staples grabbed and pinched in places better left unmentioned.

Jim and Bud were always best friends, and each instinctively trusted in the other. A year or so before the Governor Clements incident at the Harlingen airport, Bud had become very ill with kidney problems. He was eventually diagnosed with cancer of the kidney, and when chemotherapy and radiation treatments failed to shrink the tumors, doctors resorted to removing a badly diseased right kidney. For ten years, everything seemed to be okay, and Bud did fine with only one kidney.

But in 1989, Bud developed severe problems in his remaining kidney. Doctors ran a series of tests and determined that he had more tumors. The disease had also spread to nearby organs, and one tumor had already grown up into his heart. He was given only months to live. Although he quietly accepted the diagnosis, he wasn't yet ready to lie down and die. He had a few aces up his sleeve, and one of those aces was his brother. He asked Jim to hypnotize him.

Jim had gone back to school in 1980 to become a Certified Hypnotist for the Texas Rangers, and it wasn't unusual for him to travel all over the country assisting other law officers with hypnosis. Although doctors are good hypnotists, they are not good from a criminal investigator's standpoint because they tend to ask leading questions. Jim doesn't ask leading questions, and under his careful examination, victims of crime remember details of the event. Hypnotism can even help them recall very traumatic events that their conscious mind has suppressed. In 1994, for instance, he took one witness back nineteen years to remember details about the murder of an Alice police officer which the witness had long forgotten

When Bud asked for a hypnosis session, Jim readily agreed. He had already helped his daughters and their friends on many occasions cram for exams through hypnosis. He would now help his brother live through hypnosis.

Under hypnosis, a person never loses consciousness. Instead, the individual just deeply relaxes, completely at peace, with sagging facial muscles, twitching eyelids, and so on, as the subconscious mind kicks into gear. Since it also helps if the person can imagine a scene or situation as a third person spectator instead of a first person participator, Jim asked Bud if he had any thoughts on the matter.

"Yeah," Bud said. "I like the idea of Star Wars and the ray guns."

With Jim's help, Bud devised a method that had little space ships entering his system and traveling throughout his body eliminating the bad cells and shrinking the tumors with laser blasts from the ray guns. Hypnosis proves that the human mind is a powerful tool. Using his Star Wars and ray guns method. Bud had his other kidney removed, beat the cancer with his mind and chemotherapy, and gave himself three more good years of life. He died in 1992, leaving a wife and two grown sons.

THE LEONARD FREEMAN CASE

It was July 19, 1973, and Jim was involved from the outset on the case in nearby Atascosa County because the deputy sheriff and his wife had been taken hostage at gunpoint. As Jim sped to the scene, he received word on his radio that the case had escalated into a bizarre double murder with the suspect fleeing into the brush on foot. Before the fugitive would be caught and arrested, the case would involve three Sheriff's Departments, the DPS highway patrol, Chiefs of Police all along the route, the FBI, and three Rangers of Company "D."

The deputy sheriff incident happened on one of the hottest days of the year. For almost a week, there was none of the customary wind that is so usual in summer in the Hill Country of South-Central Texas, and without the wind, the humidity crept to an all-time high. It was sticky-wet, even in the shade, and anyone outdoors just wilted. The uncomfortable temperature also played havoc with the nerves, causing tempers to flare, patience to disappear, and southern hospitality to slip into low gear.

Around 1:30 p.m., Leonard Freeman, a handsome young man of twenty-eight and an ex-convict from Houston, stopped his flaming red sports car at a gas station about two miles south of the tiny town of Charlotte in western Atascosa County. After filling his car with gas, he asked the station attendant, Winston Wiley, for a piece of wiring that the attendant did not have. Freeman's behavior was so threatening that Wiley became frightened. Just as Wiley though he was about to be robbed, a county deputy sheriff drove into view. Freeman took one look at the official car, hopped into his own, and sped off with a squeal of tires in a cloud of dust.

The Atascosa County sheriff's deputy was Luis Garza, and the suspicious manner in which the red sports car had left the gas station prompted him to stop it for questioning. Deputy Garza also had his wife, Elida, in the county car with him, and while a shocked Winston Wiley looked on helplessly from a distance, Leonard Freeman somehow managed to get the drop on Deputy Garza and his wife. At gunpoint, Freeman forced the officer's wife to drive the red sports car, while he and Deputy Garza followed in the county vehicle.

Wiley raced into the gas station and called for help. He described the suspect as being about six feet tall, 180 pounds, with blond hair and blue eyes. The man was wearing a white and blue sports shirt, blue bell-bottom pants, white belt and white shoes. Moments later, sheriff's deputies, Department of Public Safety highway patrol officers, and Texas Rangers Jim Peters and Jack Van Cleve were rushing to the area from different directions, searching for the missing hostages and the lone gunman.

About a half hour into the search, DPS officers found both victims and both cars at an abandoned farmhouse several miles south of Charlotte. Elida Garza was dead at the scene. Her husband was critically wounded with gunshots in the head and shoulder. Luis Garza died without ever regaining consciousness a few hours later in a San Antonio hospital, fifty miles away.

In searching the red sports car, DPS officers discovered it was a car rented in San Antonio by a thirty-three-year-old Dallas man, Terrell Cookston, Jr. Officials also learned that Cookston had arrived at the car rental agency in the company of two other men and in a car bearing Arkansas license plates. An All Points Bulletin was issued for the arrest of Cookston on charges of murder. It stated that the suspect was considered armed and extremely dangerous, and all caution should be exercised in apprehending the fugitive. Authorities wouldn't learn until it was all over that Leonard Freeman, instead of Cookston, was driving the car.

As far as Jim knew, the only real lead was that the gunman had escaped into the brush on foot after shooting the Garzas. But, did the gunman get picked up by either of the other two men seen to be with him at the rental car agency? Jim mulled it over as he sped down Highway 140 in Atascosa County toward Charlotte to assist Ranger Jack Van Cleve at the scene. Before he reached the murder site, however, Jim received a report that a car had been stolen from a farmhouse in nearby Bigfoot.

Bigfoot got its name from the most famous Texas Ranger and frontier legend of all time, William Alexander Anderson "Big Foot" Wallace. Big Foot Wallace spent his entire adult life in the service of Texas building towns and cities, as well as Rangering and freighting across the frontier. The well that he dug by himself in Austin still stands on the corner of Congress and Pine and is known as the 'Wallace Well." He buried some of the ashes of the Alamo defenders, which he found in his first visit to San Antonio two years after the infamous battle. He was known to civilians and to the Army, to the enemy outlaws, Indians and Mexicans, as the bravest man on the Texas frontier. The State named the town that he founded after him.

Now not much more than a few houses, the Big Foot Wallace Museum, and a small post office, the tiny hamlet lies just inside the northeast corner of the Frio County limits. Suspecting that the fleeing murder suspect had stolen the car, Jim headed north to the farm, which was between Charlotte and Pearsall, about three miles inside the Frio County lines.

The lady of the house, Evelyn Mann, was very agitated when Jim arrived. In a shaky voice, she said that a stranger came to the door and rang the doorbell. Her thirteen-year-old daughter, Emily, answered the door, and Evelyn heard the man say, "I'm lost." Emily turned to call her mother, but

Mrs. Mann was already on her way to the door to give directions. Emily went to a back room, while her mother opened the door to talk to the stranger.

From the woman's description, Jim knew the man was the fleeing suspect. (To keep the record straight, the suspect will be identified as Leonard Freeman even though the authorities were looking for Terrell Cookston, Jr., as the driver of the red sports car.) Freeman was now wearing a brown straw hat, tan short-sleeve shirt, and brown shoes, as well as the blue, bell-bottom pants that the gas station attendant had reported. He pulled a gun and told Mrs. Mann to call her daughter back into the room.

The gun scared Mrs. Mann, and fearing for her daughter, she replied, "Oh, no!" She then put her hands up toward the suspect, and he fired the gun. The bullet struck the overhead door facing between the living room and hall.

"I just killed a deputy," Freeman told the terrified woman. "I'll kill you, too, if you don't do what I say!"

At the sound of the gunshot, Emily, her fourteen-year-old cousin, Belinda, and Evelyn's husband, Robert, entered the room. Freeman told them all to sit down. "Anyone else," he demanded to know. When told that no one else was in the house, Freeman ordered Robert Mann to tear out the phone. Freeman then robbed the family of all the cash that was on hand and demanded to know where the keys to the car were.

"In my purse," Evelyn Mann told him.

Freeman rummaged through Mrs. Mann's handbag until he found the keys to a 1972 green Mercury, which was parked in the garage. He next asked if there was any rope that he could use to tie everyone up. Robert Mann said he did not have any rope, and when Freeman looked menacingly down at his gun, Evelyn Mann told him that he could use her stockings. She offered to go into the bedroom and get them, but Freeman said, "No. Let Emily go and get them." He ordered the family to follow Emily into the bedroom.

Once in the bedroom, Freeman took off all their eyeglasses and tied them all up with Evelyn's stockings. He told his captives that he would put his truck into the garage and take their car. He also revealed that he had caught a man in bed with his wife and said that he had shot the man. The family was terrified, and they cooperated fully without a struggle.

Deciding he needed another change of clothing, Freeman searched through Robert Mann's closet and finally selected a shirt, necktie, and another pair of shoes. He then left the room, and the captives all thought he had left the premises when they heard the front door shut.

Evelyn Mann was not tied as tightly as the others, and she managed to free herself from her bonds, but just as she untied her husband, Leonard

Freemen re-entered the room. This time, using belts as well as the stockings, Freeman rebound the couple. He also said he would take Emily with him as a means of controlling the Manns until he got away, promising to let her go once he was clear of the area.

That really scared Evelyn Mann, and she pleaded and implored the gunman to leave her daughter alone.

"Don't take her, please," she begged. "She can't help you. She'll only get hurt, and you don't want to hurt her. Please don't do this."

"Shut up. If you do what you're told, she won't get hurt."

"She's just a baby. Please. Don't take her with you."

Evelyn Mann told Jim that after about five minutes of pleading, Leonard Freeman finally agreed to leave Emily with her family. He slammed the front door shut when he left.

At about the same time that Leonard Freeman left the farm in the Manns' car, Jimmy McClellen, a family friend, passed the Mann vehicle on the highway. The green Mercury was headed west toward Pearsall, and not recognizing the driver, McClellen decided to go to the farm and investigate. Receiving no answer to the doorbell or his knock, he opened the door and went inside, where he heard yells from the back room. Discovering what had happened, he hopped in his truck and pursued the stolen Mercury, using his mobile phone to advise the Sheriff's Department.

At Pearsall, Freeman headed north on Interstate 35, where he was finally apprehended near Natalia in Medina County by DPS officers and Ranger Captain John Wood. He was placed in the Atascosa County Jail at Jourdanton on bonds totaling 1.5 million dollars and charged with two counts of murder in connection with the slayings of Sheriff's Deputy Luis Garza and his wife, Elida.

In interviewing the suspect, Jim discovered that after shooting the Garzas at the abandoned farmhouse, Freeman escaped into the brush on foot, until he stumbled upon a residence belonging to Melvin Jones about a mile away. He broke into the Jones house by pulling a screen from a window. Once inside, he took a 30-40 Craig rifle, a 410 shotgun, brown shoes, and the hat and shirt that he had left at the Mann residence. Freeman left the white shoes, white belt and blue sports shirt at the Jones location, where Ranger Jack Van Cleve found them, still wet from perspiration and the trek through the brush. It was also at the Jones residence that Freeman stole the truck that he had left in the garage at the Mann farm. Found inside the truck was Deputy Garza's pistol.

With Leonard Freeman in possession of the red sports car and also in possession of Terrell Cookston, Jr's., driver's licence, authorities began to suspect that Cookston was also a victim and had met with foul play somewhere between San Antonio and the gas station at Charlotte.

Intelligence officers called Cookston's mother in Dallas, and she told them that she was sure that her son was all right and in good health.

Since the original All Points Bulletin was for the apprehension of Terrell Cookston, Jr., who was mistakenly wanted for the murders of the Garzas, he was arrested outside Cotulla along with Michael Hatfield of Jacksonville, Arkansas, by FBI investigators. Special Agent-in-Charge of the San Antonio office of the FBI, James Adams, said the pair was charged with conspiring with Freeman to rob the Stockman's National Bank of Cotulla.

Although all the suspects were apprehended in a timely fashion, Jim felt the same sense of remorse that all law officers feel when one of their own has fallen in the line of duty. Deputy Garza and his wife didn't deserve to die. In fact, Elida Garza had been just a bystander to her husband's loyalty to duty---an innocent witness in the wrong place at the wrong time to a crime of unimaginable horror, the murder of her husband.

THE JAMES CROCKETT BUSTER CASE

In his years as a Ranger, Jim has discovered that sometimes the pursuit and arrest of criminals has comic overtones---after the fact, of course. The crime is never humorous, and the hunt for the perpetrator is often vexing, especially if it spans several years. But the final arrest, when it does come, can be exhilarating---indeed funny---as Jim was to find out in the James Crockett Buster case.

The case began with a robbery in 1971. Shortly after 11:30 p.m. on the night of May 22, one white man climbed through an open back window of the Bus Stop grocery store in the small, mostly Mexican, town of Benavides in Duval County. Once inside, he quietly made his way over to the back door and removed the bar used to latch the door. The bar and latch method was similar in manner to the wood and latch method used to secure old-fashioned, country barn doors. The man just lifted the bar over the latch, and the door opened.

Another white man then joined the first one inside the grocery store. To mask themselves in darkness, they pulled the plug on a lighted clock, which is how the authorities determined the time of the robbery. The crooks then settled down to wait. At approximately 2:30 a.m. in the morning, they made their move.

The owner of the establishment, Amador Caballero, was sixty-six years old, and he lived alone over the store. His quarters could only be reached by a latched stairwell at the back of the building. The only people who could possibly know this were the patrons of the store---or the employees---as it was not a noticeable fact from the outside of the building. Actually, it wasn't even noticeable from the inside of the building because the patrons were not allowed in the back of the store.

Securing the door at the stairwell was a common, screen-door type latch---the kind that uses a hook-and-eye closure. The crooks apparently knew this. They also knew the exact height of the latch. Using a knife or similarly sharp object, they neatly bored holes in the sheetrock at the appropriate place beside the latch, reached through the wall, and unlocked the door. The two crooks then crept quietly up the stairs and broke into Caballero's room.

With one crook holding a small revolver to Caballero's head, the two men marched the frightened proprietor down the stairs and demanded that he open the safe. Although frightened, Caballero stalled for time, and this angered the crooks. The one with the pistol beat the store owner over the head with the weapon, almost knocking Caballero senseless.

Amador Caballero was now practically useless in his pistol-whipped state, but he dimly remembers one of the men suggested killing him. The other one refused, wanting only to get the money and escape. Working in the glow of a dim flashlight, the two crooks attacked the safe. In his semi-conscious state and with blood in his eyes from his beating, Caballero could not see the crooks very well. He did overhear one of the men call the other one "Robert."

After what seemed like an eternity to Caballero, the safe-crackers finally gave up trying to open the safe. While one stayed behind and stood watch, the other one went back upstairs and ransacked the room. He returned around ten minutes later with a cigar box full of money, approximately $4,000 in receipts from the weekend, which Caballero had planned on taking to the bank in the morning. The box also held a flashlight and Caballero's .38 Super Colt automatic.

By now, Caballero's senses were returning, and he could hear things a little clearer. "If we're not going to kill him, we need to tie him up," he heard one of the men say.

The crooks spent a few minutes searching the store for something to use. They finally settled on a couple of packages of children's jump rope. When Caballero was securely trussed, one of the men went to the front of the store and signaled someone outside with the flashlight. A few minutes later, a car drove up to the side of the building, and the crooks disappeared into the night.

Finding himself alone, Caballero managed to roll out the front door onto the sidewalk in front of the store. The store acted as the bus station for the small town, hence the name "Bus Stop" grocery, and he thought someone passing by would see him and help him. In his rolling effort, however, he managed to loosen his own bonds. He promptly summoned police.

Amador Caballero described his two assailants as being definitely Anglo in appearance and speech. Both were in their mid-30's, about five feet, six inches tall and weighed around 160 pounds. They wore long sleeved shirts, jeans, and had bandanas over their mouths. The crooks also wore western-type straw hats on their heads. Neither one spoke with any kind of accent, which ruled out practically all the population of South Texas of Mexican descent. Caballero not could give Texas Ranger John Hogg, who made the initial investigation, any information on the hair and eye color of the crooks because it was too dark in the store. Besides, his eyesight had been greatly impaired with blood from the beating.

Ranger John Hogg followed up his initial investigation with a comprehensive study of Caballero's employees. It was his opinion that the crooks must have had inside information. How else could they have known of the back stairwell with the hook-and-eye closure and just where to bore through the wall to open it? There were also two safes in the store, both in plain sight, and only the front one was ever routinely used. The crooks had chosen the front safe, totally ignoring the other one. It just had to be an inside job.

In talking with the store employees, John Hogg struck what he though was pay dirt almost immediately. Caballero had a nineteen-year-old clerk who had been working in the store for less than two months, and this beautiful young woman had an Anglo boyfriend in Houston, who called her frequently on the telephone. When Ranger Hogg questioned the young woman, she was more than reluctant to talk to him---she was absolutely petrified.

John Hogg thought he now had a good candidate for the "inside man" for the robbery and a possible suspect for one of the Anglo men involved. He requested that Houston authorities question the boyfriend. The Houston investigation, however, revealed that the young man not only worked for a respectable Houston hotel, he had not had a day off for nine days. Back to square one.

Out of curiosity more than anything, John Hogg asked the young woman if she would agree to a polygraph test. He wanted to know why she was so reluctant and uncooperative with the police. She reluctantly agreed to the test, and its results indicated that she was telling the truth about everything she said. She finally admitted that the reason she was unwilling to answer any questions was that she had never before in her life had talked to a policeman, much less a Texas Ranger. She had a real fear of police and an absolute terror of a Ranger. After the polygraph examination and the courteous manner in which she had been treated, she talked freely and fully cooperated.

After two days of questioning the store employees, John Hogg finally determined that "no employee aided in the planning or commission of the offense."

About a week later, John Hogg was chatting with Dick Moseley, a Texas Ranger assigned to the Southwest Cattle Raisers Association, Duval County Chief Deputy Sheriff Israel Saenz, and Duval County Game Warden "Chicken" Saenz about a cattle theft case going before the Duval County Grand Jury on May 27th. During the discussion, Ranger Hogg learned that the cattle rustlers lived in a house across the highway from the grocery store. The house sat on the other side of the railroad tracks that paralleled the highway and slightly to the southwest, but still in full view of the store.

A man named Pedro Ramirez owned the house, and he had a daughter who was pregnant by an ex-convict named Tito Ibanez, whose real name turned out to be Erasamo Hinojosa. Hinojosa was from Hebbronville, and although he already had a wife and children living in Hebbronville, he moved into the Ramirez house to be with his pregnant, common-law wife.

Hinojosa thus became the only apparent means of support for the entire Ramirez family.

Ranger Hogg discovered that Tito also managed a bar in Alice, and he had some Anglo associates living in Corpus Christi, who visited him often. The associates drove a two-tone station wagon and reportedly brought stolen articles to Alice in the vehicle to Tito for disposition.

Also living in the house was Pedro Ramirez's long-haired son Pedro Ramirez, Jr., known as "Cinderella." Having nothing else to do, "Cinderella" and his pregnant sister frequented the Bus Stop grocery. Since the store substituted as a bus station for the town of Benavides, it was usually the only busy establishment in the whole area. The two Ramirez siblings knew every door, lock, and safe in the building, having grown up right across the street. They also knew about how much money was apt to be in the store at the end of each day.

Tito and "Cinderella" were the two suspects in the cattle theft case that the Southwest Cattle Raisers Association Rangers Dick Moseley and Murray Potts had investigated with the Duval county Game Warden Chick Saenz. The Rangers were using a sixteen-year-old boy, who was part of the ring, as an informer. According to the boy, everyone involved was badly in need of money for attorney fees. The Rangers and Duval County authorities had decided to wait until after the Grand Jury indictment, before questioning anyone in the Ramirez house about the Bus Stop robbery for fear of burning the informer in the rustling ring.

One week after the Duval County Grand Jury returned an indictment in the cattle theft case, Jim Peters stepped into the investigation. Alice was in Jim Wells County, Jim's home in his days with the Highway Patrol. He was more like family than outside investigator, and he stood by as a polygraph examination regarding the cattle thefts in Duval County was administered to Pedro Ramirez, Jr., alias "Cinderella." Ramirez then gave Jim a statement involving Tito and two white men from Corpus Christi.

According to "Cinderella's" statement, the two white men were James Crockett Buster and Arthur Robert Thomas. Approximately two days prior to the Bus Stop robbery, Buster and Thomas went to Kingsville to confer with Erasamo "Tito" Hinojosa. Tito had decided to burglarize the store and get the safe, and he wanted the two men to help him do it.

On the day of the robbery, Buster and Thomas drove to Alice, where they met with Hinojosa and the senior Ramirez. Using two vehicles---Thomas and Ramirez in Hinojosa's green Pontiac, and Buster and Hinojosa in Thomas' Ford Falcon station wagon---the four journeyed to Benavides---to Ramirez's home, which was across the street from the Bus Stop grocery store. It took about a half hour of bickering before they all agreed to split the money taken in the robbery four ways. Hinojosa gave

Buster a .38 caliber revolver to use in the commission of the crime.

Buster and Thomas went to the store on foot, got inside, and discovered that the safe was too big for them to move. They went back to the Ramirez house and discussed the fact that the safe was too large and that they couldn't move it. It was finally decided that the two men would re-enter the store, wake the owner, and force him to open the safe. It was Buster who cut the hole in the wall, reaching his hand in through the hole, and unlatching the door at the entrance to the stairway leading to Amador Caballero's bedroom upstairs.

The two crooks entered the bedroom, woke up the elderly proprietor, and at gun point, told him to get down the stairs.

"I know what you want," said Amador Caballero, but when all three of them got to the safe at the front of the store, he refused to open it. Buster then struck him such a hard blow on the top of the head with the butt of the gun that blood ran into his eyes, and he couldn't see.

Robert Thomas went back upstairs and ransacked the bedroom, finally finding the cigar box full of money, along with Caballero's gun and the flashlight. After tying the bleeding old man up, he and Buster went to the front window and used the flashlight to signal the Ramirez house across the street that they were ready to be picked up.

Hinojosa and both Ramirezes were in the front room of the house, waiting for the signal that the robbery had gone off as planned. As soon as they saw the flashing light from the front window of the store, Hinojosa went out the back door of the Ramirez house, hopped into Thomas' Ford station wagon, drove across the street, and stopped at the side of the grocery store. Buster and Thomas then ran out the store, got into the station wagon with Hinojosa, and they all sped off to the outskirts of town.

The rest of the plan called for the senior Ramirez to take Hinojosa's green Pontiac and meet the others at a designated spot on Conception Road. After the meeting, Hinojosa hopped into the car with Ramirez, and they went to Alice. Buster and Thomas returned to Corpus Christi. Two days later, Buster and Thomas showed up at the bar in Alice that Hinojosa ran, and along with the elder Ramirez, they split the money four ways.

By Friday, June 11th, all four of the suspects had been arrested and charged with the robbery. Bail was set at $50,000 each.

James Buster and Pedro "Cinderella" Ramirez, Jr., gave written statements to Jim in the Duval County Jail in San Diego. Jim had also obtained an oral confession from Arthur Robert Thomas, who had been picked up June 9th for possession of marijuana. But Arthur Thomas was being held in the Jim Wells County Jail in Alice, and before Jim could get the oral confession down in writing, Thomas used his belt to commit suicide. The suspect hung himself from the bars of the jail at 2:00 p.m. on

June 11th.

The elder Pedro Ramirez gave a written confession to Ranger B.J. Green in Falfurrias. Hinojosa remained silent in the Duval County Jail.

Two years later, by June 1973, Hinojosa and the senior Armored were out of jail on bond, awaiting trial for their part in the Bus Stop robbery. James Crockett Buster had already been tried and found guilty, receiving fifty years in the state penitentiary. Before Buster could be transferred to the state prison system, he escaped from the Duval County Jail on the night of June 8th.

Three weeks after Buster's jail break, Jim received information that the fugitive was living and working in Amarillo. He sent a copy of Buster's mug shot, showing a handsome young man in long brown hair and blue eyes, to M. D. Rogers, the Texas Ranger in the Amarillo area. Although Ranger Rogers conducted an intensive search for the wanted man, Buster remained free.

Two more years passed before Jim again received information on James Buster's whereabouts. This time the informant was an old school mate of Buster's who had seen the wanted man in the Corpus Christi area in early October of that year, 1975. According to the informant, Buster was working as a heavy equipment operator at odd jobs with various construction companies around town. He was also using the alias of "James Chambers" and had acquired a rather expensive dope habit, which left him in constant need of money.

By December 15th, Jim had traced Buster to a construction site on the corner of Everhart and Saratoga. The fugitive was now heavier than his original 160 pounds, and had grown a mustache and beard, but he was easily recognized from his mug shot by the foreman on the site. Buster was also trying to stay out of trouble so he would not be picked up.

The foreman of the job reported that Buster, using the alias James Chambers, had reported for work the end of September. He had left November 28th, claiming his grandmother's will was being probated. The foreman also said Buster was driven to work by an uncle in a light tan-over-brown Ford, and the supervisor then provided Jim with an address.

Jim immediately went to the address and found the Ford. A check on the license plates showed that it was registered to James Chambers. There was also a 1964 Pontiac at the same location registered to Ruby Chambers. Jim already knew from his previous sleuthing that Ruby Chambers was Buster's mother's name. Buster's father, J.J. Buster, was deceased.

Jim decided on a trick to flush the wanted man into the open. He had the superintendent of the construction company call the address and try and determine when Buster, alias Chambers, would return to work. Buster, however, wasn't there, and he didn't return the call. He also didn't report back to work. Jim put the house under surveillance, which had been under surveillance many times in the past.

After the holidays, in January 1976, Jim again got with the informant in Buster's case and learned that Buster had a girlfriend with reddish brown hair, name and address unknown. Buster had been seen several times sitting on a bike rack at one of the movie theaters on South Staples street, talking to the girl, and the informant promised to try and obtain the license plate number of the light blue vehicle that Buster drove.

On February 17, 1976, at approximately 1:15 p.m., Jim was cruising along on Padre Island Drive, when he received a public service call from his informant with the information that James Crockett Buster was in a white 1960 Buick LaSabre, traveling on the same highway in the same direction. At about that same time, the Buick passed him. Jim promptly got on his radio and advised the dispatcher that he was in pursuit of the escaped fugitive, giving a description of the car and everything.

Padre Island Drive is a lawman's worst nightmare. Instead of being a straight, smooth ribbon of highway with an unobstructed view, it rolls up and down as it crosses over each side street. It does this the entire length of the city. Also, for the most part, the entry onto the expressway is AFTER the crest of the hill. This means that drivers with speeds of 55 miles per hour invariably plow into others trying to enter the system at much slower speeds. More than one ugly accident has resulted in more than one city officer wanting to dynamite the highway, thus forcing traffic engineering to correct the hazard.

As Jim whizzed over the overpasses of Padre Island Drive with his siren blaring, he hoped he wouldn't come upon a slow-moving vehicle on the other side of the hill. It didn't take him long to catch the Buick, and he got right behind the vehicle before the driver realized that Jim wanted the car stopped. They had just crossed the Kostoryz overpass heading east, and the other driver pulled the Buick neatly to the side of the road. Jim pulled in behind and was able to peacefully arrest Buster, who was a passenger in the back seat.

The Buick and Jim's Ranger car were parked at the side of the road on the downside of the hill. Although the vehicles were out of the way of traffic, they could not be seen by anyone approaching on the other side of the overpass. As Jim calmly handcuffed the cooperating Buster, he heard the approaching screams of city police units in pursuit. The sirens got louder and louder, and Jim watched in total amazement as two city patrol cars whizzed over the crest of the hill, spied the Ranger car and the Buick at the side of the road, and attempted to halt.

"They came over that hill and practically turned themselves

sideways in the road trying to stop." Jim said with a laugh, as he recalled the event. "They laid rubber from the top clear to the bottom, cars fishtailing all the way. And when they did get stopped, they came running up with guns drawn. I asked them what in the tarnation they thought they were doing. 'We heard that a Ranger was in pursuit of a dangerous criminal, a jailbreaker.' responded one all out of breath, 'and we thought we'd lend a hand.' Now, I'm not one to turn down any help, but it was all I could do to keep a straight face."

Jim turned the prisoner over to the city police, and after questioning the others in the Buick, released them. James Buster was subsequently transported back to San Diego and turned over to Sheriff Raul Serna for processing.

THE ROSHARON JAIL BREAK

It was mid-July in 1973 when Jim received yet *another* phone call to help solve a jail break which had occurred the day before at the Darrington Prison in Rosharon. Expecting little in the way of leads, he quietly listened to the details being transmitted, jotting down an occasional note for future reference on the pad he kept next to the phone for that purpose. The more he heard, however, the more he grinned, shaking his head in the familiar understanding of one who already knows the answer but still can't believe what he is hearing. When the caller finally paused, Jim chimed in with the name of a suspect. It was the first and only time in his whole career that identifying an accomplice was as easy as pie, and he did it without ever once having to leave his desk.

The jailbreak turned out to be a complete comedy of errors from beginning to end for the crooks. It began when Robert Graham was arrested in Robstown, just west of Corpus Christi, for a crime he had committed in Kerr County. The robbery by assault eventually netted him twenty years in the state penitentiary in Rosharon, near Houston, only like most inmates, Robert didn't like jail. Shortly after he arrived at the prison, he got with two other inmates and devised an elaborate scheme of escape. An integral part of their preparations involved playing basketball in the gymnasium each and every night to throw suspicion off the guards---and to establish a routine.

While in the gym, they began to "collect" pants and tee-shirts belonging to the guards. When they had enough for all of them, they dyed the shirts black with shoe polish, and then hid the entire stash somewhere outside on the grounds. They also managed to secure a ladder, a board, and some rubberized tape, which they wrapped around the board until it was well-padded, reasoning incorrectly that the insulated board, when thrown over the energized wires atop the fence surrounding the prison, would prevent the alarm from going off. These items they also hid outside on the grounds. When it came time to escape, their plan was to wear the stolen clothing, lean the hidden ladder against the fence, throw the padded board on top, and be gone before anyone would be the wiser.

Having all their gear together, it remained only to find an accomplice on the outside to help with the guards. One of the prisoners chose a girlfriend named Susan Fields, who lived in nearby Houston. Robert Graham chose an old buddy of his from Corpus Christi, Robert Walters, and Walters recruited Ray Tamez to help.

On July 25th, Ray Tamez made the four-hour drive to Houston and conferred with Susan Fields, giving her instructions for her part in the prison break. He also gave her money to rent a car to be used as a decoy on the night of the planned escape, in case the guard at the gate became suspicious. Two days later, Susan met with Robert Walters, who identified himself to her only as "Hector." Walters drove off in the rental car, and when he brought it back one hour later, it sported a bogus set of license plates.

Everything was now ready. At the planned time, Susan was to drive to a certain spot at the prison at a certain time of night and wait for the guard to come and investigate. As soon as the guard was at her car, she was to flash her lights as a signal to the men in the gymnasium that the guard was with her. To give the men inside the prison enough time to escape, she was to pull out a map, claim she was lost, and ask for directions.

On the night in question, everything went just as planned. Susan drove up to the prison, got the guard to come to her car, flashed the headlights, engaged the guard in conversation for a little while, and then drove home to Houston. But for some reason, the warden didn't let the men play in the gymnasium that night. It was all for nothing.

Susan Fields thought her part in the jail break was finished---until she received a phone call from Robert Walters instructing her that she had to repeat the performance the next night because the escape hadn't come off as expected. She reluctantly agreed. This time, instead of driving a rental car, she drove up to the prison in her own Volkswagon. She changed the plates on her car with plates from a Volkswagon van.

Things didn't go well for anyone this time. There was a different guard on duty, and he wouldn't have anything to do with Susan when she pulled up. He just walked up to her and said, "Go on. Get out of here," and went back to his post.

Meanwhile, she had already flashed her lights, and the men in the gymnasium thought she had the guard under control. They raced across the prison yard and threw the ladder up against the wall. Robert Graham climbed the ladder, laid the insulated board over the wires, and the alarm immediately went off. Graham went over the wires, and the other two men froze at the fence. The roving guard fired two shots at Graham, saw him fall, get up, and then run into a grain field. Robert Graham hightailed it through the field and down the road on the other side to where Robert Walters was waiting for him in a yellow Buick. Graham hopped in, and the two men drove off into the night.

Susan had problems with the escape, too. When the siren went off announcing the jail break, it frightened her so badly that she threw her car into reverse to turn around, only she backed into soft dirt and got the car stuck. Not able to free the vehicle, she abandoned it---forgetting her handbag lying on the seat. It was only after she got out to the main road that she remembered her purse, but by then, she was too scared to return and retrieve it. She hitchhiked back to Houston with a car full of hippies.

Naturally, the prison authorities found her car and her handbag, traced her, and had her arrested.

Susan immediately confessed and gave the authorities all the details. She described the accomplice from Corpus Christi, known to her as "Hector" and who had furnished the bogus license plates, as being "five feet, nine inches tall, 180 pounds, green eyes, light brown or blond hair, about thirty, good-looking, well-dressed, did not curse, talked like he was influential and had a lot of money. He drove a yellow Buick."

The next day, Jim got the phone call from Ray Sandlin, an investigator for the Sheriff's Department in Angleton, Rosharon's neighbor down the highway. Sandlin explained that Robert Graham had made a successful prison break. He then explained what the girl accomplice had said, giving Jim a full description of "Hector." When he was through, Jim immediately said, "Robert Walters."

"Really?" The Rosharon investigator was absolutely flabbergasted.

"Yep," said Jim into the telephone, grinning from ear to ear. "We have a few famous crooks here, and we all know who they are. When something happens, we know who to interview." He then sent the Rosharon investigator a picture of Robert Walters, and sure enough, he was the man. Warrants for Robert Walters' and Ray Tamez's arrests were then issued for "aiding a prisoner to escape."

Finding the fugitives proved to be just a matter of patience. All of them had many friends in the Corpus Christi area, and it was just a matter of time before they were spotted by the authorities. Ray Tamez, in fact, was found in the Jim Wells County Courthouse in Alice doing construction work. Investigators decided to wait until he crossed back into Nueces County before arresting him, and he was put under surveillance. Somehow, he was tipped off because he managed to slip surveillance and went into hiding.

On August 15th, Jim and Captain Ken Bung of the Corpus Christi Police Department arrested Robert Walters. The fugitive had pulled up to the stop light at South Staples and Everhart directly in front of the Ranger vehicle.

"Some days you get lucky," Jim laughed.

Ray Tamez turned himself in to authorities in Angleton a week later, and Robert Graham was apprehended not long after that.

Robert Walters was convicted of aiding a prisoner to escape and was given five years in the Department of Corrections. Susan Fields received five years probation. Robert Graham got an additional three years tacked onto his sentence. Ray Tamez received fifteen days in jail and a fine.

Later, when Robert Walters was in the penitentiary, Jim went and talked to him about the George Randolph Farenthold murder. Walters told

Jim why it was committed, how it was committed, and then gave a statement.

THE RANDY FARENTHOLD MURDER CASE

In all of Jim's years as a Texas Ranger, there was probably never a more widely-publicized murder investigation than that of George Randolph Farenthold, multi-millionaire playboy step-son of gubernatorial candidate, Frances "Sissy" Farenthold. When Randy's body was found in the surf off Mustang Island, shocked Texans everywhere demanded a quick ending, but it wasn't to be. Before his death was finally solved, it involved literally hundreds of investigators, half a dozen or so investigative agencies, no clues, theories by the score, and a reward that approached one million dollars. It was Jim Peters who probably provided the most evidence leading to a solution of the case, and it was Jim who finally brought Randy's killer back to Texas for justice. It's a case no one involved will ever forget.

It began on Monday, June 6, 1972. That morning, elderly Port Aransas fisherman Roy Wilson* and his helper, Joe, expected just another routine day. As they did every day of the week before the sun peeked over the horizon, they drove in Roy's battered old pickup truck down the packed sand of Mustang Island beach and searched for any signs of bait fish in the surf. Their usual custom after Roy found what he was seeking was to park the truck, drag a large beach seine down to the surf, wade into the shallow water pulling the seine, make a large circle, and then tow the fish-laden net ashore. Roy would sell the catch to charter and pleasure boat captains and pay Joe. Over the years, he's captured tons of bait fish in that manner.

This morning, however, was different. It was a little past 6:00 a.m., and the sun had already topped the horizon before Roy finally spotted what he wanted in the surf. The two men would have to hurry if they expected to sell their catch to early-morning boat captains. The charter boats left at 8:00 a.m. sharp for their first excursions of the day.

Roy parked his truck just out of reach of the tide, and along with Joe, waded into the gentle waves with the big net. They walked in their customary circle, dragging the heavy seine, and as the net filled with mullet and became hard to tow, it snagged on something heavy in the water. The old fisherman stepped gingerly out to see what it was. Peering into the clear water, he recoiled in horror. Sightless eyes in a bloated face stared back at him through the mesh of the seine.

The two men struggled to drag the corpse to shore, which was no easy task because of the condition the body was in. After stooping down to examine it closely, Roy left Joe guarding the discovery, jumped in his truck, and sped back down the beach to the Port Aransas Police Department.

At that time, Port Aransas was a small beach community of about 3,000 permanent residents, and the Police Department shared a facade with City Hall. Roy parked in front of the building, entered, and reported to the dispatcher on duty, Sergeant Paul Olsen. He told Olsen of finding a body in the surf on Mustang Island, and then added for definite clarification, "and it wasn't no accident, either. The man's been beat, cut, and tied up with wires and chains...and there's a concrete block wired to his neck!"

Sergeant Olsen stared at Roy like he was crazy, but the old man was a well-known character and had a reputation for being nobody's fool. Olsen got up and walked into the inner office where the Chief of Police, Jim Wright, was sipping his morning coffee. "You're not going to believe this," Olsen began, and then filled his chief in on the details as Roy had told them.

Chief Wright listened dumbfounded. Violent crime never happened in Port Aransas. He hurried to the outer chamber, talked a few moments with Roy, and then instructed the old fisherman to lead the way to the body. He jumped in his patrol car and followed the old man's battered pickup truck down the beach.

At precisely where Roy said it would be, Jim Wright bent over and examined the mutilated corpse. It was a gruesome sight to behold. Not only was the face cut, bruised, bloated, and chalky white from being immersed in the sea, but wire and chain were wrapped tightly around the neck---the other end of the chain being secured to a 40-pound concrete block. Yet, even through the distortion and grotesque appearance, the face looked vaguely familiar.

My God! thought the Chief. *It's Randy Farenthold.* He raced to his patrol car and radioed Sergeant Olsen with the news. The Sergeant notified both the Nueces County Sheriff's office and the County Medical Examiner, Doctor Joseph Rupp.

By 8:00 a.m., the area was teeming with police and medical officials from Port Aransas and Corpus Christi. Several of the public officials present agreed that the corpse looked like Randy Farenthold, but no one could actually be certain because of the advanced state of decomposition. One deputy, however, made a prophetic statement, "If that IS Randy Farenthold, there's going to be hell to pay."

The coroner ordered the body removed to Corpus Christi, and ambulance attendant, Don Moore, who would later become a Port Aransas police officer himself, drove it to the Nueces County Medical Examiner's office. By nightfall, the coroner had a verdict. The body found in the surf at Port Aransas was, indeed, that of George Randolph Farenthold. It was the coroner's opinion that the victim had died of a combination of strangulation, beating, asphyxiation, and drowning.

George Randolph Farenthold, or Randy as he liked to be called, was Corpus Christi's favorite playboy millionaire. Oh, there were other millionaires in the "Sparkling City by the Sea," but none had the charm, the good looks, or the connections that Randy had. He had friends by the

117

Captain Alfred Young Allee, Sr. Jim's first Ranger Captain.

Taxas Ranger Company "D" 1971. Standing left to right: John Hogg, Jack Dean, Glenn Krueger, Joaquin Jackson, Jack Van Cleve, L.T. Carpenter, Bill Nelson. Sitting left to right: Jim Peters, Captain John Wood, Sgt. Bob Werner, Jerome Preiss, B. J. Green, and Art Rodriguez.

Implements of Jim Peter's successful career, his guns, badge, and knife.

Jim's family. Lydia and their two daughters, Shelly (left) and Janna around 1993.

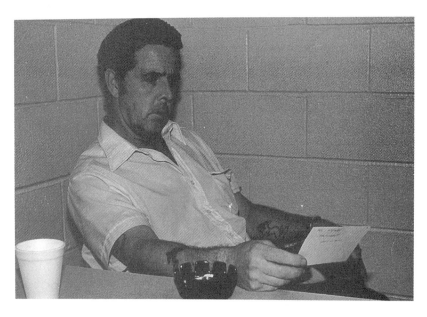

Henry Lee Lucas looking at the photo of a murdered girl.

Age : Mid 30's
White male

grayish with dirty yellow hair

medium completion

light grayish eyes

Tattoo inside right
forearm, only 6"to
8"could be seen
from under shirt
sleeve. aprox. ½
to3/4 inch wide
running parallel
to his arm.

6" 200"

AGGRAVATED KIDNAPPING

1-29-83

M.C. PETERS
DPS HARLINGEN

DPS sketch of one of the Loman's kidnappers.

thousands, acquaintances by the score, and no apparent enemies---or so everyone thought.

His grandfather was the late Rand Morgan, the wealthiest industrial businessman for miles around. When Randy turned twenty-one in 1961, he inherited Morgan's cotton and maize farms, and several large cotton gins all over South Texas. One of the largest of the gin complexes was on Rand Morgan Road, located just outside the Corpus Christi city limits on the northwest side of town. Much to the surprise of others in the business community, Randy leaped whole-heartedly into the company and ran it with a firm hand. He seemed imbued with business acumen, and it wasn't long before he had multiplied his considerable fortune many times over.

Randy married and fathered two children, and to all outward appearances, he seemed a devoted parent and husband. But trouble brewed on the horizon. The more successful he became, the more time he spent pursuing his leisure activities of gambling, pigeon shooting, and sports fishing. Although things were friendly and he kept in close contact with his family, there was first a legal separation from his wife, and then a divorce.

In 1970, Hurricane Celia changed his life forever. The windy lady blew ashore between Corpus Christi and Port Aransas with peak wind gusts estimated at more than 210 miles per hour---no one knows for sure as all wind barometers blew away. She damaged or destroyed practically everything in her path. One of her casualties was the Farenthold cotton gin on Rand Morgan Road. It was completely destroyed, and that seemed to be the turning point in Randy's life. He did not rebuild the gin. Instead, he shucked the business world altogether.

Randy was an avid sports fisherman, and one of his memberships was with the Port Aransas Boatman's Association. His pride and joy was a 35-foot yacht, *THE LOLLIPOP*, which he kept docked at the island community, and his presence around town soon became a common sight to the local islanders. In fact, his transformation became so complete, that the locals looked upon him as one of their own, which is no easy feat in an island community where anyone in coat and tie is looked upon with suspicion. Randy took to wearing worn tee shirts, old faded jeans, and sneakers without socks.

Although extremely wealthy, Randy had several things going for him with the Port Aransas island community. Foremost among them was that he never "put on airs" with the local folks. He always treated everyone with such open friendliness that he achieved a reputation as "just a good ole boy." Randy was also one "hell of a fisherman," and it gained him the respect of all the boat captains in the whole area. The islanders vied with each other to work on *THE LOLLIPOP*.

It seemed inconceivable to everyone that Randy Farenthold could be murdered. The Saturday before his body was found, the Farenthold family celebrated Sissy Farenthold's entry into Texas politics. She had narrowly missed becoming her party's gubernatorial candidate, and it was a sign of the changing times in the Lone Star State. Although Randy's absence at the party was duly noted, no one ever suspected that at that very moment, miles away on the Texas Riviera, as the Gulf Coast around Corpus Christi was known, he was being brutally murdered, his body being dumped into the sea. Everyone just assumed he had gone deep sea fishing---the bill fish were running---and that he would show up later that night. When his body was found Monday morning...well, as the deputy had said, "all hell broke loose."

Nueces County Sheriff Johnnie Mitchell was on vacation when Randy's body was pulled from the surf. He had just won re-election in a particularly arduous political campaign and was looking forward to a few days of rest and relaxation before returning to Corpus Christi and the influx of summer visitors. When he learned the identity of the victim, however, he caught the first plane back to personally take charge of the investigation. He knew the Farenthold family was sure to apply pressure from every quarter for a quick arrest in the case.

Sheriff Mitchell assigned investigators Ted Jolly and Lester Manson to the case, and they began on Mustang Island trying to trace Randy's last hours. It was a monumental undertaking from the beginning. The tourist season was just beginning, and already, thousands of visitors were in Port Aransas for fishing and swimming in the warm Gulf waters. Men, women, and children milled everywhere up and down the main thoroughfare, and cars were bumper to bumper at the ferry landing---both entering and leaving the island paradise. The two officers just stood on the steps of city hall and stared aghast at the situation. Randy's killer could be anyone.

Deputies Jolly and Manson decided to start their search along the waterfront dock area. Before the day was over, they had interviewed sailors, fishermen, boat captains, bartenders, waitresses, waiters, and service station attendants. They were confident they had traced every movement Randy had made in the last week of his life. Nowhere did they turn up the name of anyone who would want to kill him. Randy Farenthold seemed to be well-liked and admired by everyone in town.

At the same time the sheriff's deputies were conducting their investigation, Jim was doing sleuthing of his own. Even though one of the issues on Sissy Farenthold's ticket had been the abolition of the Texas Rangers Organization---probably the single, most important reason why she lost the election---Jim gave the case everything he had. His attention to

125

detail missed nothing.

Jim conducted his investigation in practically the same manner as the sheriff's deputies. He went to Port Aransas and interviewed hundreds of islanders, gleaning as much as possible about the last few days of Randy Farenthold's life. He learned that in the previous week, Randy had participated in a deep sea fishing tournament in New Orleans and had then brought *THE LOLLIPOP* back to Port Aransas, where he had it hauled out of the water to repair some minor hull damage.

On June 2, Randy had been seen around his beach house. He had also gone to a swank nearby restaurant for dinner, and so meticulous was the investigation that Jim learned what Randy had ordered from the menu. Randy spent the night at his beach house, got up early the next morning, and had breakfast at a local cafe. He had then gone down to his boat and helped the boat captain repair the damage, spending the remainder of the day at the dock.

On June 3, Randy had driven down the beach to Padre Island and had entered Corpus Christi via the John F. Kennedy Causeway, voting before the polls closed. From there, he went to his elegant Corpus Christi home, showered, and changed clothing. His next stop had been the Corpus Christi Yacht Club, where he enjoyed two drinks around 6:00 p.m., before driving to his ex-wife's home for dinner with her and their two children. He left that residence around 8:00 p.m. and headed for a local nightclub.

Randy had spent an aimless night on June 3. He went from one night spot to another before becoming engaged in a crap game which witnesses claimed had netted him several thousand dollars. It could have been a motive for murder, but Jim learned that all the men in the crap game were wealthy and in the same social class as Randy. Furthermore, Randy had really only won several hundred dollars, not thousands as reported, and the sheriff's deputies had already found the money from the game where Randy had carelessly tossed it---in a dresser drawer in the master bedroom of his house.

One puzzling aspect to the case concerned the finding of Randy's car keys in the grass in front of his house. His car was parked neatly in the driveway. Had he been accosted before reaching his front door, or just as he was leaving? Jim thought it might have been when he had returned home, but how to account for the money from the crap game in the dresser drawer? Perhaps, Jim reasoned, the money in the dresser drawer wasn't from the crap game after all. Suppose it was Randy's "mad money," money he routinely kept on hand all the time? It was also possible that Randy had been home, left the money, and had then been accosted as he was leaving for somewhere else. It would be months before Jim would know which theory was correct.

Jim learned that Randy had received a phone call from a woman prior to leaving the last nightclub. Thinking she might have lured Randy home to his house, where he had then been abducted and killed, he tracked her down and interviewed her. It was a false lead. The woman in question had only called and asked Randy to join her for a drink, which he had politely refused. When Jim checked, her story held up.

Randy Farenthold had met his killer sometime in the early morning of June 4th...someone who hated him enough to hack him with a knife, beat him viciously with a club, and then garrote him with wire, before chaining at least one 40-pound concrete block to his neck and dropping him into the Gulf of Mexico. But who? And why? The thirty-two-year-old Randy was liked and admired by everyone.

Jim sent the chains, wires, and concrete block to the Crime Lab in Austin for analysis, but it proved to be fruitless. Items of that nature were so common that they littered practically every boat yard and dock on the Gulf Coast from the Mexican border to the tip of Florida. Jim then turned his attention to an expert on coastal tides, in an effort to discover exactly where Randy had been dumped into the sea.

The scientist contacted the coroner's office and obtained the weight and measurements of the body, along with the weight of the chains that had bound the body to the concrete block. Knowing that Randy had died in the early hours of Saturday morning, the tide expert consulted his charts. In his opinion, the body had been tossed into the water at the mouth of the jetties, which border the ship channel running between St. Joseph and Mustang Islands.

The Port Aransas side of the jetties are always packed with fishermen from the crack of dawn until shortly after the sun sets, and the only activity in the area after dark is usually from the shrimp boats headed out for their harvest of the ocean floor. Pleasure craft seldom clear the harbor at night. Even the big, commercial shipping vessels normally "lay to" off the jetties at night, preferring to maneuver the ship channel in daylight. Jim knew Randy's body had probably been dumped by a shrimp boat. But which one? All of them denied any knowledge in the matter. In fact, they all seemed more than willing to take the law into their own hands the moment Randy's murderer was caught. Everyone in Port Aransas felt the same way.

Meanwhile, the two sheriff's deputies from Nueces County, Ted Jolly and Lester Manson, were also busy with the shrimp boats. They intensively questioned the crews of two boats, learning only that another shrimper had left Port Aransas for Houston around the time of the killing. The two deputies then journeyed to Houston to question the suspect, but it turned out that the shrimper had only gone to Houston to voluntarily check himself into the Veterans Administration Hospital for narcotics addiction. Another dead end. Things took a strange turn of events when the Federal Bureau of Investigation entered the case. It turned out that Randy Farenthold was a key witness scheduled to testify in federal court on a fraud case involving a Corpus Christi contractor with alleged ties to the Mafia. The trial was set to begin four months away---in October.

According to the FBI, Randy had been approached in 1969 by contractor Bruce Bass with a get-rich-quick-scheme of buying short-term U.S. Treasury notes at a huge discount from a Mafia source in Houston. Bass claimed that he was unable to raise the cash on his own, but he offered to cut Randy in as a partner if Randy would finance the plan.

Randy knew Bass from years of associating in the same "by-invitation-only" gambling and pigeon shooting clique that also involved others of wealthy, independent means. Although the two were acquaintances, they were not close friends, but for some unknown reason, Randy still agreed to the proposition. He put up $100,000 to purchase $166,000 worth of bonds. His instructions were to withdraw the money in cash, check into a Houston hotel, and wait for his contact. The bills were to be in small denominations with non-consecutive serial numbers.

Randy did as instructed, and presently his contact arrived. The "Mafioso" type asked to see the money, satisfied himself that it was all there, and the two men sat down to discuss the transaction. In the meantime, Randy had already called down to Room Service for some soft drinks and ice, and when a knock sounded at the door, he naturally assumed it was the waiter with the drinks. He opened the door, and in rushed a man in a Batman costume, brandishing a sawed-off shotgun. "Batman" robbed Randy of his money, and the Mafioso guy of $10,000---money which Randy said that he never saw.

This angered Randy, and he called Bruce Bass with plans of calling in the police. Bass, however, talked him out of it. Bass and a companion then placed a call to Las Vegas, Nevada, and claimed they talked with a highly placed Mafia official who promised to listen to Randy's story. If the official believed what Randy said, he would then recover the stolen money and also sell Randy double the amount of the bonds.

Somewhat mollified, Randy returned to Corpus Christi, secured yet another $100,000, and boarded a plane to Las Vegas with the money. During the journey, however, he came to his senses, and as soon as the plane landed, he went straight to the police. He told them everything. The police officials referred him to the Federal Bureau of Investigation, where agents took his statement and promised to investigate. Randy then returned to Corpus Christi, and when Hurricane Celia blew away his cotton gin, committed himself full-time to the gambling, pigeon shooting, and sports fishing activities that he so loved.

Meanwhile, the Special Agent-in-Charge of the Corpus Christi branch of the FBI, Penrod Harris, was hot on the trail. He had a copy of Randy's statement, and after a thorough investigation of the charges, presented everything to the U.S. Attorney's office. Early in 1970, Bruce Bass and a Corpus Christi accomplice were indicted for fraud. The charges also named two men from Louisville, Kentucky, as co-conspirators. After numerous delays by lawyers for the defense, the trial was scheduled to begin in October 1972.

With Randy Farenthold the key witness, prosecutors thought they had a sure thing. He was an upstanding citizen of the community with family members highly placed in State politics. Furthermore, he insisted on testifying against Bruce Bass and his associates. He made a powerful witness. The prosecution, however, failed to take into account the power of Randy's adversaries. When Randy reported death threats on his life if he persisted in testifying against Bass and his associates, authorities failed to take them seriously. It turned out to be a colossal mistake.

It now appeared to Jim that he had, at last, stumbled over the motive for the murder. He concentrated his efforts on Bruce Bass and his associates. The four men in the indictment, however, had iron-clad alibis for the time of the murder, but that didn't faze Jim. He reasoned that the murder could have been committed by a hired "hitman."

By now, the Port Aransas area literally swarmed with federal investigators. They found nothing more than what the sheriff's deputies or Jim had found. The FBI then expanded its investigation to include New Orleans where THE LOLLIPOP had been entered in the fishing tournament the week prior to the murder. Every participating fisherman, every boat captain and dock worker who had even the remotest contact with Randy was interrogated and released. Hotel desk clerks, waitresses, bellhops, bartenders, maids...no one was overlooked by the FBI. New Orleans turned up an absolute blank.

The FBI then sought out a banker in Georgia, a man who was involved in the gambling click that Randy belonged to. The banker testified that it was his practice to fly a bunch of the gambling members to the Bahamas, and they would gamble on his plane, spend a couple of days in the sun, and fly back. During the investigation, however, the FBI became highly interested in all the money that the banker was spending, and the man eventually ended up in the penitentiary for embezzling a lot of money from several banks. Things just went on this way, turning all these weird rocks over, but nothing led to the apprehension of Randy's killer.

When the federal authorities decided to look for any shadowy character in Randy's past that might have borne him a grudge, they travelled the Gulf Coast from Cozumel, Mexico, to Carabel, Florida, stopping and interrogating people in hundreds of places. They questioned yachtsmen and shrimpers, jet setters and the downtrodden, running the social gamut from the fabulously wealthy to the unemployed. They expended thousands of investigative hours and learned only one thing--- Randy Farenthold had been well-liked by virtually everyone, and they all wanted to see his killer brought to justice.

Meanwhile, right after Randy's body was found with no trace of his killer, the Farenthold family prepared to issue a news statement with the offer of a six-figure reward for the arrest and conviction of Randy's slayer. Sheriff Johnnie Mitchell talked them out of it---temporarily anyway. The Sheriff feared the announcement would bring an onslaught of false tips and interference from the general public, especially thrill seekers. He may as well have saved his breath. Everyone in the Coastal Bend area attempted to help, reward or no, and investigators from all the agencies involved found themselves stumbling over each other as they tracked down each lead and false clue.

The murder car was finally found abandoned in a maize field off Weber Road in the far southwestern part of Corpus Christi. Chemical tests of the trunk proved it to be the vehicle which had transported Randy to the dock for his final journey to his watery grave, but the owner of the car had reported it stolen. The owner also had an iron-clad alibi. In fact, no one could be found who could even be suspected of driving the death car.

Finding the murder car also presented more problems. To get the body into the trunk required two or more people. Randy stood five feet, ten inches tall, and he weighed 250 pounds. He was healthy and strong, in the prime of life. It seemed unlikely to Jim that any one person could have subdued Randy and inflicted the terrible damaged that he had suffered. Furthermore, one person could not have lifted the body from the trunk and carried him onto the boat---unless the killer was some kind of gigantic weight lifter.

Things took another weird twist when Bruce Bass called the police to his home, pointing in terror to his front door where someone had left a crudely lettered note: "YOU WILL GET YOURS." Some investigators believed it was just a ruse to put lawmen off the scent, but others believed that it was a genuine threat from Randy's friends on Mustang Island. The islanders, all 1,218 of them, would have done just about anything to see Randy Farenthold's murder avenged.

By the time the fraud case was due to come to trial in October, there was still no indictment in Randy's murder. And without the key witness, the charges against Bruce Bass and associates were dropped. The four co-

conspirators scattered.

As the years passed, Jim worked the case at every free moment that he had. His gut feeling told him that Bruce Bass had something to do with the murder, even if Bass's iron-clad alibi did put him somewhere else at the time. It remained only for Jim to find the evidence which would point to Bass's guilt. Jim was not alone in his belief. As he searched for the missing clue, the Nueces County Sheriff's Department, the FBI, the Corpus Christi Police Department's Organized Crime Unit, and the Nueces County District Attorney also continued to work the case. No one lost track of Bruce Bass.

There also continued to be false leads pouring in from the community in response to the reward offered by the Farenthold family, which now approached one million dollars. Every one was methodically checked out. One promising lead claimed Randy had been killed by a hired killer from Mexico, only when Jim checked into it, the suspect could not be found and the story could not be verified. Jim eventually chalked it all off as a red herring.

By this time, there were so many investigators from so many different investigative agencies that keeping up with the traffic of paperwork seemed all but impossible. Jim finally decided it was time to try yet another tactic. A friend of his, Ken Bung, a Lieutenant in the Corpus Christi Police Department assigned to the Organized Crime Unit, called him early one morning, suggesting that they interrogate a prison inmate in the state penitentiary, who might be able to shed some light on the Farenthold investigation. The two lawmen journeyed to Huntsville, near Houston. The inmate had admitted to killing twelve people---"they all deserved killing, but I never picked on any officer"---but he was only convicted of killing two. Although the prisoner readily agreed to talk to the officers, he wasn't able to help in any way.

Disappointed, Jim and Ken left the penitentiary. They hadn't gotten very far before Jim's intuition kicked into gear. "Ken," Jim said, "Robert Walters is up here. He may be able to help us. Let's go talk to him while we're here."

"Sure," replied Lt. Bung. What did they have to lose?

Jim reached for the radio and called the Huntsville headquarters, known as "The Walls," to find out which prison Walters was in.

Robert Walters was in jail in Rosharon for his part in the Robert Graham jail break, and the lawmen drove over to the prison to interview him. He didn't say anything, other than to "let me think about it." Two weeks later, he sent Jim a letter. "Come back. I want to talk to you," he wrote.

Jim and Ken Bung drove back to Rosharon, and Robert Walters gave them an earful. "I'm not interested in any reward money,"

Walters said. "I'm also not interested in getting out early. I'm doing my time, and I'll be out soon. This is the way it went down."

Walters said that Bruce Bass had come to him and had asked him to set everything up for the hit. According to Walters, Bass had told him to rent two cars, buy a boat and motor to transport the body out into the Gulf, and buy a chain and the big concrete blocks which were used to weigh the body down. Bass then had him buy a navigation map, rent a boat slip in the water at Port Aransas, and rent a boat barn stall in Corpus Christi. Walters then explained how Bass got rid of the boat and the stolen murder car---the whole works. With this information, Jim and the Corpus Christi Organized Crime Unit began to corroborate everything Walters said.

Meanwhile, the unthinkable happened. It was now 1975, and Bruce Bass was involved in a serious automobile accident. As he lay in guarded condition, close to death, police officers, who were so close to arresting him, became frantic with worry. They were almost in a state of sheer panic. "If he dies," one of them remarked, "we'll never close the case." "Yeah, I'd give that guy blood if it'd induce him to give us a statement."

When Bruce Bass, the prime suspect, finally recovered from the accident and was released from the hospital, he left Texas for Grand Junction, Colorado. He rented a two-bedroom apartment for $250 a month under the alias of Ponders.

Jim and officers of the Organized Crime Unit were finally able to put all the evidence together, and they gave it to District Attorney William B. Mobley. In March 1976, Mobley laid it before the Grand Jury. The panel members spent three months reviewing the evidence. Just before its session was due to expire in July, they requested, and received, a three month extension to continue the study of the evidence. On September 8, in a sealed indictment, the Grand Jury charged Bruce Bass with the murder of Randy Farenthold.

The indictment was passed on to the District Attorney's office, and a warrant for arrest was issued for Bruce Bass. Grand Junction, Colorado, authorities then arrested Bass without incident. He waived extradition proceedings, and on September 10, Jim and two members of the Organized Crime Unit flew in a Department of Public Safety plane to Grand Junction and escorted Bruce Bass back to Texas.

On the way back, the plane stopped in Lubbock, Texas, to refuel, and Jim escorted the prisoner to a comfortable chair in the lounge, where they could wait. Bass, who hadn't spoken one word to Jim since the officers had picked him up, suddenly turned and said, "Peters, as skinny and frail as I am, do you think that I could kidnap Randy Farenthold, put him in the trunk of his car, take him out there, take him out of his car and put him into another car, transfer him from car to car, take him out there off Weber Road, beat him with a pistol and choke him to death, put him back in the car, take him over to Port Aransas, put him on a boat, take him out in the Gulf and lift him out of the boat with all those chains and concrete?"

Jim looked Bruce evenly in the eye and said, "No, but I know you had it done. They got Randy when he got home. They kidnapped him in his driveway and put him in the trunk of the car. They transferred him from one car to another, and you ordered it."

Robert Walters, in his talks with Jim, also named another person with Bass, and although all the law enforcement officers knew the other person with Bruce, the man was never prosecuted and his name cannot be given. Several years later, this other man died from a heart attack.

Robert Walters was given immunity for his cooperation in breaking the case. He said that he and his brother, Donnie, had gotten everything together for Bruce Bass. At the time Jim interviewed Walters in Rosharon, Donnie was in a federal penitentiary in Kansas, and Robert wanted to talk to Donnie.

"Can you make it possible for me to talk to my brother?" Walters asked Jim.

"Sure. Be glad to," Jim replied. It was a call from a prisoner in a state penitentiary to a prisoner in a federal penitentiary in another state.

"When we told the FBI about it later," Jim laughed, "they said, 'That's impossible. There's absolutely no way that it can be done.' I said, 'Oh yeah? I'm a Texas Ranger, and Rangers can do anything.'"

Bruce Bass stood trial for the murder of Randy Farenthold and was given thirteen years in the state penitentiary. Shortly after he was released, he was shot and killed by some of his unsavory associates.

When it came time to testify against Bruce Bass in federal court, Randy Farenthold had refused to back down, and he was murdered because of it. District Attorney William Mobley spoke for all lawmen everywhere when he said, "...to kill any witness in another case is about as bad as you can get...."

THE RICHARDSON MURDER CASE

Tied in with the Randy Farenthold murder case, because of the same investigators, informers, attorneys, and killers, and loosely tied to Jody Martin Parr, because she was once married to him, is the murder of Corpus Christi millionaire oilman William Asher Richardson, Jr. When Jim helped solve the Randy Farenthold case, he inadvertently solved the Richardson case, too.

It began around 9:00 p.m. on the night of August 1, 1971, when wealthy oilman, William Richardson, pulled the family's motor home into the driveway of his fashionable residence in the Country Club Estates on Corpus Christi's southside. He parked the vehicle in its customary place at the front corner of the house, close to the front door, and then chuckled as his wife and ten year old step-son gratefully scrambled out and bounded up the walk. The family had just returned from a weekend pigeon shoot in McAllen, and everyone was bone tired. Although it was still light enough to see outside, he couldn't wait to get inside the house and get some sleep.

Stretching and yawning after the three-hour drive, he turned on the kitchen light of the motor home, walked to the bedroom, retrieved his gun and a few other personal items, returned to the kitchen, turned off the light, and stepped out into the early darkness. Moments later, he lay sprawled in the driveway, shot at close range by unknown assailants.

When she heard the gunshots from inside the house, Shirley Richardson screamed. She ran toward the door, but Mary Chavez, the family's maid, grabbed her and stopped her from going back outside. Shirley then ran to the telephone, but found it was dead. Racing hysterically into the bedroom, she grabbed a shotgun, and again headed toward the front door. This time, her young son, James LaBarba, and Mary Chavez both prevented her from going outside. She and James finally exited out the back door, raced across the back yard, climbed over the fence, and ran to neighborhood houses for help.

The house directly behind the Richardson house belonged to an anesthesiologist. Doctor James Cottingham had just gotten home from work and was eating a late dinner when he heard four shotgun blasts. He dropped his fork and raced for the stairs, intending to see if he could look out the bedroom window over the back fence into the Richardson property. Halfway up the stairs, James LaBarba pounded on the patio door and breathlessly cried that his stepfather had been shot.

Cottingham immediately grabbed a breathing device and climbed the fence to try and help Richardson. He knelt beside the wounded man and tried to revive him, but soon realized it was hopeless. Richardson had been shot in the head and body at close range. Blood and tissue lay everywhere.

134

As Dr. Cottingham knelt beside the dead man, applying first aid in a futile attempt to revive Richardson, a car pulled into the driveway. Out jumped Jerry LaBarba, James's father and the former husband of Shirley Richardson. And Jerry carried a gun.

Doctor Cottingham, not knowing at first who it was, jumped back over the fence, but upon recognizing Jerry LaBarba, he returned to the Richardson yard and continued with his administration to William Richardson. James had called his father from the Cottingham house, and Jerry took only moments to respond.

A few minutes later, Corpus Christi Policeman D. L. Kennedy arrived, followed by more police and an ambulance. The scene was gruesome. Richardson's bloody and mutilated body lay right beside the camper's door. Bits of brain, body tissue, and blood littered the side of the trailer and pooled in the driveway. An autopsy would later determine that he had been shot in the head and body at close range with four blasts from a shotgun.

There appeared to be only two witnesses to the murder, Mary Chavez and James LaBarba. Chavez, who worked for the Richardsons as a maid and babysitter, told authorities that she had seen a strange man around the house four times that evening. The first three times he appeared to be canvassing the house, but on the fourth time, he was with another man. She saw two men run across the lawn with "long guns" in their hands toward the place where Richardson was cut down by shotgun blasts. One of the men was tall and skinny, and the other was short and stocky.

James LaBarba said he also saw two men, and gave descriptions matching those of Mary Chavez. The tall man was wearing sunglasses and a ball cap. James added only one other enticing piece of information. The tall, skinny man had a mole on his cheek.

The investigation of William Richardson's murder lasted one month with the police interrogating witnesses, suspects, and informers by the score. Their investigation was compounded by Richardson's membership in a highly selective gambling and pigeon shooting clique, which held high stakes games in various towns all across South Texas and neighboring states. He had just been to a pigeon shoot in McAllen and had come away with $3,000 in his pocket from the gambling that accompanied the shoot. Any person in the clique could have wanted the oilman dead. He was an excellent shot and an astute player in the gambling games. With so many towns and jurisdictions involved, Jim Peters was part of the investigation from the outset.

When the police finally determined they had enough evidence, they indicted two men for the murder, which they claimed was a murder for hire. The suspects, Thomas Odis Hammond, forty-two years old, and Sam Mena, thirty-seven years old, were both from Fort Worth, and both had previous police records.

In separate trials, conducted a year later, a series of statements and contradictions abounded to confuse the jury. The first man to be tried was Thomas Hammond, and District Attorney William Mobley went about methodically placing Hammond at the scene of the crime. He had Shirley Richardson, Mary Chavez, and James LaBarba testify. Then he called Dr. Cottingham and Jerry LaBarba. Next came the investigators, the medical experts, and even James's elementary school principal.

Mobley also put two policemen, Sergeants Larry Sherwood and G.E. Burch, on the stand to testify that they saw a Fort Worth man, who allegedly arrived in town to kill Mary Chavez because she was a witness. The two policemen were inside the Richardson house at the time the hitman arrived and watched as the man canvassed the property. Sergeant Burch then remained inside the house, while Sergeant Sherwood followed the suspect. The alleged hitman left town before doing anything, and six weeks later, he was found in the Fort Worth area with six bullets in the head.

No matter how detailed District Attorney Mobley got with the various witness, the defense attorneys, Richard Bradshaw and Douglas Tinker, managed to cast doubt on the proceedings. They questioned Shirley Richardson extensively about the pigeon shooting and her husband's role in it, asking her if he didn't make his living at the pigeon shoots. Shirley stated, "Generally speaking." Attorney Tinker then asked her about the gambling that took place at the McAllen pigeon shoot and about whether her husband had argued with a "*colombaire*," or live pigeon thrower, at the meet. Although she denied knowing anything about the argument, she said there had been gambling in the motel room of a Georgia banker.

The defense attorneys attempted to keep James LaBarba from testifying, claiming that he was not a "competent witness." When Judge Vernon Harville said the boy would be allowed to testify, Attorney Tinker told the youth that he was not "going to pick on you." Later, the boy's principal was subpoenaed to bring James's school records to court. A clinical psychologist, Dr. Richard Austin, Jr., then testified that James had been treated from 1968 to 1971 for a "learning problem," and that he had also been brought to him for treatment after the murder because the boy was "anxious and upset."

The defense attorneys were determined to place their client, Thomas Hammond, somewhere else at the time of the shooting. They brought in witness after witness to testify that Hammond was in Fort Worth on the day in question, even though a witness had placed Sam Mena in a Valley hotel on July 30th, 1971. They also used a State's witness to show that a drive from Fort Worth to the Valley would take seven-and-a-half hours at a minimum.

One of the most interesting pieces of testimony came from Jim's favorite informer, Strawberry. Strawberry, serving a ten-year prison term at a prison farm in Huntsville for assault with intent to rob, had been a cellmate of Thomas Hammond and Sam Mena in the Nueces County Jail at the time of the latter two's arrest. When the Richardson murder had occurred, Strawberry was out of the penitentiary on an appeal bond. While awaiting his appeal hearing, he committed another burglary, got arrested, and was placed in the cell with Hammond and Mena.

On the witness stand, Strawberry told District Attorney Mobley of an alleged assassination plot to kill Mary Chavez. He admitted that he had contacted a Fort Worth man, Tommy Gibbs, on instructions from Hammond and Mena. He was to instruct Gibbs to kill Mary Chavez, and it had been Sam Mena who had asked him to get Gibbs to do it..

When Attorney Mobley asked Strawberry if Hammond ever said anything about killing the maid, Strawberry replied, "He said that's the only chance they would have. She was an eyewitness." Strawberry then conferred with his court-appointed attorney, Kenneth Yarbrough, before admitting that police officers the year before had asked him to get information on Hammond and Mena while in the cell with them.

In his testimony, he admitted that after sharing a cell with the two men for three weeks, he was out of jail because the burglary charge was dismissed "for lack of evidence." It was after he was released that he had contacted Gibbs and pointed out Mary Chavez's house to him, while two policemen had watched from inside the house. Sergeant Sherwood had then tailed Gibbs, while Sergeant Burch remained in the house.

In a hearing outside the presence of the jury, District Attorney Mobley also questioned a retired Houston policeman, B. Steward Baker, about a murder investigation he had conducted in 1959 for which Hammond was convicted. Hammond had a sawed-off shotgun, but did not use it in that burglary. According to Baker, Hammond confessed, stating that the motive was robbery. Hammond and three other men had viewed the scene prior to the murder and had "laid in waiting."

Attorney Mobley wanted to present Baker's testimony to the jury to show similarities between the Houston killing and the Richardson killing, but since constitutional rights warnings were not required in 1959 by the U.S. Supreme Court and they are today, Judge Harville ruled Baker's testimony to be in a gray area and would not allow it into evidence.

An FBI firearms expert, Richard J. Poppleton, testified that the four shotgun-shell hulls found at the scene were all fired by the same "automatic or pump-action shotgun," which ejects hulls from a slot on the side of the shotgun. James LaBarba had previously testified that the men he saw shoot his stepdad had used "over and under" shotguns and opened or "broke" their guns, apparently to eject the four spent shells. Mobley then asked the expert if the four spent hulls could have landed where they were found by police after being ejected from an automatic or pump action shotgun if the killers had stood where James LaBarba had claimed he had seen the men who killed his stepfather. Poppleton said it would be impossible, which prompted Mobley to claim the spent shells were a plant. But not finding the murder weapon left that testimony up in the air.

Eventually, with so much confusing and conflicting testimony, the jury reached no verdict. Without a verdict in the Hammond case, Sam Mena was not prosecuted. William Richardson's murder remained unsolved, and that's how things stood---until Jim and Ken Bung made their historic trip to Huntsville to talk to Robert Walters about the Randy Farenthold murder a few years later.

During the interview with Walters on Farenthold, Walters gave Jim a statement on the Richardson murder. According to Walters, Bruce Bass and his partner had shown up at his apartment complex August 1, 1971, with a scheme to kill William Richardson that afternoon when he came in from his pigeon shoot in McAllen.

Walters said that the two men were supposed to bring him the shotgun that they would use in the murder, and he was supposed to dispose of it for them. The two men were then going to rush home "so we can be home when they call us about the news."

Walters went on to explain that Bruce Bass was involved in the gambling clique. In fact, there was a whole group from the Corpus Christi area involved in the action long before William Richardson became a part of it. The man in charge of much of the activities was an influential banker in Georgia, which the FBI later arrested and prosecuted for embezzlement.

Bruce Bass used to play a prominent role in the gambling activities, but Bass started using narcotics quite heavily, and he got where he couldn't shoot very well because of the effects of the drugs. He was quietly, but purposely, put aside and replaced with Richardson. Then, as his habit became worse, he was also cut out of the gambling games and again replaced with Richardson. When that happened, it was the last straw, and the reason he allegedly killed Richardson.

According to Walters, Bass had approached him and asked, "Are you going to be home tonight?" and then explained what he wanted. Walters had answered, "I think so. My wife and I talked about going to a picture show, so if I'm not here, leave the shotgun on top of the storage box outside the apartment, and I'll dispose of it when I get home."

Walters then said that he and his wife didn't go to the picture show, and "they came by and gave me the shotgun after Bruce said he killed him.

138

I dismantled the gun and threw the bolt down a storm sewer. I then took the rest of it and threw it off a bridge into the water in Oso Creek."

It was great news for Jim. As soon as he could arrange it, he and several other officers searched the Oso Creek for the shotgun to corroborate the statement. However, due to the elapsed time involved, the bottom of the creek was covered in about three feet of mud. It came clear up to the knees of the searchers and was so thick and so mucky that the lawmen never were able to locate the gun to corroborate Walter's statement.

Bruce Bass was tried for the Randy Farenthold murder, and that was it. He received thirteen years in the penitentiary, got out, and was shot to death not too long afterwards. He was never tried for the Richardson murder.

'Richardson was eliminated because Bruce was mad," Jim said. "Even though two men were arrested for the Richardson case, we never could prove they did it---until up jumped Robert Walters with his confession. But, we never could find the shotgun to corroborate his statement, and without the shotgun, it was only a story."

Officially, the William Asher Richardson, Jr., murder case remains unsolved.

JODY MARTIN PARR

Throughout his law enforcement career, Jim encountered the mighty George Parr and members of his extended family on many occasions. And it was always to the advantage of the Parrs. They were a powerful and corrupt political machine, holding the reins of Duval County since the turn of the century. They also always considered themselves above the law, or at least on the same level with it, and they weren't about to let anyone forget it. Especially Jody. The plight of the beautiful, tragic woman touched people all over the State. Knowing the Parr family as well as he did, after years of butting heads with them, no one was more moved by Jody's predicament than Jim.

Jody's life reads like a fairylike gone sour. She was born in Oklahoma in 1934, one of three daughters of Eben Martin and his wife, and lavished with lots of love and attention as only doting parents could give. Through her mother, she was a direct descendant of Nancy Ward, known by the Indian name of Guigau, and Nancy was one of the few women leaders known to have participated in high Cherokee councils. Jody's Cherokee heritage showed in her features, and she grew up tall and slim, having the high cheekbones of top fashion models. With the unusual mix of blonde hair and brown eyes, she was the most beautiful woman in South Texas. Jody would later claim it was her Cherokee blood that kept her going.

The Martin family moved to Corpus Christi when Jody was in the second grade, and the city became her permanent home. But Jody was a shy child, and to overcome her shyness, she began modeling fashions at several local department stores. By the time she graduated from the old Corpus Christi High School in 1950, she was as outgoing and vibrant as a person could be.

Jody immediately entered local Del Mar Junior College after high school, and she met William Asher Richardson there. The man was charming and attentive and absolutely enraptured with the beautiful Jody. Two years later, in 1952, after graduating from the College, she and Richardson married in a lavish wedding ceremony attended by hundreds of friends and family members. A year later, when it was obvious that the marriage wouldn't take, Jody and Richardson divorced.. She decided to return to modeling and quickly became a top model for Lichtenstein's Department Store, a Corpus Christi landmark since 1875 when Sol Lichtenstein supplied Ranger Captain Leander McNelly with anything he needed to tame the outlaw-controlled Nueces Strip.

Jody liked modeling for Lichtenstein's, and her years at the store became her introduction to the world of high fashion. In 1960, she opened her own boutique, calling it "Jody, Inc." It did well, earning her much prestige throughout the community, but Jody was restless. She wanted more from life than a nine-to-five workday routine. She wanted marriage and a family. She wanted love.

After five years with the exclusive dress shop, she sold the firm for a huge profit and turned to travel. On one of her trips, she met Archer Parr, Duval County Judge, nephew of George Parr, and the heir apparent to the mighty Parr political machine of Duval County.

Archer Parr was the semi-mystery man in the Parr Regime. He was like his uncle when it came to politics and authority, but people found him disconcertingly unfathomable with his charm and graciousness. He was respectfully literate, reading more than just the hunting and quarterhorse magazines like his uncle, but he preferred speaking the "double-meaning-riddled Spanish idiom" of the poor peons in the area rathen than good English. He loved travel, and he was rich, yet he lived in a one-story concrete-block ranch house that had all the appeal and charm of a maximum security prison (although few prisons have chicken coops inside the yard.) As a rancher, he pursued quality with over 700 head of prized, South-Texas-bred Beefmaster cattle. And yet, much to the utter disgust of other Duval cattlemen, he also fed 1,200 Spanish goats. He enjoyed beautiful women and beautiful places, and his frequenting of both had labeled him a playboy in Corpus Christi society.

To Jody, he appeared to be all she wanted in a man: rich, famous, and well-connected. But she really didn't know what she was getting into when she started dating him. After learning that she planned on becoming Archer's fourth wife, her friends warned her that she was handling snakes. She was naive of the way things were run in Duval County, they cautioned, but she "poo-pooed" all the advice her friends gave her. After a whirlwind romance, she and Archer married in Rio Grande City on July 12, 1969. They alternated living between Archer's 1,600-acre ranch, just west of San Diego in Duval County, and a town house condominium on the fashionable southside in Corpus Christi.

For awhile, Jody and Archer were a happy couple, and in February, 1973, Jody found herself pregnant for the first time. It was all she had ever wanted, and she was elated. Three months later, to celebrate the occasion, she and Archer flew with friends to Acapulco, Mexico, but the celebration was short-lived. Jody miscarried while they were there, and the loss depressed her terribly. Archer, more gifted at handling Spanish goats than depressed women, just ignored her. They quarreled, said bitter things, and Jody cried that she wanted out of the marriage. Archer completely agreed.

But hot tempers have a way of cooling, and once back in Corpus Christi, they again talked of having a baby. Duval County politics, however, got in the way, and Jody was no match for it. It reared its ugly head on June

24, when Archer did their income tax. He was working on their joint statement, and he wanted her signature to a document she believed was inaccurate. "It did not," she would later testify, "acknowledge the fact that once a month, a county official delivered an envelope containing $5,000 in cash to Archer. He called it a love letter from the taxpayers."

It was their final argument. The next day, she filed a divorce petition in Nueces County's Domestic Relations Court. Archer Parr promptly responded by filing his own divorce petition July 3rd in the 229th District Court in San Diego, the seat of Duval County politics, where the Parr family had held the reins of government for more than sixty years. What followed next was a legal tug of war to determine where the divorce case would be tried. It lasted nearly a year.

Jody's lawyer, Jack Pope, at first refused to believe all the things Jody was telling him. But later, after Duval County had charge of the divorce case, after learning that Archer had talked his creditors into filing against the couple's community property and that a Parr-linked lawyer, Emilio Davila of Laredo, had been named the court-appointed Receiver and was systematically confiscating all of Jody's property and none of Archer's, Pope tried to move the case to Nueces County. He never succeeded.

The lawsuits began coming in from every direction. The First State Bank of San Diego filed suit in the Duval County Courthouse against both Parrs to collect $125,000 on a promissory note. That was promptly followed by the Alamo Lumber Company of Alice filing suit to collect $8,534. Next, others intervened in the bank suit, claiming debts of more than $100,000. Duval County filed suit against both Parrs, claiming each of them owed the County $220,000. Even Jody's town house furniture was sold during the complex legal battle.

With millions of dollars at stake and so many suits involved, a court order was finally issued to place the estate of the estranged couple into receivership. They were prohibited from distributing any of their estate before the debts were settled.

Jody Martin Parr owned jewels and furs worth approximately a quarter-million dollars, and she sold some of them to get money to live on and to pay lawyers. Emilio Davila, the Court Receiver, had taken everything she had in her town house---her clothes, the furniture, even two dozen filet steaks and ten bottles of wine that were in the house. She later acquired a hard, metal Army cot, a card table and chair, and a black-and-white television set from a friend.

With Archer and his receiver-friend breathing down her neck for the rest of her jewelry and fur collection, but ignoring Archer's own jewelry, furs and horses, she filed a Federal Bankruptcy Petition, which removed her property from the hand of the State Court and effectively shielded her from any more of that type harassment. But this action infuriated the 229th District Court, which was under Archer and George Parr's domain, and it retaliated in force.

First, District Judge Magus Smith of Edinburg sentenced Jody in October 1973 to a ninety-day jail term for selling her property against court orders. The judge said she could clear herself if she'd provide detailed information on the sale, and if she would also give Emilio Davila her $20,000 engagement ring and her Cadillac. She refused.

Judge Smith then increased the jail term to 150 days for failing to appear in court and purging herself of contempt. And by this time, Jody did have a contempt of the Duval County legal system. She said that she feared for her life if placed in the Duval County jail. Her sister feared for her also. When Jody was finally incarcerated in the facility, her sister, Bonnie White, kept vigil in a car outside the courthouse. George Parr visited Jody that first night and invited her to stay at his house. Fearful of what would happen to her at Parr's house, Jody refused the offer.

Meanwhile, Jack Pope was in Austin obtaining her freedom, and by the time the Texas Supreme Court granted a Writ of Habeas Corpus three days later, the U.S. Attorney in Houston, Anthony J.T. Farris, had wired Duval, warning them that Jody had been subpoenaed as a Federal Grand Jury witness. The unwritten message was that they expected her to be alive and well when they needed her.

The Texas Supreme Court later overturned the contempt sentence, but new contempt of court charges were then levied, only Nueces County Sheriff Johnnie Mitchell refused to serve it. In fact, so touchy was the situation that Sheriff Mitchell refused to involve his office in any way in any of the proceedings. It was finally decided that the Texas Rangers would take charge, and Captain John Wood asked Jim to serve the warrant. Jody later said it was the best thing Archer had ever done for her, as it got her introduced to Rangers John Wood and Jim Peters. She didn't know how to handle the boys in Duval, but the Rangers were men; she didn't have to handle them.

Jim's involvement in Jody's plight began in the late afternoon of June 4, 1974, when Kenneth Yarbrough, an attorney who represented District Judge Magus Smith of Edinburg, delivered a bench warrant for Jody Martin Parr to him in Corpus Christi. The bench warrant was from Duval County, and it ordered Jody Martin Parr to be returned to Duval County to answer charges of contempt of court. The Nueces County Sheriff's Office, under orders from Sheriff Johnnie Mitchell, had refused to serve the warrant or any type of warrant on Jody Parr, and a local judge had decided that the best way to handle the situation would be to turn the warrant over to the Texas Rangers. Ranger Captain John Wood had agreed, and the judge made the warrant to the Texas Rangers.

Jim was about four or five blocks away from Jody's condominium on Santa Fe Street when he pulled his car to the side of the road and carefully re-read the terms of the warrant. He knew that Jody Parr did not want to be returned to Duval County. She had an intense distrust and fear of the County's legal system, mainly because Archer Parr was the County Judge and George Parr was his powerful uncle. Jim understood Jody's reasoning only too well. He himself had come up against the powerful Parr machine many times in his own career.

Jim knew also that Jody Parr had made several statements concerning Duval County, and one of her quotations was, "I'm still waiting, and they are trying to arrest me on old charges of Archer's, charges which have already been thrown out by the Texas Supreme Court. I am not going to go." On another occasion she had said, "I have barricaded my door and will shoot anyone that tries to come in."

Jim felt that forcibly arresting her at her own home would be a mistake, that she would either hurt someone or herself in her desperate attempt to remain clear of Duval County. As he studied the document, he looked for any loophole which would keep him from taking her there. When he found it, he took a deep breath of relief. She might eventually end up in the Duval County Jail in San Diego, but for right now, she did not have to go there.

Jim laid the warrant on the seat beside him. Nowhere did the document say to place her in the Duval County Jail. That was where she definitely did not want to go. After deciding what would be the best way to meet the needs of public interest, he knew the smart thing to do was to call her attorney and ask him to surrender her. He placed the call.

"She's not going to go to that jail," warned Jack Pope, Jody's attorney, in listening to Jim.

"Well, Jack," replied Jim, "nowhere does it say on this warrant that she has to go to the Duval County Jail. She just has to be brought to the court. You pick the jail, and we'll do it."

Jack Pope and Justice of the Peace Mike Westergren, who was also representing Jody Martin Parr, made arrangements to surrender her on Wednesday, June 5th, at the Texas Supreme Court Building in Austin, if the Texas Rangers would agree. That arrangement was fine with Jim and Captain John Wood. The two Rangers met the attorneys and Jody Parr at 3:00 p.m., where she surrendered herself peacefully on a Writ of Habeas Corpus filed in the Texas Supreme Court.

The Court denied the Writ, and she was then taken by DPS plane to Corpus Christi, where Nueces County Sheriff Johnnie Mitchell refused to keep her in his jail. Sheriff Mitchell did agree, however, to keep her

144

overnight. The next day, she was transferred to the Jim Wells County Jail in Alice, and on the following day, she was removed to San Diego, where she was to begin serving ninety days in the County Jail of Duval for contempt of court.

Since Jody had such a deep mistrust of Duval County, the Sheriff of Jim Wells County made arrangements with Judge Magus Smith for her to serve the ninety days in his jail. She was then carried back to Alice to begin her sentence. At all times she conducted herself as a lady, and Jim was very much impressed with her demeanor.

By this time, Jody was broke---financially, materially, and emotionally. Jack Pope once again obtained her freedom by getting the Texas Supreme Court to grant another Writ of Habeas Corpus, but even he was becoming financially strapped. He'd already sold off some prized land investments to pay his living expenses, and once he came close to having his telephone disconnected for non-payment. Still, he kept hoping that one of the higher courts would tell the Duval court to quit playing Contempt and Receiver and get on with the divorce.

A hearing was scheduled for June 19 in Austin, and Jody also faced additional contempt charges set for a hearing before Judge Smith on June 28 for "failure to appear in court." She admitted to reporters that 'they are going to stack eight or nine charges against me, and I'll get about two or three years in jail.' Jim followed her predicament closely, wishing there was some way he could help.

Jody's despair was deepening into a mood of terminal resignation. The Federal Court said she'd have to pay $25,000 in administrative costs just to get her furs and substantial jewelry collection back. If she could repossess them, she could sell them, pay her lawyers, pay her family, pay her friends---and live. But she hadn't the money to buy them back. At one time, she made a statement that she had been close to a nervous breakdown, but she pulled herself out of it, determined to win without compromising her integrity. She claimed her "bullheadedness" came from her Cherokee blood, but it still wasn't enough to save her.

All through the night of June 12, Jody wrote letters. She wrote twenty-six letters to her friends, to her attorneys, to her mother and father, her sisters, even to casual acquaintances, neighbors, and newsmen. In most cases the letters were to thank someone for help or for offering assistance. In others, she reminisced of past good times. Most were pleasant, even light, but there was no mistaking her intentions. She said that she had lived a good life, that she was happy, and not to grieve for her. At 7:00 a.m. on the morning of June 13, she put a .25 caliber pistol to her head and pulled the trigger. Jody Martin Parr was dead on arrival at the hospital---a forty-year-old victim of a political machine she couldn't handle.

When Jim arrived at the scene, the poverty she was forced to live in completely horrified him. There was absolutely nothing in her condominium that belonged to her: the Court Receiver had taken everything---every stick of furniture, her clothing, her food, everything. All that remained had been donated by family and friends, and it was a meager assortment of cheap odds and ends.

Jody's suicide sparked remorse throughout the area. Many attorneys from some of the most prestigious law firms who had turned Jody down in her appeals for help sent word that they were sorry, but it was a terribly hollow gesture sent far too late. Some said they felt shame that such a travesty of justice could occur in their own backyard, and others vowed it would never happen again. Judge Magus Smith went into seclusion for three days, and acquaintances said word of Jody's suicide had shaken him. Attorney William Bonilla made a statement: "It was a bad day for the administration of justice. I hope the bar association of the respective counties and the State Bar never forget what happened today." Jack Pope talked of giving up the practice of law---his ideals had been shattered.

Upon learning of Jody's suicide, Archer disappeared, and a few of her friends were vastly relieved. They were afraid that if he showed up at her funeral, her mother or someone else might kill him, and that would spoil everything. They wanted him in jail and it looked as if they might get their way. A few weeks prior to Jody's suicide, a federal court had convicted him of lying to a grand jury and sentenced him to prison terms totalling ten years. He was also fined $60,000. The conviction came after he was renominated in an uncontested election for another term as County Judge. The federal judge who had tried the case, in a rare exercise of judicial prerogatives, had even specified the jail: Leavenworth, Kansas. Maximum security.

George B. Parr was also convicted of income tax evasion and sentenced to five years. On April Fool's Day in 1975, George Parr's body was found in the Julian pasture on the old family ranch, Los Horcones, south of Benavides. He had shot himself with a .45 caliber revolver, the bullet going completely through his brain and exiting through the open left front window of his car.

The office of Duke of Duval was vacant for the first time in sixty-three years.

Later, Ranger Captain John Wood obtained the gun that George Parr had used to kill himself. Jim acquired Jody's gun. Jim later gave the .25 caliber weapon to his Captain, John Wood.

"Duval County has always thought it was above the law," Jody once wrote a friend. At her funeral, the minister, Lester Roloff, had said, "The next judge she stands before, she will get justice and mercy."

"All she ever wanted was a divorce she never got," Jim said quietly.

THE MY JUDY II AFFAIR

Although the culprit was never brought to justice, Jim's crafty sleuthing solved the disappearance of the *MY JUDY II*, a seventy-four foot, steel-hulled, shrimp boat which disappeared from her moorings in the dead of night one weekend in December 1974. The owner claimed it was stolen. The insurance company wasn't so sure. Their attorney contacted Jim to investigate. What Jim discovered was another comedy of errors adventure from beginning to end.

No one will ever know for sure, but the case probably began in the early 1970's when the United States Government, in a misguided sense of duty, tried to help refugee Southeast Asians establish homes along sea coasts all across America. The plan was to provide fishing boats at ridiculously low interest rates for these immigrants to make their livings. And it was probably a good plan, in general. But for many localities, the idea tragically backfired. One such locality was the tiny fishing village of Port Aransas.

The main---perhaps only---problem with the Government's plan was that with newer boats and better equipment, the refugees became too much competition for the local fishermen. It forced the locals to either go out of business altogether, or go heavily into debt by updating their equipment and buying new boats. In the fishing mecca of Port Aransas, the local fishermen totally resented the situation.

Although it can't definitely be said that the competition was the linchpin in the *MY JUDY II* affair, it most assuredly played a big role. Sometime on that December weekend in 1974, between the 12th and the 16th, the big shrimp boat slipped her moorings and went to sea for the last time. The owner said someone took her, but when no trace of her could be found anywhere up and down the Gulf Coast, it was Jim's contention that the boat had been taken out into the Gulf and sunk for insurance purposes. It was one thing to suspect deliberate sabotage, however, and quite another to prove it. Jim had to find the boat's watery grave before charges could be brought against anyone, and he sunk his teeth into the task with great determination and gusto.

Jim began his investigation in the normal manner by first interviewing the owner and obtaining a description of the boat. The *MY JUDY II* was a trawler, seventy-four feet long, white with blue trim and black rigging---a steel-hulled ship with all the newest engines and equipment money could buy. Even her miles of netting were almost new, having only been in the salt water less than a year before her disappearance. She was so beautiful that she stood out like a queen among her shabby sisters at the dock. Her value was $150,000, and it put her owner heavily into debt.

The owner insisted that the boat had been stolen, and as Jim questioned dock hands and sailors in the immediate area of the boat's mooring, he worked under the initial impression that the owner was probably right. The boat was the envy of all who saw her, and any number of people wanted her. Still, two questions kept bothering Jim. If the *MY JUDY II* had been so admired and desired, how could anyone expect to steal her and get away with it? A new boat of her type stood out so conspicuously that no one would have been able to disguise her to use her. It made no sense to steal her because she would have been recognized by fishermen all up and down the coast. Yet, if theft wasn't the reason, what was? The questions nagged at the back of Jim's mind.

In the off chance that the boat really had been disguised and tied up in some shallow back bay, Jim got with the Harbor Patrol and Coast Guard, asking them to be on the lookout for any vessel matching the general size or description of the *MY JUDY II*. Then, after a day of searching the area himself with no sight of the missing boat, he gave in to the nagging voice inside his head.

His intuition told him that the boat had been scuttled, for whatever reason he could only guess, although insurance money stuck out like a sore thumb. With that in mind, he proceeded to interview every fisherman and dock hand along the wharfs and docks in the whole general area. He struck pay dirt almost immediately when he began asking the right questions. Instead of seeking the boat and the people who stole her, he asked who would profit the most if she disappeared completely.

Fishermen have a unique fraternity. Not only do they know everyone in the fishing business for miles around, they also know everything there is to know about everyone's business in the fishing business for miles around. The only real problem is that they are a close-knit fraternity, and outsiders are looked upon with suspicion. Jim could feel the underlying current, the tenseness of mistrust when he was around. Although he was no stranger, having questioned many of the same people in the Coast Guard murder case and the Randy Farenthold murder case a few years earlier, no one really wanted to talk. Just as he was about to start elsewhere, he made friends with an old salt in one of the popular sailor hangouts by buying the old man a beer.

Jim learned from the shrimper that the owner of the *MY JUDY II* had four shrimp boats. Two had already been seized for non-payment of bills, and papers had been drawn to seize a third one. The only reason the papers were not drawn against the *MY JUDY II was* because of the lien still on the boat. Desperate for cash, rumor had it that the owner had hired someone to scuttle the *MY JUDY II* at sea.

Jim understood shrimping, and he knew the owner of the *MY JUDY II* had to be heavily in debt. It costs a lot of money to operate a shrimp boat.

The fuel costs alone are astronomical, since a shrimp boat trolls all night and sometimes all day with its nets out and the engines running. Adding to the financial worry are also the maintenance costs on the engines and hydraulics, the boat upkeep, netting repairs, fish holds, and so on. Nowadays, shrimp boats must also include turtle excluder devices (TEDs) on their nets because several endangered species of turtles inhabit the Gulf waters. Installing and maintaining the TEDs are an added expense, not to mention that the skipper has to bring his nets in often to ensure he hasn't trapped dolphins or porpoise. The whole operation cuts down on the catch. To top it all off, unlike the charter fishing boats who take paying customers, the shrimp boats rely solely on their catch for their income.

Asking carefully pointed questions, Jim quietly learned that all the electronic equipment had already been removed from the boat, as well as one of her engines. An old engine had then been installed, but on the second trip into the Gulf, the crankshaft had broken. The owner promptly filed an insurance claim stating that the "new" engine had failed, but he had not yet been paid. As the plot thickened, so did Jim's determination to find the missing boat.

Once Jim satisfied himself that the boat was genuinely missing, and suspecting that the owner had something to do with her disappearance because the owner seemed in a mighty big hurry for the insurance company to settle the claim, he began questioning characters in shrimping communities up and down the coast. He also notified all agencies to be on the lookout for the missing boat.

The insurance company posted a $5,000 reward to be paid to the first person furnishing information leading to the location and recovery of the missing shrimp boat. As a result of the reward, an informer called the insurance company's attorney with an enlightening story. He said that he and his wife were fishing at the jetties around 11:00 p.m., and they observed the *MY JUDY II* going through the jetties approximately sixty feet astern another shrimp boat. The informer gave the attorney the name of the other boat. The informer was also under the impression that the missing boat was being towed by the first boat because of the close distance, but he could not see a tow line between the two boats. In Jim's earlier investigation, he had already discovered that the first shrimp boat in the two-boat lineup witnessed by the informer as going through the jetties that night was also a boat owned by the owner of the *MY JUDY II*.

Another informer after the reward also called and said that he had seen the *MY JUDY II* going out to sea without any lights.

On February 1, 1975, Jim received information from Drug Enforcement Agency Officer Ed Courtney of Corpus Christi that they had an informant in New Orleans in possession of a newly painted shrimp boat, approximately seventy-four feet long. According to Agent Courtney, there was no earthly way that the informer could have obtained the money to purchase such a big boat. Courtney advised Jim that one of the DEA agents in New Orleans would investigate. Although the informer was, indeed, squatting on a large shrimp boat garnered by ill-gotten means, the boat was not the *MY JUDY II.*

Six days later, another lead led Jim to a nurse at the hospital in Aransas Pass. She said that her daughter, Debbie, had met a man named James Falloway* and had run off with him to Texas City. From there, the couple had gone to Mobile, Alabama, to live with Debbie's grandmother. Debbie told her mother that Falloway had been the captain of a shrimp boat that had been taken into the Gulf and sunk at the owner's request. The owner had been a friend to the owner of the *MY JUDY II.* The scuttling of the other ship boat had been for insurance purposes, and Falloway was to get a "cut" of the money after the insurance company paid. Supposedly, he was to have captained the *MY JUDY II*, only he had gone to the public health service hospital in Galveston for an operation.

Jim checked with the hospital in question, and hospital authorities revealed that Falloway had checked out of the hospital around 3:00 p.m. on that Friday, December 12th. He had not returned until Monday morning. It was the time frame of the *MY JUDY II's* disappearance. Jim also discovered that Falloway was wanted for aggravated assault on an officer, having attacked a DPS Narcotics Agent in a courtroom in Sinton, but had jumped bail. Jim sent the information to the Mobile Police Department, requesting that Falloway be arrested and detained for extradition to Texas.

Two weeks later, Jim and a deputy sheriff from San Patricio County were in Mobile, Alabama, to escort Falloway back to Texas for trial. While there, Jim talked to Debbie, and he learned that Falloway and Debbie had spent the time of the *MY JUDY II's* theft in a motel in Galveston. While escorting Falloway back to Texas, Jim had the information verified by the prisoner. Falloway also confirmed Debbie's information to her mother about the mysterious shrimp boat that had sunk while he was captain, stating that the sea cocks had accidentally been left open. According to Falloway, the boat sank, and he and the crew had spent five-and-a-half harrowing hours in the water before being rescued. He was supposed to have been the captain of the *MY JUDY II*, but had to go to the hospital in Galveston. By the time he had returned to Aransas Pass, the *MY JUDY II* had been stolen. He did say, however, that he was very familiar with her gear, and he saw all the electronic equipment sitting on the dock.

Two days later, Jim learned of David Grant*. Grant was in the Nueces County Jail for possession of marijuana, and he was being held without bond because he was a parole violator. Grant offered to give Jim the details of what happened to the *MY JUDY II*---for a price. He wanted Jim to see what could be done about the charges pending against him and also help him collect on the reward money. Although Jim made no promises, David Grant decided to talk anyway.

Grant said that a friend named Bennie Martinez* had taken the shrimp boat into the Gulf of Mexico, opened the seacocks, waited for the boat to sink, and then returned to the dock in another boat which had followed the doomed ship out to sea. The *MY JUDY II* had sunk just outside the twelve-mile limit at night.

Bennie was already well-known to the police, having been in and out of jail on a variety of miscellaneous charges for years. He was a heavy user of heroin and had pulled several burglaries, including a safe job where he was apprehended towing the safe down the street behind his car. He was a likeable, friendly fellow, always in need of money, and always willing to do just about anything to get it. The word on the street was that he had disappeared shortly after the *MY JUDY II* had mysteriously vanished. Supposedly, he had stolen the boat with two other men at the owner's request.

Jim began hunting for Bennie, and the first place he went to get information on the suspect was the Corpus Christi Police Department. To his surprise, he discovered that the Corpus Christi police already had a warrant for arrest for Bennie on theft charges unrelated to the *MY JUDY II*, only Bennie had fled the State. Bennie chose as his sanctuary, an Indian reservation somewhere in Washington State, which effectively shielded him from the clutches of any South Texas law.

Deciding that the suspect would sooner or later contact his mother or she would contact her son, Jim obtained the mother's address and went to see her. He asked, "The next time you hear from Bennie, would you have him call me collect at my house?" He
then gave the woman his home telephone number.

The woman agreed, and in March 1975, Jim got the call.

"Bennie," he said, "I need for you to help me bring an end to this case. I know you took the *MY JUDY II* shrimp boat out in the Gulf and sunk it. I know who hired you to do it, and I know why the man who owned the boat had it done. If you come down here and help me find that boat, I'll see what I can do about the cases pending against you."

Bennie Martinez listened carefully to everything Jim had to say, but he wasn't sure he wanted to return to Texas. It took several days of negotiating before Bennie finally agreed to cooperate.

"I'll have a plane ticket sent up there to you," Jim told the fugitive, "and you'll fly to Houston where I'll pick you up. Then we'll have a leisurely drive back to Corpus Christi where we can talk and visit. Along the way, we'll also stop for a nice meal of rock shrimp in Port Lavaca."

Bennie was suspicious. Corpus Christi has no direct flights into the city and no matter what airline Jim put him on, he would have to change planes in Dallas. Once back on Texas soil, what would prevent him from being nabbed by authorities the moment he deplaned in Dallas? Also, he couldn't understand why Jim wanted him to fly to Houston and then drive south to Corpus Christi. If the "Sparkling City by the Sea" was to be the ultimate destination anyway, why not just fly there in the first place?

"It's because I want to talk with you," Jim said. He then went on to explain that no one knew Bennie would be changing planes in Dallas for Houston, so no one would be waiting to seize him the moment he deplaned. And once in Houston, Jim could take him before a Houston magistrate, which by law, Jim had to do. The Houston magistrate would then read Bennie his rights and turn him over to Jim for the journey south. They could enjoy a leisurely drive and chat, stopping along the way for a nice lunch in Port Lavaca.

"But if you come straight into Corpus Christi, I'll have to take you before a Corpus judge. Then, you'd be arrested, put into jail, and everyone would be wanting to get at you. I wouldn't have a chance to talk to you."

Bennie agreed, and everything happened just as Jim said it would. Jim met the plane in Houston, read Bennie his rights, took him before a Houston magistrate who again read Bennie his rights, and on the journey south, stopped in Port Lavaca where they had a nice meal of rock shrimp.

"I didn't believe you, Jim, but now I do," Bennie said. "I just knew when the plane landed in Dallas, someone would be there to arrest me. What do you want to know?"

Bennie gave Jim everything. He said that he and two friends had been hired by a man named Eddie Salazar* to steal the *MY JUDY II* and sink her in the Gulf of Mexico. Bennie also confessed that Salazar had been hired by the owner. As he talked, some of what Bennie said seemed almost like a comedy of errors. It was all Jim could do to suppress a big, belly laugh.

Bennie revealed that all three of the thieves knew that some places in the Gulf waters around Port Aransas were not deep enough to hide a boat the size of the *MY JUDY II*, and they almost got into a shouting match and fight trying to decide which would be the best place to take the ship for the sinking. One of the men wanted to head straight out to sea, figuring they'd reach deeper water sooner than by sailing up or down the coast, and the sooner the boat was sunk, the sooner they could escape possible detection from snooping trawlers in the area.

Bennie liked the idea, but the third man pointed out that commercial fishing also occurred straight out the jetties, and the chances of being discovered by at least one boat were practically guaranteed. Although shrimp boats don't generally cluster when they cast their nets, if one boat had good luck, others were sure to follow suit. Odds were that the three men could end up right in the thick of night fishing just as they were hacking holes in the boat.

Also, the men wanted to sink the *MY JUDY II* near one of the sunken liberty ships. Two liberty ships had already been sunk in the Gulf near Port Aransas as an artificial reef, and a third one was planned to be sunk between the other two in a few days. If the men could get the shrimp boat close enough, it would become part of the reef. There was risk in that plan, however, because of all the charting and mapping by the Texas Coastal and Marine Council in placing the third liberty ship.

The three men finally decided to take the shrimp boat a little up the coast before heading out to sea. They had discovered a place on the charts which indicated deep water, and it was a spot where no one would accidently find her, especially fishing trawlers plowing the sea with their monstrous fishing nets. The grave was also out of the mainstream shipping lanes and away from the offshore drilling routes where most of the boats associated with those activities had sonar and would be apt to stumble over the wreck, causing an investigation.

On the night of the theft, the seas were running very high, and they almost called everything off. Transferring from the *MY JUDY II* to the standby boat in high seas was deemed too dangerous. But Bennie needed the money, and he finally decided to risk it. His father was a shrimper, and he used to help his dad on the boat all the time. He had lots of experience boating in rough seas.

The two accomplices slipped aboard the *MY JUDY II* around midnight, started the engines, and silently headed up the coast toward Port Lavaca, following Bennie in the other boat. They followed a predetermined course that would take them into deep water and away from major boat traffic. At the designated spot, the men opened the seacocks so the *MY JUDY II* would sink. They then tied the two boats together with a half-inch-thick line, and stood by on the other boat, watching and waiting for the doomed ship to go under.

But the *MY JUDY II* had a mind of her own. She didn't sink right away. She floated, decks awash, slightly beneath the water with most of her riggings above the sea. And there she stayed...and stayed...and stayed.

After waiting more than two hours with no signs of further sinking, Bennie reboarded the *MY JUDY II* in an effort to determine why she still floated. Apparently none of them had taken into consideration that the *MY JUDY II* had been a *working* shrimp boat, that she had been decked out to keep shrimp fresh. He found about ninety bars of slowly melting ice in the hold which kept her afloat.

Bennie returned to the standby boat, and the seas were so rough that the trip back scared him. At one point, the half-inch rope between the two boats snapped, striking him in the chest and knocking him down. At approximately 4:20 a.m., the men abandoned the *MY JUDY II* and returned to port, leaving the doomed ship still floating low in the water.

The next night, the three men returned to the area of the *MY JUDY II*, and during the night, ten or twelve other shrimp boats entered the area. Sending out their nets, the three men disguised themselves as part of the fleet, all the while listening anxiously to the radio traffic between the boats. It was during this time that they overheard alarming news.

It seems that one of the other boats, while dragging its nets in the water in the dark night as it trawled south, was suddenly blinded by a spotlight from a boat trawling north. The southbound boat captain shone his spotlight back. The northbound boat captain then came on the radio and told how he had just narrowly missed hitting a big steel-hulled boat with decks under water, no lights, and no one in sight. According to the northbound boat captain, the big boat was definitely sinking. The boat captain also said that he was very familiar with the *MY JUDY II*, and "it looked like it was the *MY JUDY II* that was under water." Everyone else in the fleet was then made aware of the sinking vessel and steered clear of her.

By morning, the *MY JUDY II* had finally gone down. Bennie told Jim that while waiting for the ship to sink, they took Loran readings. Unfortunately, he could remember only one of the readings, but he did remember that the ship sunk in nineteen fathoms of water.

Jim spent several months attempting to locate the grave, exhausting agencies and clues one after another. The Naval Air Station in Corpus Christi promised to check the site with divers if the area could be pinpointed more accurately. A seismograph boat had recorded the bottom of the Gulf southeast of Port Lavaca, and Jim obtained copies of their charts. No luck. A charter fishing boat captain reported a sunken wreck about 300 feet inshore from the first liberty ship, but Jim was unable to find it when he looked for it. The sinking *MY JUDY II* could have drifted in any direction as she went down.

Using the Loran reading that Bennie gave, which was in an area of the Gulf where one mile of travel equalled about one fathom of water, and knowing that the boat lay in nineteen fathoms, Jim finally took Bennie to Rockport in early 1976. They boarded a Parks and Wildlife boat piloted by Game Management Officer E.L. Billings. They went approximately twenty miles southeast of Port Lavaca to the suspected area with depth finders and side-scan sonar. Although they searched a four mile square area of the Gulf, they could not find the sunken boat.

Next, Jim approached the owners of the fishing boat *SCAT CAT* in Port Aransas and made arrangements for them to loan the boat to him for one day. The *SCAT CAT* is one of the largest charter fishing boats in the entire area. It is equipped with depth finders, side-scan sonar, fish finders, Loran, and several other pieces of high-tech electronic gear guaranteed to find fish for the paying customers. On that day, the captain was Gene Williams*, an experienced seaman trained in the use of the side-scan sonar. FBI Agent John Newton and Texas Ranger Morgan Miller from Victoria also came along.

John Newton originally grew up in Victoria---for many years, his daddy was the DPS chaplain---and he and Morgan Miller were already fast friends long before they became brothers-in-law. Both are professional divers, and each had been in law enforcement for many years. They had made many dives as lawmen. They now planned to dive together on the wreck as soon as it could be found.

It didn't take long to get back out to the area Jim believed to be the grave of the sunken shrimp boat, and after a couple of passes, they heard the welcome "ping-ping, ping-ping, ping-ping" that signaled a wreck on the ocean bottom. The sunken vessel was a steel-hulled ship, about the right length for it to be the *MY JUDY II*, and it was lying on its side. All the lawmen needed to prove that it was the missing shrimp boat was to read the name on the boat. And they had that all worked out. The divers would go down and read the name on the bow of the boat.

Sometimes, the best laid plan can go awry at the most inopportune time, and that's exactly what happened. Newton and Miller dove on the location, but the visibility was only two feet at the bottom. The current was also running very swiftly. They were unable to leave the anchor chain and search for the boat.

Arrangements were next made with the *SCAT CAT* for June 17, 1976. On the arranged date, several divers were on hand, including two men from the FBI with underwater cameras. But the weather turned sour with high winds and seas running about ten feet, and the trip was cancelled. A week later, another attempt was made with the *SCAT CAT*, but this time there was a different captain, and they found nothing. It was the lawmen's opinion that there may have been a deliberate attempt to keep them from relocating the vessel and diving on it.

Agent Newton then came up with a solution. He said he would make arrangements to get another ship, and they'd all go back out at another time. Before he could arrange it, however, the statute of limitations ran out on the crime.

Although Jim had signed confessions from Bennie and his two accomplices who had sunk the *MY JUDY II*, and he knew who had hired them to do the job, and he had a wreck on the ocean floor matching the size of the *MY JUDY II*, he never did prove that the wreck was, indeed, the *MY JUDY II*. And with no photographic evidence as proof, no warrant for arrest was ever brought against anyone.

The lack of a satisfactory solution didn't faze Jim. Being an ardent fisherman, he says with a grin, "Oh, well. It makes a great fishing reef."

A LITTLE BIT OF RANGER FUN

The Texas Rangers as an organization are world known as "hard riding, fast shooting, and always getting their man." So fierce and fearless is their reputation, that people often forget that beneath the tough outer exterior lies a man capable of appreciating life's finer things---like humor. Of course, Ranger humor is unlike any other in the world. It's often dry, creeping up on the unwary like chiggers in the backwoods, and jokes are always told with straight faces. But it's also every bit as outrageous as possible without compromising dignity---dignity being the one ingredient every Ranger is careful to protect. Most of the time, that is.

One of the best ways to appreciate Ranger humor is when they are all together telling old war stories and reliving past exploits, such as the Ranger reunion held every summer at Fort Fisher in Waco. As many active and retired Rangers as possible usually attend, many with their families, and all kinds of shenanigans are possible. The best of Company "D" Ranger humor, however, is always saved for themselves. Most of the time, it surfaces at the mandatory firearms qualifications held every year at the famous Y-O Ranch in Mountain Home near Kerrville.

Every Ranger has to qualify on any pistol or gun that he uses, and Jim's preferred weapon of choice is a .45 caliber automatic. It is also the preferred weapon of most of the other Rangers, and there is a very good reason for this. A .38 caliber weapon will not stop a man, unless the Ranger is extremely lucky and hits a vital, critical organ on the first shot, whereas a .45 caliber weapon will. This was proven in the Philippines during World War II when the enemy soldiers, high on drugs of one kind or another, sustained shot after shot from a .38 caliber weapon and still charged the American soldiers. Sometimes, it took six or more bullets to bring the enemy down. When the U.S. military finally switched to a .45 caliber weapon, the enemy went down---and did not get back up.

Most Rangers also use automatic weapons and not a revolver. Jim explained it this way. "A cylinder only holds six bullets, and after firing all of them, you must stop and reload. Suppose you are in the middle of a shootout when that happens? The criminals use an automatic weapon because it is faster to inject a clip full of bullets than to stop and reload a cylinder. Why shouldn't we have that advantage?"

There are qualifying shooting ranges all over the State, but a favorite for the South Texas Rangers is the Y-O Ranch, northeast of San Antonio about ninety miles. The ranch has a wild and woolly history, being part of the Taylor faction of the largest, longest-running range war in the history of the United States---the Sutton-Taylor feud. In fact, the Schreiner family only acquired it because, as Charles Schreiner, III, put it, "the kids were getting big enough to become targets."

For the historian, the Sutton-Taylor feud began in South Carolina two generations before the Civil War where the two families had border disputes over their neighboring lands. Eventually, members of both families moved to Georgia and then to Texas, incredibly always settling on neighboring property. Since the land---in Texas anyway---was not fenced, the Sutton cattle mixed with the Taylor cattle and created maverick herds bearing the brand of neither outfit. Ownership of the mavericks only added fuel to the fire which finally flamed out of control when Buck Taylor sold at auction for Bill Sutton horses that turned out to be stolen.

Taylor got into trouble for it, and he blamed Sutton. The two men went to war, and it eventually incorporated virtually everyone in three counties with literally thousands lining up and taking sides. Such notable men like cattle baron Shanghai Pierce opted for the Suttons, and John Wesley Hardin came to the aid of his Taylor cousins. The Texas Rangers rode ramrod on the feuding factions for many years, mainly under Ranger Captains Leander McNelly and Lee Hall in the 1870's, but they were never able to end the war. The feud gradually died out when the youngsters started getting shot.

The Y-O Ranch was acquired by Charles Schreiner III's great-grandfather, Charles Schreiner, who was also a Texas Ranger. The elder Charles Schreiner made quite a reputation for himself as a cattleman in Kerr County, acquiring the title of "captain" when he commanded a home guard of "minute men" to protect the life and property of Central Texans from menacing Indians in the 1860's and 1870's. It was a title he carried for the rest of his life. He was also a United States Deputy Marshal and served as Treasurer of Kerr County for over thirty years. Several of his merchandising institutions still stand today in Kerrville, as does the Schreiner Institute, a high school and junior college he founded in 1922.

Charles Schreiner had a deep and lasting respect for the Texas Rangers, and it wasn't only because he was once part of the organization. In a twenty year period between 1870 and 1890, he shipped more than 300,000 head of Longhorns from his Kerr County hub of operations, cattle which might otherwise have been stolen or lost to marauding Indians and cattle rustlers if not for the protection provided by the Rangers. Out of respect for the men, and in all the generations since, the ranch has been open to the Ranger organization any time the Rangers need it.

Today, the Rangers always stay in the small houses on the ranch, either the old school house or a bunk house or one of the old foreman houses, which are all fairly close together like a family-gathering encampment. Most of the buildings have three or four rooms in them, all decorated in the old Ranger paraphernalia with saddles and tack, antlers,

Mexican blankets, and such, and the Rangers just pick and choose at will. Located in the center of this encampment is a flagpole about twenty feet tall.

Each year, the Rangers gather at the ranch for three days, and all kinds of mischief happens while they are there. Glenn Krueger from Beeville and Joaquin Jackson from Uvalde (later Alpine) were usually right in the thick of it with antics that would make an outsider wonder if they even liked each other.

Jim remembers one year that the two men were just like monkeys, always at each other doing something. It was during the rifle target exercise that Joaquin Jackson struck with his *coup de grace* The rifle targets were set back in the dense brush, and the idea was to walk down the grassy, winding road, spy a target, turn, and fire. It took ten, maybe fifteen minutes to make the trek. During Glenn Krueger's walk through the target field, Jackson tied a smoke grenade to Krueger's car, fastening it to a rock in such a fashion that when Glenn drove off, the pin would be pulled, smoke would start, and the car would be filled with the noxious cloud---not to mention the surrounding area.

It would have been the perfect coup, only when Krueger backed his car around and the smoke grenade went off, it startled him so badly that he slammed his foot down on the accelerator instead of the brake. The car leaped forward like one of the frogs in California's Calaveras County jumping frog contest.

Texas Rangers have magnificent reflexes, and it only took a fraction of a second for Glenn Krueger to get his car back under control, but it was a fraction too long. The moment the car lunged forward, it bounced over a pointed rock which punched a hole in the oil pan. Krueger had no choice. He drove crazily back to the ranch headquarters in a cloud of foul smoke, dripping oil in a steady stream on the dusty road behind him.

Back at the ranch house, one of the ranch hands assessed the damage, pulled the oil pan, and welded it so Krueger could get back to town.

That wasn't the end of it. Krueger decided on revenge, but he had only that one night in which to do it because the weekend was over and everyone would be leaving the next day. Unfortunately, that night the Rangers gathered around with a few toddies, telling old war stories, and generally enjoying each other's company until late into the evening. Furthermore, when everyone decided to retire around midnight, Joaquin Jackson decided to remain up reading.

Joaquin Jackson always stayed up late, but this time, he was later than usual getting to bed, and Glenn Krueger was beginning to think his planned revenge would have to wait until the next year. Finally, around 2:00 a.m. in the morning, Krueger heard the familiar snores emanating from Jackson's room. Stealthily, like a cat on paddy-paws, Glenn Krueger slipped into the room and stole the other Ranger's pants. Krueger then tied the pants to the line of the twenty-foot tall flagpole with dozens of tiny little knots, and ran the garment up the pole for the whole world to see.

Early the next morning, all the Rangers went to eat in the camp cook house. All, that is, except Joaquin Jackson, who was sleeping late after staying up into the wee hours of the morning. Jim remembers being almost finished with breakfast when Joaquin walked in madder than a hornet kicked from its nest.

Joaquin Jackson is a big man, taller than Jim, and he had on an old, ratty pair of camouflage pants that someone had stashed in the trunk of a car. The pants came nowhere near fitting the big man. The cuffs ended just below the knees, the legs were slit clear up the thighs, the crotch was all ripped out, and there was absolutely no way Jackson had them secured around the waist. He looked positively hilarious, and everyone just burst out laughing.

"All right!" he thundered. "Where are they?" His eyes bored holes into Glenn Krueger.

"Where are what?" Krueger asked with just the right touch of innocence in his voice.

What turned out to be the icing on the cake, Jim didn't learn until later. Joaquin Jackson had brought only that one pair of pants for the weekend, and when he woke up to find them missing, he naturally assumed someone was playing a trick on him. He tore the bunkhouse apart searching for them---checking under all the bunks, under the furniture, behind the chairs, in the closets, everywhere---and when he couldn't find them, he didn't know what to do.

He thought about borrowing a pair of Jim's pants. Joaquin Jackson is six feet, six inches and 245 pounds, and although Jim was close to Joaquin in height, Jim barely topped 200 pounds---he was as lanky a Ranger as he was a Highway Patrol officer. Jackson knew Jim's pants really wouldn't fit, but they would do in a pinch until he could find his own. The problem was that in order to get to Jim to ask for a pair, Jackson first had to find him, and that meant walking around outside in his underwear, unless he could come up with something else.

Sitting on the edge of the bunk, pondering how to handle the situation, Jackson suddenly remembered seeing an old pair of camouflage pants in the trunk of one of the cars. The car was just outside the bunkhouse. Throwing caution to the wind, he decided to run out in his underwear and get the pants. No sooner had he covered half the distance to the car when he heard a woman laughing hysterically. He turned around to see a lady sitting in a truck, staring at him as he raced across the compound half naked. Stopping dead in his tracks, he turned and raced back to the cabin, slamming the door as he crossed the threshold. He stayed inside, peeking out the window until the woman drove away, getting madder and more frustrated with each ticking second. By the time he was able to race to the car for the ill-fitting garment, he was ready to wring someone's neck. Later, after all the teasing and laughing died down, someone finally told him where his own pants were, and he retrieved them from the flagpole.

It wasn't unusual for Joaquin Jackson and Glenn Krueger to try and "out best" each other on the pistol range, either. During pistol practice, six or seven men normally compete at the same time, and usually Jackson and Krueger would manage to be together. Both men are super good shots. Jim remembers one occasion when Glenn Krueger was shooting at his target, and Joaquin Jackson was off to the side, shooting at the same target. Only Jackson was deliberately hitting it on the extreme outside edges to make Krueger think his shots were bad.

On still another occasion, Glenn Krueger and Joaquin Jackson got after it in the game room at the ranch. Charles Schreiner always treats the Rangers wonderfully when they are at his ranch, and in his game room, he keeps all kinds of interesting amusements for the men. There is a pool table, shuffleboard, chess, television, and so forth. His game room is also decorated in old Ranger lore just like the bunk houses where the Rangers stay during their visits. It has mounted deer heads, old Ranger pictures on the walls, old weapons, saddles and tack...even a Gatling gun.

That particular night, Krueger was shooting pool while Jackson was standing around visiting and smoking his cigar across the room. Jackson always smoked big stogies, and if it went out, which it sometimes did when he was busy talking, he would just chew on the end of it. As the night progressed, he quietly and nonchalantly moved about the room until he was able to sidle up behind Glenn Krueger, all the while carefully puffing out big plumes of cigar smoke. Jim knew something was up by the way Jackson painstakingly kept the cigar smoking.

Krueger also knew Jackson was up to something, but he was also right in the middle of shooting pool. To stop the game and acknowledge Jackson was to spoil Jackson's surprise, whatever it was, and Krueger didn't want to do that. Part of the joke was not to ruin each other's fun. Krueger also wanted to get it over with so he wouldn't have to worry about Jackson cropping up with something else later in the evening. His mind worked furiously to find a way of turning the tables on Jackson---make Jackson the brunt of the joke instead of himself.

As Jackson got closer, some of the hubbub in the room died down. Several other Rangers knew something was coming, and they stood watch with big grins on their faces. Glenn Krueger heard the quiet around him, and he tensed himself for the worst. He didn't have long to wait.

Joaquin Jackson surreptitiously lit a firecracker with his cigar, stood at Krueger's side as if to watch the next pool shot, and carefully slipped the smoking cylinder into Glenn's hip pocket the moment Glenn reached over to make a shot.

Without turning his head or taking his eye off his planned shot or even so much as batting an eyelash, Glenn Krueger reached his right hand around to his hip pocket, retrieved the smoking firecracker, flipped it out into space with a flick of his middle finger, and made his pool shot---just as the firecracker exploded with a loud boom!

Joaquin Jackson looked crestfallen, and everyone just roared.

Joaquin Jackson, before he moved to Alpine, was the Ranger at Uvalde, and he was always stopping by the court houses on his drives throughout his territory to visit with the secretaries who worked for the county judges. One secretary in Laredo, Connie Rowland, tells of the time that the big Ranger showed up with ugly scratches all down his left arm as if he had been in some kind of cock fight or something.

"Joaquin," Connie asked, "what happened? Who did that?"

"Well, Shirley did it," Joaquin answered with an embarrassed shrug of his massive shoulders.

Shirley is Joaquin's five foot, two inch, ex-Marine wife, and according to Connie, the tough little lady led the big Ranger around by the nose. Whereas Joaquin took guff from no one, Shirley took none from him. The two are a matched set.

Joaquin Jackson always wears tan long-sleeved shirts, tan britches, and western boots, and he's always prided himself on not getting hurt. Everyone actually believes that the big Ranger would sooner break someone's arm than to allow himself to get so much as a scratch. So, when he rolled up his sleeve and showed Connie all the red welts, she was astounded. So apparently was Don Joaquin, the big Ranger's son, who was six-years-old at the time.

"Don Joaquin," the big man said ruefully, "wants to take me to school for 'Show and Tell.'"

LINDA

Every lawman knows that unless a suspect can be apprehended quickly, chances are that he will escape punishment---that's assuming, of course, that he travels the road straight and narrow and stays out of trouble. It's this way because the justice system, in all its infinite wisdom, has put statutes of limitations on most crimes. And for the lawman who works the case to a conclusion, as well as the victim who lives with the crime day in and day out, the "statute-of-limitations" rule stinks. Such situations happened to Jim several times, but the one that irked him the most was Linda's case. It took him five years to solve and by then, the statute of limitations had run out. Consequently, the suspect was never prosecuted for kidnapping and raping a child.

At 3:30 p.m. on September 4, 1979, twelve-year-old Michael Sanders* got home from school. Putting his key in the door lock, he grinned as he heard the excited whimpers of the family's dog on the other side of the door. Stepping inside, Pepper, the two-year-old, salt-and-pepper, toy Schnauzer, jumped all over him, ecstatic with glee.

Spying his ten-year-old sister, Linda*, asleep on the sofa, Michael shushed the dog, laid his books on the dining table, went to the kitchen, made a snack, and left to play with his friends. When he returned at 5:00 p.m., he found the door to the apartment unlocked. Linda and Pepper were gone. Gone also was the dog's leash. Assuming Linda was out walking the dog, he thought nothing more of it---until his parents came home and Linda remained missing.

The family immediately instituted a search of the area. With Linda's mother waiting anxiously by the telephone, her father hopped in the car and and made a methodical search up and down all the streets for miles in all directions. Michael and his friends began to systematically comb the area on foot. They contacted all Linda's friends, searched the school grounds, checked the convenience store at the end of the block, and the Dairy Queen three blocks away. In short, all the places the kids used as hangouts were checked and then checked again. No one could remember seeing Linda or the dog that afternoon. At 11:00 p.m., frantic with worry, Linda's father finally notified the police.

Corpus Christi Police Officer J. F. Salazar responded to the missing person report. He drove to Linda's home in Flour Bluff on the extreme south side of the city and met with Linda's family. From Linda's father, Officer Salazar learned that Linda was four feet, eight inches tall, weighed about ninety pounds, and had long, blonde hair and blue eyes. Never in her whole life had she ever run away from home, and her family didn't believe she had done it this time, either. Nor was she having trouble at school. She was a dutiful child, always telling where she was going if she expected to be gone more than a few minutes. It was also Linda's custom to walk the dog every day.

Officer Salazar learned that Linda had been to the dentist shortly before returning home from school, and her brother Michael knew it, which is why he let her sleep on the sofa instead of waking her and talking to her. When he left to play, she was wearing a white tee-shirt sporting a large face on the front, and blue shorts. Presumably, that was what she was wearing when she left the house. Also, if she had any money, it was just enough for a soft drink or candy bar. It was everyone's opinion that the little girl left home to walk the dog and that she had every intention of coming back.

It was approaching midnight when Officer Salazar finished gathering information from Linda's parents and neighbors. Other officers were already in the area conducting the search. A half hour later, the manager of a popular all night restaurant in the heart of Corpus Christi near Padre Island Drive noticed a little girl with a dog on a leash come into the building. She was very upset, appeared to be in great pain, and she had blood running down her leg. She told the store's manager that she was looking for her daddy. The manager promptly assisted her in calling the police and her parents.

The police immediately picked up the child, who turned out to be the missing Linda, and transported her to Memorial Medical Center's emergency trauma unit. Notified on his radio that the missing girl had been found, the officer in charge of the case, Sergeant Gary Garrett, arrived five minutes later. Linda and her mother were waiting for Sgt. Garrett in a private room prior to medical treatment, and there, snuggled deep in her mother's arms, still in pain and still bleeding slightly, Linda told the officer a horror story. Linda said that it was around 4:30 p.m. when she awoke from her nap. Deciding to walk Pepper, she got the dog's leash and headed toward the nearby convenience store a block away for a candy bar. As she walked across the parking lot to the store's entrance, an anglo woman sitting alone in a silver-colored, four-door Mercury with a burgundy interior and a CB antenna on the center of the trunk called her over to the car.

The woman was about thirty-five years old, five feet five inches tall, and chubby. She had dark brown, collar-length hair parted in the middle and brown eyes. There was also a scar resembling a smallpox vaccination on the right side of her face just to the right of her mouth. The woman was fashionably dressed in a three-piece pants suit---vest, jacket, and pants---blue and white in color.

"I've lost my dog," the woman said. "Will you help me find it?"

The woman then asked Linda what she was planning on doing in the store. Upon learning that the little girl intended to buy a candy bar, the woman asked Linda to buy one for her, too. She reached into her handbag and gave Linda the money.

Linda went into the store, bought two chocolate bars, and returned to the woman in the car.

"Get in the car, Honey, and we'll drive around and look for my dog. It would be worth one hundred dollars as a reward if we find him." The woman's voice was coaxing.

"I'm not allowed to ride in cars with strangers," replied Linda.

"Don't be stupid, Honey. I'm not going to hurt you. All I want to do is to find my dog. Get in, now, and we'll drive around and look."

Linda got in the car with Pepper, and the woman drove around a little bit before returning to stop behind the convenience store and picking up a man. The man was also white, younger than the woman, and very skinny. He stood about six feet tall, had blondish-red hair which he wore in an Afro style, long sideburns, and a mustache. He was dressed in a blue and white cowboy shirt, blue jeans, shoes, and black belt.

The man showed Linda a hundred dollar bill and said they were looking for a lost dog. After driving around the area for several minutes, he had the woman drive to a large grocery store on Padre Island Drive several miles away where he could go inside and get change for the large bill. He said he wanted to reward Linda for her trouble and that they would take her home as soon as he got the change for the bill.

When the man emerged from the grocery store, he got behind the wheel and headed the car in the general direction of Flour Bluff where Linda lived, only after going about two miles, he turned off the highway, drove through several residential neighborhoods and emerged on Ocean Drive headed north toward downtown Corpus Christi.

Ocean Drive parallels the Gulf of Mexico and is one of the most beautiful streets in the city. It is lined with swank mansions and palatial homes and landscaped with swaying palm trees and flowering shrubs. It flows from the North Gate of the Naval Air Station and continues to downtown Corpus Christi where, when the street curves along the Gulf, it changes its name to Shoreline Drive. As Shoreline Drive, it continues to the Harbor Bridge where it becomes Highway 181 to Portland and points beyond on the other side of Corpus Christi Bay. Millions of tourists each year travel the scenic beauty.

The man never stopped in Corpus Christi. He drove over the Harbor Bridge and continued on to Victoria, about ninety miles up the coast. When reaching a motel on the outskirts of Victoria, he pulled up to a room with the number "29" on the door. The door to the room was painted orange.

As Sgt. Garrett listened to the little girl's story, he was positively

166

amazed that she could remember so many details with such accuracy. Although she was also obviously in a lot of pain and the doctor was waiting impatiently to treat her, she insisted on telling the officer everything. She wanted the man and woman caught and punished immediately!

Inside the motel room, Linda continued, they watched television for a little while before the woman went next door to a fast food hamburger place and obtained something for all of them to eat. After eating, Linda was allowed to watch television for about an hour before the woman forced her to take a shower. While she was bathing, the woman took her clothes and hid them.

Linda was terrified. The woman had said that the man had just gotten out of jail for murder and had only been in Corpus Christi for two weeks. She thought the man was going to kill her and not finding her clothes when she got out of the shower only convinced her of it. She spied a terry-cloth bathrobe hanging on the back of the bathroom door and she put it on.

The man then tied Linda spread-eagled to the bed, undressed himself, and proceeded to fondle and rape her. The woman also undressed down to her underwear and took Polaroid snapshots of Linda's attack. Each time Linda tried to scream, the man put his hand over her mouth until she couldn't breathe. He also held a knife to her throat and kept repeatedly sticking her with it until she thought she was going to die.

After the ordeal, the man and woman cleaned up the room. Linda was unable to tell Sgt. Garrett what the suspects did with the sheets or the bathrobe or any of the other items used in the attack.

"They made me get dressed, put me in the car, and said they were taking me home."

Instead of taking Linda home, the suspects dropped her off at the restaurant in downtown Corpus Christi, telling her that her daddy was waiting for her inside the store.

At this point, the doctor interrupted Linda's testimony and adamantly insisted on treating the little girl immediately, as she was bleeding more profusely and he was afraid she might go into shock. Linda was rushed into surgery and underwent several hours of extensive repair to her genitalia and internal organs.

Although he had only talked to her for about five minutes prior to her surgery, Sgt. Garrett had gleaned a wealth of information about Linda's attackers. During the attack, the man had called the woman "Sherry," and at one time, Linda had seen the woman wearing designer eyeglasses with the initials "SH" on them. Linda had also said that prior to the attack the man had left the motel to fill the car with gasoline. Taking Linda's clothing to be used for evidence, Sgt. Gary Garrett contacted the police in Victoria and advised them of the situation, asking that they try and locate the motel where the attack had occurred, and possibly the gas station where the car had been filled.

Approximately an hour later, the Victoria Police Department called Sgt. Garrett with the news that one of their detectives had located the motel. It was on the Houston Highway on the north side of town, and it did have an orange door just like Linda had said. The manager said the occupant of room "29" was driving a silver Mercury, and there had been three people in the car, but when checking the registration cards, there was no license plate number indicated for the vehicle.

The home address provided, which was for a residence in Baytown, proved to be fictitious. The police were also never able to trace the car to a gas station in the Victoria area, and consequently, a possible credit card lead never materialized.

The Victoria police made a crime scene investigation of the motel room. It had two double beds, and both were neatly made up. The room was all in order. The double bed nearest the door had both pillows stacked one on top of the other, and it appeared that someone had been sitting on the bed. The other bed nearest the bathroom was completely made, but when officers checked it further, they discovered it had no sheets and no mattress pad. All the towels in the bathroom were also missing.

With two investigative agencies involved, Jim entered the case. He immediately issued an "all points bulletin" to all police agencies in the State with descriptions of the suspects and the vehicle wanted in Linda's attack. He also contacted Bill Milner with the Crime Analysis Service in Austin and requested that the analyst search Austin records for anyone fitting the description or modus operandi.

Jim was stunned at the results the Crime Analysis Service reported. The Houston Police Department advised that they had six cases involving the same subjects in the Houston area. Wharton had one, and Baytown had one. None of them had been solved!

As soon as Linda was out of surgery and had recovered from the effects of the anesthesia, Sgt. Garrett resumed questioning her. He obtained a police artist's sketch of both suspects, and Jim forwarded them to the Crime Lab with a special request that they be placed in the next printing of the Crime Analysis Bulletin. He was determined to put an end to these suspects' raping sprees.

Then began the tedious process of trying to catch the suspects. On September 17, Jim interrogated a prisoner in the Aransas County Jail whose physical description matched Linda's male attacker. The inmate already had numerous arrests for similar offenses and was in jail because he had been caught chasing a ten-year-old girl down a street in Port Aransas while armed with a knife.

Jim showed Linda a mugshot of the prisoner, and while she did agree that it somewhat resembled her attacker, she was sure he was not the right man. As other mugshots arrived from the Crime Lab, Jim took each to the little girl for identification. None of them was the man who had raped her.

On September 18, a promising lead appeared when a barber in Victoria approached Texas Ranger Morgan Miller with suspicions that the male suspect just might be his ex-brother-in-law. Several of the area's newspapers had shown the artist's sketch of the wanted suspects complete with the physical descriptions Linda had given police, and the barber, Ron Wheedlin*, thought the man resembled Paul Dutton*.

Wheedlin told Ranger Miller that Dutton had been married to his sister, but that his sister had recently divorced the suspect. Wheedlin further advised Ranger Miller that Dutton used to live in Houston and was formerly the vice-president of a bank. Although the barber thought the suspect might have moved to the Virgin Islands, he knew for a fact that Dutton and his dark-haired secretary, who worked for the same company as Dutton, had been in Victoria around the first of the month.

Ranger Miller contacted Jim with the news, and Jim immediately followed up by obtaining a Texas driver's license on the suspect from the Crime Lab. According to the license, Dutton still lived in Houston. He did not, however, have a criminal record. Jim also discovered that Wheedlin's sister had replied to the allegations against Dutton by saying, "I wouldn't doubt it. He is capable of it." The sister also stated that Dutton had a silver Mercury.

Jim took the driver's license photograph to Linda, but the little girl could not identify the man as her attacker. In fact, although the man resembled her attacker somewhat, she was certain that he was not the right man.

Back to square one.

Two weeks later, Ranger Morgan Miller again contacted Jim with another good suspect. This man, Barry Williams*, had been picked up by the police for weaving all over the highway in a customized, 1976 Ford van. The man was a white male, tall at about five feet, ten inches, and had brown hair, brown beard, and brown eyes. Although the physical description didn't match Linda's description of her male attacker, Ranger Miller wanted Jim to have the information because of what was found in Williams' car during the police search.

Victoria County Sheriff's Deputy Robert Acree had arrested Williams shortly after 1:00 a.m. in the morning for driving while intoxicated. The vehicle was then inventoried, and all kinds of lewd and unsavory-type property turned up. Apparently, Williams lived part-time in his van because it contained a considerable amount of personal belongings and household goods.

Among the items that officers found were several pounds of marijuana, a glass vial containing a substance field tested and suspected to be hashish oil, and an assortment of marijuana smoking paraphernalia. The suspect had about 500 publications ranging from the conservative *Playboy* magazines to explicit, hardcore pornographic magazines. He also had ten 8mm pornographic films, eight artificial sexual devices, two Polaroid cameras and approximately 200 Polaroid pictures taken of young women engaged in various sexual acts. Officers found a loaded .22 caliber pistol, several realistic-looking water pistols, and a five-gallon container crammed with a large sum of money in loose change and rolled wrappers.

Jim obtained photographs of this suspect, but he held no real hope that Linda would identify the man as her attacker. The man did not fit the description. Sure enough, Linda said Williams was not the man.

That's how things stood for several years. Suspects came, and suspects went, and Linda grew older. Although it was beginning to look as if her attacker wasn't going to be caught, she never lost hope that someday he would be punished for his crime. At all times, she remained willing and eager to cooperate in any way with Jim and the police.

Jim never once lost hope in Linda's case, but the statute of limitations was fast running out on the two crimes of aggravated kidnapping being investigated by the Corpus Christi police, and aggravated sexual abuse offenses being investigated by the Victoria police. When the break finally did come in 1984, it was purely by chance.

It was also too late.

In May of that year, FBI Agent Karl McLeon was in Victoria looking for a federal fugitive, Harry Roger Wilson*, who was supposed to be in hiding in the general area. While obtaining information from the Victoria Police Department, Agent McLeon learned from an informant at the jail of a man bearing a name similar to the wanted fugitive. According to this informant, the man had kidnapped a girl in Corpus Christi, taken her to Victoria, and had raped her.

In checking out the name, Agent McLeon discovered that this second man closely matched the description of the male wanted in Linda's kidnapping and rape case of 1979. He immediately contacted Jim with this information, adding that there was absolutely no connection between his wanted federal fugitive, Harry Roger Wilson, and the suspect in Linda's case, Harry Arthur Wilson*, other than names. Agent McLeon also advised that he personally saw Harry Arthur Wilson's ex-wife, Rebecca*, in Victoria, and the woman closely resembled the female suspect in Linda's

170

case. (Note: the reason the federal fugitive is not identified here is because his name is the same as the rapist in Linda's case, and Linda's rapist escaped prosecution.)

By this time, Linda had moved to Duncanville, Texas. Jim obtained photographs of Harry Arthur Wilson and Rebecca Wilson, and armed with about a dozen other photographs closely resembling the Wilson pair, he drove to Duncanville to present them to Linda.

Linda immediately picked Harry Wilson from the photographs. When shown another set of ten pictures of men without moustaches, one of which was of Harry, she again had no hesitation in identifying the suspect as the one who had raped her and threatened her life. She signed and dated on the back of both pictures that she identified the man in the photographs as her attacker. She could not, however, identify any of the women's pictures as the woman called "Sherry."

Linda then gave a written statement to Jim that Harry Arthur Wilson was the man who had kidnapped and raped her on September 4, 1979. Included on the document was a statement made to Linda by her attacker, "If you don't shut up, I'll kill you." The document was witnessed by Ranger Captain Bob Mitchell.

Next, Jim got with Sgt. Gary Garrett, the chief investigator on Linda's case in Corpus Christi, and the two men went to Victoria to interview Rebecca Wilson. The woman stated that her ex-husband was into bondage and child pornography and that sometime in 1969 or 1970 while they lived in Lubbock, he had gone too far with a little girl because the child had gone into a coma and died. She divorced Wilson in 1971, moved to Victoria, and tried to begin another life, only she claimed that Wilson found out where she was and continually pestered her to help him.

According to Rebecca's story, during the latter part of 1979, Wilson had wanted her to help him with some pornographic movies involving a little girl in Victoria. She said that she flatly refused to help. Rebecca then admitted that her ex-husband later showed her a picture of a nine- or ten-year-old child tied to a bed, blindfolded, and with a cattle prod on the bed beside the girl. The girl was also bloody. Rebecca said that Wilson claimed the child had given him a hard time. He had never told Rebecca where the child came from or who else was in the room with him. Rebecca claimed to be afraid of Wilson and agreed to testify against him.

In checking Rebecca's story, Jim was never able to identify any child dying in Lubbock with the descriptions that Rebecca gave. Maybe the story never happened? Might not Rebecca be a liar? He just didn't know, but he proceeded on the assumption that Rebecca had been truthful, even if he couldn't find substantiating evidence.

He contacted Linda's mother and asked for photographs of her daughter at about nine to ten years of age to be used in a lineup for Rebecca to identify. Rebecca Wilson, after looking at several photographs of little girls all similar in age and description, picked Linda from the lineup as being the little girl she had seen spread-eagled and tied on the bed in a pool of blood. She then signed a sworn statement to the same.

Jim decided it was time to go to the Crime Analysis Lab in Austin and meet with Analyst Bill Milner. A search of the criminal file on Harry Arthur Wilson revealed not only that he did have an arrest record, but also that his correct name was really Arthur Harry Wilson*. Jim then got with Sgt. Garrett of the Corpus Christi Police Department and went back to Duncanville to obtain a second, corrected statement from Linda using Wilson's correct name in the statement. He took no chances that the suspect would slip through his clutches due to a mix-up in names!

When the two lawmen returned to Corpus Christi, and since the statute of limitations had passed on the original aggravated kidnapping and aggravating sexual abuse charges, a warrant of arrest for attempted murder was filed on Wilson. By this time, Wilson lived in Lubbock, and the warrant had to be processed by the Rangers and DPS Intelligence in that part of the State. By January, 1985, Arthur Harry Wilson was in the Nueces County Jail awaiting trial.

The statute of limitations had run out on the original charges, and although Jim, other law enforcement officers, and the District Attorney tried every way they could to have the suspect prosecuted for attempted murder, there was never enough evidence to convince a jury. Arthur Harry Wilson walked back into society a free man.

172

THE LOMAN RV KIDNAPPING CASE

The new year of 1983 began in terror for a Colorado couple spending their vacation in South Texas. Velma and Ronald Loman from Denver, Colorado, intending to enjoy the fascinating beauty of the beach on Padre Island National Seashore, were rudely kidnapped at gunpoint by two men on the morning of January 25. The men were part of a group of five adults and two children camping in a van in the sand dunes several yards away. Before it was all over, it took the intervention of two Nations, a dozen different law enforcement agencies in two States, and Jim to apprehend the culprits and bring them to justice.

Padre Island is a hauntingly beautiful expanse of wilderness with possibly the most unique history of anywhere else in the United States. Each year, it attracts hundreds of thousands of visitors to its beaches and salt water activities. The longest coastal barrier island in the world, it extends 113 miles from Corpus Christi Pass, which once separated it from Mustang Island in the north, to the Mansfield Channel, or Mansfield Cut as the locals like to say, in the south. Along the way, the pristine sands bear such names as North Beach, Malaquite Beach, South Beach, Little Shell Beach, and Big Shell Beach.

Separating it from the mainland is a shallow waterway known as the Laguna Madre, a virtually tideless waterway open to the Gulf only through man-made Mansfield Channel on the south. As no rivers drain into the Laguna, its only source of fresh water is from rainfall which is always plentiful along the Gulf Coast. Bird Island Basin, one of the finest waterbird sanctuaries in the nation, is at the north end. The Basin is a mecca for fun-seeking windsurfers year round.

Before Padre Island became the fascinating, exciting drama of adventure that it is today, it was used primarily for cattle ranching. It held several advantages: there was no need for fences, it had good grassland and ample fresh water, and the narrow geographic profile simplified the job of herding cattle. Its first cattle baron was a Spanish friar, Nicolas Balli, son of Dona Rosa Maria Balli, the first "cattle queen" in Texas. Because of her attention to detail, she ended up owning one-third of the lower Rio Grande Valley, including the land on which the present-day cities of Harlingen, McAllen, and Edinburg are now located. Part of her land holdings also included the island, which was then known as Isla Santiago. What most people don't know, however, is that the Balli family predates Texas. Long before the Pilgrims landed at Plymouth Rock, long before Stephen Austin started his Colonies, the Balli family was already here. Descendents today include Jimmy McAllen of the vast San Juanito Ranch/McAllen Ranch near Linn.

Padre Balli brought in the island's first settlers. He called his settlement Rancho Santa Cruz. The area is now frequently referred to as the Lost City, although some of the ruins are still visible on South Padre Island. Padre Balli died in 1816, but even before his death, locals had started referring to the island as "Padre's Island." Hence, it's present name as Padre Island.

In September 1962, Lady Bird Johnson, wife of then Vice-President Lyndon Baines Johnson, designated the center section of the island as the Padre Island National Seashore, administered by the National Park Service. Aside from a visitor center and other amenities at the northern end of the seashore, which is the only car entrance, most of the area has been left as Nature dictated. There is no entrance at the Mansfield Cut, and that area lying in the middle can only be accessed with a 4-wheel drive vehicle.

On Monday, January 24, 1983, Velma and Ronald Loman left their campground in Port Aransas for the National Seashore. They selected a campsite about one-half mile south of where the paved road ends. It was about 200 feet south of a toilet that was located by a picket fence in the dunes. They noticed a tent at the north end of the picket fence with a man sunbathing near the tent, but thought nothing of it. Although it was a little cool for local folks to be sunbathing, the Lomans thought the man, like themselves, was a visitor from a northern climate. The January weather felt wonderful compared to the freezing cold at home.

The Lomans parked with their twenty-five foot, light tan motor home facing the water. They disconnected their tan Audi, which they pulled behind the motor home, and sat back to enjoy the beach. The next morning, they took an early walk down the beach, picked up a few sea shells, admired the water birds, and returned to the motor home to fix breakfast. After eating, they got in the Audi and drove south to the "4-Wheel Drive Only" sign. Spying two old ladies in a van stuck in the sand, they drove about one hundred feet south of the sign and helped pull the ladies free.

As they drove back toward their motor home, they noticed that they had company near their campsite. A car was now parked on the beach, and a young woman carrying a big bag walked near the car. The woman drew their attention because the bag was of a woven kind similar to the type sold in tourist stalls in Mexico. It had a multi-colored liner like a bath towel.

The Lomans thought the woman belonged to the car. She was of medium height, had long brown hair and a tan jacket. The woman walked past the car, however, toward the direction of a light blue van parked up in the dunes. At the van were two men with big, bushy beards.

After returning to the motor home and doing the dishes, the Lomans decided to visit the Park's Visitor Center and use the phone. They drove to the Center, signed the register, looked around, but did not use the phone. Returning to the motor home, they were in the middle of their lunch when they saw two men exit the sand dunes about 200 feet south of them. The men walked to the water, turned, and walked north up the beach in the direction of the motor home. When the men got near the camper, they walked straight up to it, past the window, to the door.

Ronald Loman answered the knock on the door. One of the strangers pointed a big, black revolver at Loman and said, "I'll kill you, you motherfucker." Both men then entered the home.

The man with the gun was a white male, about thirty years old, and stinking to high heaven as if he hadn't had a bath in his entire life. He stood about six feet tall, weighed 200 pounds, and had long, shoulder length, greyish-yellow hair. He also had a very heavy, very thick beard down to his mid-chest. He wore blue jeans, white tennis shoes, and a brown leather jacket with sheepskin lining. On the right inside forearm was a tattoo about six inches long and one-half inch wide.

His partner was also a white male. The man was shorter, about five feet, ten inches tall, and weighed somewhere in the neighborhood of 180 pounds. He wore a gray, hooded sweatshirt, blue jeans, and some type of tennis shoe. His hair was dirty and long, blond in color, and he kept it hid in the hood of the dirty sweatshirt. The Lomans also said he wore gold-rimmed glasses with clear lenses, had a thin moustache, and had a brown beard about four inches long. The beard was not as heavy as the first man's beard.

The strangers directed the Lomans to sit down, and the one with the big pistol warned, "I'll kill you if you make one move. This .45 makes a big hole."

The Lomans were terrified. When the strangers pulled the shades, the Lomans pleaded with the men to take whatever they wanted and leave.

The intruders, however, showed no inclination of obeying. Instead, the shorter man bound Ronald Loman with a piece of black wire that he had brought with him. He instructed Loman to lie face down on the floor with his arms behind his back, and he tied the fifty-six year old man at the wrist with the wire. The stranger then tied Loman's knees with a belt, and tied his elbows back.

With Ronald Loman incapacitated, the strangers turned their attention to the terrified fifty-four year old Velma. They trussed her up with cut pieces of towels and then began searching the place.

The two men eventually found an expensive diamond ring belonging to Velma Loman, but they stated, "We don't want to take anything of sentimental value." Laughing, they threw it back into the drawer. In fact, the men did not take any jewelry, watches, or anything of sentimental value, but they did take bank, Sears, and oil company credit cards. They also took $800 in American Express travelers checks in the name of Velma Loman and an additional $650 in American Express travelers checks in the name of Ronald Loman.

After a thorough search of the camper, the short man went outside and found a length of yellow, plastic rope on the beach. When he returned to the motor home, Ronald Loman complained about the wire cutting off the circulation in his wrists. The short intruder promptly tied Loman's arms down by his sides with the plastic rope and let the older man sit up. Both Lomans were then gagged.

The short man left the motor home, and the tall man began playing with Velma Loman. He cut off her bra and fondled her, putting a filet knife belonging to her against her temple. When he was tired of terrorizing her, he said, "I ain't going to rape you. I just wanted to scare the hell out of you."

The tall man finally helped her sit up. He then placed the Lomans back to back and blindfolded both victims. After rummaging around through the camper, he asked, "Which one of you has high blood pressure." After learning that the medication belonged to Velma Loman, the intruder removed her gag, gave her the pill, and gagged her again.

About this time, a Park Ranger drove up and parked near the motor home. The tall intruder then became very nervous. He put the gun to Ronald Loman's head and promised to kill both him and the ranger if the ranger came inside. Fifteen minutes later, the ranger drove away, and the Lomans heard him say that he was giving speeding tickets on the beach. The short intruder then returned.

By now, the Lomans had no earthly idea of what was going to happen to them. The intruders did not seem to want to hurt them and appeared to be concerned about their health, but they were talking of selling the motor home in Mexico for several years' supply of cocaine. They used foul language, corresponded with each other by note, yet they still appeared courteous to the Lomans. It left the Lomans terrified.

The strangers finally made coffee, opened cans and jars, and drank wine. They then lounged in the motor home's living area, as if waiting for someone or something to happen. Calling the Loman's credit cards "plastic," they boasted that they could buy plane tickets around the world with one of them.

The intruders went in and out the motor home many times, and the bound Lomans could not keep track of time. All of a sudden, the Lomans heard a girl's voice, but they told Jim later when he questioned them that they didn't know when the girl entered the camper. She was just there.

Apparently the intruders were waiting for the sun to do down because after it was dark, the girl and one of the men started the motor home. They drove out of the parking spot, but after driving only a short distance, they stopped. A dog barked, and the Lomans heard the girl say, "I hear a dog. Is that ours?"

"No," replied the man, and the voice sounded to the Loman's as the voice of the tall intruder. "It's a coyote." It was followed by, "I wish that motherfucker would move."

The kidnappers drove to a store about fifteen minutes away. The girl got out, immediately came back, and said she'd forgotten the money for cigarettes. The Lomans heard the tinkle of coins. The girl got back out and came right back saying the store was closed. They drove a short distance to what was apparently the next store down the road where the girl again got out, this time buying cigarettes. They then drove over the high bridge of the John F. Kennedy Causeway because the Lomans could feel the motor home pulling.

About an hour later, somewhere down the road, the kidnappers pulled in to get gas, but the pumps were on the wrong side of the motor home. The male kidnapper cussed and left the station, stopping at another one further down the road. After leaving that gas station and approximately an hour later, they again stopped. This time the Loman's heard the kidnappers rummaging around in the motor home for the jack. When Ronald Loman asked if the flat was on the Audi being towed, a man said, "No. We have to have a car to get away in." The flat was apparently on the vehicle they were following.

At some point, the Lomans were allowed to use the rest room, and the girl kidnapper struck up a conversation with Velma. The girl confided that she didn't wear panties because she could not afford them. She also said that she had bad legs. "Take Valium," she advised, "because it is good for bad legs." She later rubbed Ben Gay on Ronald Loman's back and Velma Loman's shoulders.

The Lomans told Jim that they never saw the girl, but they got the impression that she was small. She had a strong southern accent, but she said she was not from Texas. The Loman's also believed they were travelling south because they overheard phrases of "Mexico" several times. There did not appear to be much traffic on the road they were driving and no apparent indication of cities or towns, which is consistent with the ranch land of extreme South Texas.

Somewhere close to Brownsville, they began to travel on a very rough road. There were trees hitting the motor home, and Ronald Loman could see street lights and red/green lights out the top of his blindfold. When they stopped moving, the girl began packing food, saying, "I'm going to eat."

The tall man had Ronald Loman lie down on the floor. He said,

"I'm going to have to knock you out. I'll hit you so you won't get hurt." He struck Ronald Loman four times and Velma Loman once with a pistol. Both Lomans faked being unconscious, but neither one was knocked out. They heard the kidnappers disconnect the Audi, drive it up beside the motor home, and put the towbar in the car. The kidnappers then drove off in a vehicle that made a loud, distinct noise.

As soon as the kidnappers were gone, the Lomans escaped from the motor home. They locked it, got into the Audi, and drove to the nearest telephone for help. They had no earthly idea where they were, only that there were other vehicles in the area and that it appeared to be some sort of parking lot.

On the morning of January 26, Jim received a call from a lieutenant in the Brownsville Police Department stating that both Lomans were in the Brownsville Medical Center Hospital with injuries to their head caused when they were struck with a pistol. Jim also learned that the motor home and Audi had been found at the Brownsville Airport.

Jim called his brother Bud in Harlington. Bud was very familiar with the area around Corpus Christi, and as a Trooper with the Department of Public Safety, he immediately went to the Brownsville Medical Center Hospital to interview the Lomans, hoping to learn exactly where the kidnapping had originated. From the description he obtained from the Loman's, Bud called Jim and told him the victims had been taken from Malaquite Beach.

After learning that the kidnapping had occurred on the National Seashore, Jim contacted Tommy McDaniels, the Park Supervisor at the National Seashore, advising him of a crime in his territory. Jim also called John Newton, the FBI Agent-in-Charge in Corpus Christi.

The next morning, Jim and Padre Island National Seashore Park Ranger Anne Anderson questioned several people in the area of the kidnapping. They learned from a man visiting from Wisconsin, who had camped a short distance south of the Loman's motor home, that a light blue, older model van had been in the area. The van contained three white men with beards, two women, two children, and a dog.

Another camper from Illinois had been on the beach for several months. He had pitched a tent at the north end of a dune rehabilitation area. This area was distinguished by a red picket fence, approximately one hundred feet long, along the dune line. It was also near a toilet, and he was apparently the man the Loman's remembered seeing sunbathing on the day they arrived on the beach. This witness remembered a middle-aged couple in a motor home towing a car parking just south of the toilet.

The next day, the witness was gone most of the day, but when he returned in the late afternoon, he went outside to watch the sunset from a

178

dune near his tent. He observed the motor home start up, pull out onto the beach a short distance, and stop. The lights were out, and since it was dusk, it struck him as being odd.

A short while later when he was in his tent, he heard a vehicle pull up outside. He left his tent to see what was going on. It was dark, around 7:00 p.m., and the vehicle was a light blue van, older model, with a distinct, noisy-sounding muffler. The van had Colorado license plates and had been on the beach a few days. The Illinois man had had several contacts with the occupants, which he said gave him the "creeps."

The man from Illinois provided Jim and the park ranger with good descriptions of the occupants of the van. There were three men, two women, two children, and two dogs. He said that they were from Alma, Colorado, and that they had been doing a roofing job there. They had told him that they were looking for a boat captain as they wanted to go sailing to the Antilles.

National Seashore Park Ranger Paul Eubank also remembered a man from Alma, Colorado. While on patrol on January 22, Eubank received information that a man was bothering people by trying to solicit a ride in the Malaquite Beach parking lot. Eubank questioned the man who was about five feet, six inches tall, in his early twenties, with collar-length light brown hair, and thin short beard. The man wanted to go to the 7-11 store to buy cigarettes. Eubank asked for identification, and the man showed a Colorado driver's license identifying him as Alan David Frank.

Paul Eubank gave the man a ride to the Park boundary and along the way, he learned that the man was only going to be around for a few more days. "He mentioned that he had written Betty Crocker to inquire about baking at the 12,000 foot elevation, and Betty Crocker said that no one lived at 12,000 feet. He thought that was funny."

At 3:30 p.m. on the 26th, a woman attempted to cash one of the American Express travelers checks in the name of Velma Loman. The teller at the savings and loan in Pharr, a small town about 100 miles west of Brownsville, refused to cash it when the woman signed it differently than it was originally signed. The teller asked for identification, but the woman was only able to provide a bank credit card---nothing with a picture identification to verify the signature. The teller said the woman was about thirty years old, slightly chubby, reddish-brown hair done up in pigtails, and wearing blue bibb overalls. The description matched that given by the man from Illinois as being one of the women in the blue van.

Jim and Park Ranger Anne Armstrong then went to Brownsville to interview the Lomans, who were now staying at a motel while their car and motor home were being processed for evidence. The tall kidnapper had told the Loman's that he had been a Marine and talked about Viet Nam. He claimed he had been arrested before by the FBI and would not be taken again. The Loman's said the man was very anti-government.

Jim put Velma Loman under hypnosis, and obtained a good description from her of the suspect. Before the Loman's left for Colorado the next day, he asked them to stop at the Department of Public Safety Headquarters in Harlingen and let his brother Bud draw an artist's sketch of the tall kidnapper with the gun.

Jim then got with FBI Agent Bob Dixon at the Brownsville Police Department and helped process the motor home and car for latent prints and evidence. Among the evidence gathered were a blanket with blood on it, several pieces of towels, some black and yellow cord, a belt, a knife, and two .45 caliber long Colt shells that had not been fired. When asked about the unfired shells, the Loman's said that they were unloaded from the gun before the kidnappers struck the Loman's in the back of the head. Apparently, the kidnappers had dropped two of the shells and had not noticed them.

All of the evidence gathered from the motor home, including the fingerprints, was turned over to FBI agent Bob Dixon, as the case was going to be prosecuted as a federal case because it happened on the National Seashore. Agent Dixon bagged it into one of those large plastic trash bags, took it back to his office, and set it on his desk. That night, the cleaning lady allegedly picked it up and threw it away with the rest of the trash. However it happened, all the evidence disappeared.

Jim next contacted Deputy Marshal Tim Kuretich of Alma, Colorado, and asked for his assistance in locating individuals matching the kidnappers' descriptions. Kuretich interviewed people in the Alma area and reported back with the information that the blue van with Colorado plates belonged to Alan Frank. He also provided a list of people who were known to associate together with Alan Frank. They had all left together around January 16th bound for Texas. The van was a 1965 light blue Chevrolet with a "banged up body on it."

According to Deputy Kuretich, the people in the van were:

1. Alan David Frank, five feet, three inches, 140 pounds, thirty-three years old. Frank had blue eyes, brown hair, a suspended Colorado driver's license, and was wanted on a misdemeanor charge for an outstanding traffic violation.

2. Morrice David Dehart, about six feet, 190 pounds, in his mid-thirties. Dehart had yellow-gray hair, a long, full beard, and liked to wear a Civil War-style white cap. He had also once been a former military paramedic.

3. Harry Reynaldo Tester, five feet, ten inches, 175 pounds, about twenty years old. Tester had dirty blond hair and had recently started growing a beard. He sometimes wore glasses. He was also known to hang around with Dehart most of the time.

4. Terril Ahhea Knox, age thirty-one, 177 pounds. She had long dark hair below her shoulders which she wore in braids over her ears. She had two children.

5. Brian Knox, male about three years old, sandy hair.

6. Geoffrey Boyer, male about five or six years old.

7. Bruce Lee Keller, five feet, nine inches, early twenties. He had long dark hair, slender build, no facial hair, and was known to have left with the group in the van.

Armed with this information, Jim scoured the Valley for individuals bearing these descriptions. He discovered that after the kidnappers had abandoned the motor home in Brownsville on the 26th of January, they had headed west toward McAllen where they bought gas with one of the credit cards at a small service station in Pharr. On Valentine's Day, Jim journeyed to Pharr with the artist's sketch his brother had drawn of the tall kidnapper, and when he presented it to the service station operator, the attendant positively identified it as the person who had bought the gas using the stolen credit card.

Jim then got with Ranger Frank Horger and drove to Hidalgo to confer with Angel J. Logarda and Reynaldo Garcia Duran with the Mexican Immigration at Reynosa, Mexico. After searching their records, the Mexican agents located entry documents on five subjects and their vehicle. The five, Frank, Tester, Dehart, Knox, and Keller, all showed destinations of Mexico City. Their entry documents would expire in ninety days.

Chief Inspector Blackwell with the U.S. Customs at the International Bridge in Hidalgo was then advised of the situation. He ran a computer check on all U.S./Mexico entry points and was able to determine that the blue van had not recrossed the border back into the United States. He entered the vehicle into the computer for all border crossings.

Jim next contacted Lt. Joe Cantu of the McAllen Police Department and he, in turn, contacted Captain Victor Garcia Carmova with the Mexican Federal Highway Patrol. After advising Captain Carmova of the vehicle, the credit cards, travelers checks, and gun that the kidnappers might still possess, Carmova said he would call Mexico City and notify the Highway Patrol along the routes from Tampico to Mexico City to locate the suspects.

On February 15, Jim conferred with Assistant District Attorney Bill May at the Nueces County Courthouse in Corpus Christi and, based on the evidence Jim provided to him, Bill May filed on all five subjects for kidnapping. The next day, Jim issued a bulletin. It read in part, "Subjects are considered armed and dangerous."

By March, the kidnappers were still invisible in Mexico. Jim again journeyed to the International Bridge at Hidalgo and conferred with U.S. Customs Agent Bill McFarland. Agent McFarland stated that the subjects had not crossed back into the United States and that the vehicle was still entered into the computers at all border crossing from Texas to California. The ninety day Mexican permit was due to expire April 26.

When Jim returned to Corpus Christi, he learned from FBI Agent John Newton that suspect Morrice David Dehart was a deserter from the U.S. Army.

On May 21, Harry Reynaldo Tester returned to the United States, crossing the border at Nogales, Arizona, near Tucson where his mother lived. He was then picked up and interviewed by the Federal Bureau of Investigation. According to Tester, he did not learn of the kidnapping until long after the fact. He had stayed with the van during the abduction of the Lomans, and he only knew that Terry Knox and Morrice David Dehart were driving friends to the airport in Brownsville. When he saw Dehart pay for gas with a credit card in Tampico, Mexico, he had asked Dehart where he had gotten it because prior to that time, Dehart did not have a credit card.

Dehart had replied that he had ripped someone off in Texas and that was how they had gotten as far as Tampico. Tester said he had objected to Dehart's actions, but his objections prompted Terry Knox to state that he "was too innocent and would have to some day face up and dirty the slate." Knox also said, "You think Brownsville was to drop off friends? Well it wasn't."

The group stayed in Tampico for two weeks and then travelled to Vera Cruz where Morrice Dehart confided to Tester that he didn't like having it on his head that he might have killed someone. When Tester pressed Dehart for details, Dehart told him, "I cold-cocked the motherfucker, and I might have offed him."

While in Vera Cruz, Tester observed Morrice Dehart destroying credit cards by tearing them in half and throwing them in a trash can. The group stayed in Vera Cruz for several weeks and then went to Emillio Caranza, Vera Cruz , where Terry Knox, her two children, and Alan Frank decided to stay. Harry Tester, Morrice Dehart and Bruce Keller then went on to Palenque, Chiapus, Mexico, by hitchhiking. Bruce Keller then left for places unknown.

Harry Tester and Morrice Dehart remained in Palenque for a couple of months and then hitchhiked to Porto Escondito, Oxaca, Mexico, where Dehart left saying he was headed for the Caribbean. At that point, Tester phoned his father for train fare to Nogales, Mexico, and his return to the United States. He also told the authorities that his family's heirloom Colt .45 caliber revolver, Patent Date 1871, Manufactured Date 1907, was in the van, but he though that the gun had been stolen when the van was broken into in Mexico.

By the end of May, Morrice Dehart was known to be in California.

He made a phone call to Harry Tester, and when he learned that the FBI wanted to talk to him, he expressed a desire to turn himself in to the authorities. He never did.

In August, Terry Knox hitchhiked back to the United States. She contacted a public defender in Sacramento, California, who contacted the FBI, and she gave a statement to the FBI regarding the kidnapping and robbery of the Loman's. Agent John Newton in Corpus Christi then conferred with U.S. District Attorney Robert Berg and agreed to grant Knox immunity for her testimony. State charges of Aggravated Kidnapping were also dismissed after she testified in federal court.

By December, Alan David Frank was under arrest in Colorado. Bruce Keller, Harry Tester, and Terry Knox were not arrested and agreed to testify against Alan David Frank and Morrice David Dehart. Frank received seven years in the Federal Penitentiary on Aggravated Kidnapping charges. Morrice Dehart remained at large. Whether he was later arrested and was prosecuted for his part in the kidnapping is not known.

For Jim, it was a job well-done, which had spanned many months and had involved cooperation from officials on both sides of the Border. And when it was all over, he took his customary deep sigh of relief---before delving whole-heartedly into the next case.

HENRY LEE LUCAS

Never in the annals of crime has there ever been anyone more despicable than the serial killer. Shortly after he closed the Loman kidnapping case, Jim found himself embroiled in one of the most notorious murder investigations in the world. It spanned years and was never fully resolved, but for Jim, other Rangers, and police departments across the Nation, it explained an incredible number of previously unsolved, heinous crimes. The suspect was Henry Lee Lucas.

For Texas, it apparently began on June 11, 1983, in the tiny town of Montague, located about halfway between Dallas and Wichita Falls and having a whopping population of 400. On that date, Henry Lee Lucas became the most infamous prisoner ever to occupy the tiny County Jail. It was a fluke the way it came about, but before it was all over, Lucas would confess to the murders of more than 650 people, most of them young women. Although he later would retract his confessions, Lucas cleared up some unsolved murders in the South Texas area.

It began for Montague County Sheriff W.F. Conway, better known to his constituents as "Hound Dog" because of his reputation as a tenacious investigator, on September 18, 1982. A well-known, harmless, old lady named Kate Rich had disappeared from her old, frame house in nearby Ringgold, about five miles from the Oklahoma border, shortly after Lucas and his companion, Becky Powell, had stayed with her. Since the old woman had nine children, it took awhile for family members to determine that she was actually missing and not staying with one of them.

A frantic daughter finally called Sheriff Conway, and he drove straight out to the house. He found the old woman's dog and some of her fifteen cats locked inside, and the smell was atrocious with dried feces and urine everywhere. A half-completed quilt lay draped over a chair as if Kate Rich intended to came right back to it. But of the old lady, Sheriff Conway found nothing. There was no way of knowing how long she had been gone, but his gut instinct told him that she had met with foul play. Since Henry Lee Lucas and Becky Powell were the last known people to be at the house, Conway believed the pair had something to do with the old woman's disappearance.

On September 27, with the eighty-year old woman still missing and no real leads to her disappearance, Conway called an old friend of his, Texas Ranger Phil Ryan. He told the Ranger that things just didn't look right, that he suspected the old woman had been murdered. It would become the start of an investigation that would shock the nation.

Throughout the coming months Ranger Ryan and Sheriff Conway worked hard to piece together Henry Lucas', Becky Powell's, and the missing woman's relationship. Conway discovered that after leaving Kate Rich's house on September 16---at the request of two of Kate's daughters--- Lucas and Becky went to the House of Prayer, a religious commune in nearby Stoneburg run by Ruben Moore, a roofing contractor and minister.

Moore, it turned out, had gotten the pair a handyman's job with Kate Rich a few weeks earlier. Moore told the investigators that after returning to the commune, the pair spent the night. They then left the next morning for the small town of Bowie where they intended to buy some clothes. Moore also said that Lucas returned late the following evening sans Becky, claiming she had run off with a truck driver. The following morning, September 19, Lucas drove out of the commune, apparently for good. Lucas did mention, however, that he wanted to stop and say goodbye to Granny, which is what he called Kate Rich.

No one saw or heard from Henry Lucas or Becky Powell for one month. Around 11:00 p.m. on the evening of October 17, Kate Rich's house burned to the ground by a fire that appeared to have been intentionally set. Henry Lee Lucas was also back at the House of Prayer.

By now, Sheriff Conway and Ranger Ryan decided they were looking for two missing people, Kate Rich and Becky Powell. Unfortunately, they had no evidence to arrest Henry Lucas---until Phil Ryan learned the following summer, on June 10, 1983, that Lucas had been in possession of a pistol. In Texas, convicted felons cannot possess firearms, and Lucas had been convicted of killing his mother in Michigan in 1960. The next morning, a warrant was issued for Lucas' arrest, and the two lawmen drove out to the House of Prayer to serve it.

Henry Lucas spent just four days in jail before he passed a note to the jailer to give to the sheriff. "I've been killing ever [sic] thing I can for the past ten years," he wrote. What followed has written Lucas into the pages of history as possibly the worst serial sex-killer in the world.

Lucas confessed to killing Becky Powell in an empty field outside Denton. He said they had hitchhiked to a truck stop, since his own car didn't have license plates and he was afraid to drive it, and a trucker then gave them a ride to Denton. There, in a field where they spent the night, he had gotten into a fight with the fifteen-year-old, stabbed her to death, had sex with her---he liked having sex with dead things...people, animals, it didn't matter---before cutting her body into nine pieces and stuffing them into two pillow cases. His first idea was to bury the cases, but the ground was too hard, and all he had was his knife. He resorted to removing the gory pieces from the sacks and scattering them all over the field.

He said he then returned to Kate Rich's house and asked the old woman to go to church and then help him look for Becky. He had told the old woman that Becky had run off with a truck driver, but that he thought

185

he knew where she was. Instead of turning south to church, however, he drove north into Oklahoma where he bought a case of beer for himself and a soft drink for Kate. Returning to the Ringgold area, he drove into an old campground near the cemetery, stabbed the old woman to death, had sex with her, and then hid the body in an old drain pipe that ran under the road. A month later, he retrieved the body from the drain pipe, stuffed the putrefying flesh into two plastic garbage bags, and burned the bags in a stove at the converted chicken-barn apartment he and Becky had once used at the House of Prayer.

Lucas led officers to the two death sites, and investigators recovered Becky's body parts and what was left of Kate Rich from the ash heap at the House of Prayer.

As word got out, other investigators began arriving with questions of their own about unsolved murders in their jurisdiction. Lucas, although more than willing to cooperate and confess, laid down a few ground rules. First, he refused to talk to anyone unless a member of the Montague staff or a Texas Ranger was present. Second, any descriptions he gave had to be sent to the area pertaining to the crime.

In all his life, Henry Lee Lucas possessed only one real talent, an uncanny memory almost bordering on total recall. He remembered everything---dates, places, people...practically everything he saw or heard. He readily volunteered to help solve hundreds of murders along the highways and byways across the nation. He claimed he killed on I-35 from Michigan to Laredo, on I-10 from Florida to California. He left victims down the eastern seaboard and scattered throughout the western states. Everywhere he went---he was a total drifter---he killed.

Lucas admitted he killed little girls, beautiful women, and old ladies. Some he killed with knives. Others he strangled or bludgeoned to death. Most of his victims were hitchhikers, and others he snatched off the street. Many begged for their lives and struggled. Others died soundlessly, in total shock at the situation. Always, Lucas killed them for sex. "I just crave women all the time," he said.

But as helpful as Lucas professed to be with the authorities, he was also something else. He was a consummate liar and braggart. Finding himself in the national spotlight after nearly half a century of anonymity, he lied over and over again, claiming murders that investigators knew for certain were committed by someone else. Trying to sort the truth from his fiction was an enormous task. Later, his attorneys would claim that he killed only his mother, Kate Rich, and Becky, that all his confessions to other murders were just lies. This, naturally, incensed a lot of good officers who put in tons of hours and hard work on their cases.

In August, 1983, Lucas was transferred to the Williamson County

Jail in Georgetown just north of Austin to stand trial for the murder of a woman authorities called "Orange Socks," because she was never identified and orange socks were all that she was wearing when she was found. While he was there, Travis County authorities made arrangements to "borrow" him to help solve a string of unsolved murders in the Austin area. Jim was next to get his turn to interview the killer about several grisly crimes that had occurred in the Corpus Christi area.

Henry Lee Lucas wasn't much to look at. He was of average height, slim, with brown hair and one brown eye, the right one. In 1943, while trying to make a swing with a grapevine, his brother Andrew cut at the vine with Henry holding it. The knife slipped, and Andrew sliced across Henry's nose and left eye. The accident punctured the eyeball. Later, when the eye was almost, but not quite healed, Henry's exasperated school teacher struck out at another student with her metal-edged ruler. Henry got in the way, and his injured eye ruptured.

Henry was fitted with a glass eye, but the work was not well-done. It hung askew in the socket and that, coupled with the droopy lid, was enough to embarrass him. He made it worse-looking by not keeping it clean. In fact, throughout his life, Henry didn't keep any part of himself clean. He seldom took baths and abhorred washing his teeth. It was all investigators could do to keep from gagging from the smell whenever they were cooped up with him.

Henry Lee Lucas gave Jim a statement in May 1984. He said that during the last part of December, 1975, he and Ottis Toole, his partner in crime for much of the killing and Becky Powell's uncle, were in Corpus Christi. At the time, Lucas owned a 1968, green, Ford station wagon, and they were driving around looking for action.

Late one evening, they saw a girl walking on the sidewalk in a residential area. Lucas pulled across the street in front of her and stopped. Both men got out of the car, and Lucas pulled a gun, pointed it at the girl, and told her to get in the car. They put the woman in the front seat between them, turned the car around, and drove down Padre Island Drive until they reached the beach road which led to Mustang Island. They turned left onto the road, drove approximately three to four miles, turned onto a sandy, dirt road and stopped.

"Ottis and I had sex with her," Lucas said in his statement. "Ottis and I drank beer and smoked pot. The girl smoked pot. She had long, blonde hair, was white, about sixteen or seventeen, five feet, five inches, about 125 pounds, dressed in blue jeans, western-styled shirt, and blue jean jacket. I think some cowboy boots. We stayed there about an hour or a little longer. We left and drove back toward town on the beach road approximately one mile. I stopped the car on a side road, took her out of the car on the driver's side. Ottis got out, came around the car, and we walked across the road.

"After we got on the other side of the road at the edge of the grass, I shot the girl one time on the side of the head with a .22 pistol. After she fell on the ground, Ottis and I picked her up and moved her to the tall grass. She was laying face up with her clothes on. I walked up and put the gun down by her right hand. I told Ottis I wanted it to look like a suicide. I wiped the fingerprints off the gun. The gun was fully loaded, except the one shot which had killed her.

"We then drove back to Corpus Christi. On the road between Corpus Christi to San Antonio on June 21, 1984, Texas Ranger Jim Peters showed me a photograph of a girl. I identified the girl as the one I had shot in the head in December 1975. Jim Peters told me the girl was Katherine Lucille Roberts.

"On June 21, I went with Ranger Peters and Deputy Hardeson to the area where we had sex and where I killed her. I pointed out the location completely."

Katherine Lucille Roberts was found in the grass by an employee of the Texas Department of Highways while mowing the right-of-ways. She had been shot once in the head and was lying exactly where Lucas said. There is no possible way Lucas could have known so many details unless he did the crime. So, too, for the murder of Estella Montoya. She was found stabbed several times in the chest and left naked in a ditch on the Welder ranch with only her shoes and socks. When Jim showed Lucas a photograph of her, he confessed that he did it. He then took Jim right to the exact place, described the murder scene, how he did it, and described the shoes and socks around her ankles just like she was found.

But Lucas also confessed to murders he did not do just to get the attention. One unsolved murder that Jim questioned Lucas about concerned Hortense Arbregon, aged fifty-three, found under the Harbor Bridge, which links Corpus Christi to the small town of Portland on the other side of Corpus Christi Bay. Lucas said he did it, but he couldn't provide complete details of the crime, which appeared to Jim to be totally out of character to Henry's fantastic memory. Jim firmly believes it was a lie. Lucas also confessed to the murders of Karen and Wanda Kirk, a mother and daughter duo from Bastrop, Texas. Lucas said he killed them in June of 1977, four miles south of the National Seashore Park Ranger Headquarters on Padre Island in the four-wheeled drive area of soft sand by shooting them with a .32 or .38 caliber weapon. Again, he could not provide complete details of the crime.

"It was a lot of bull," Jim said.

Of the twelve unsolved murders in Corpus Christi that Jim

questioned Lucas about, Henry apparently committed two of them. Although he confessed to killing several of the others, Jim believes that it was all a lie. He also confessed to Jim that he committed seven other murders near Corpus Christi, south of the city, but when Jim investigated the allegations, none of it could ever be substantiated.

It was frustrating in this fashion for every investigator across the State who got to question Lucas, and especially so after his lawyers had him recanting his confessions. One crime he said he committed and which was included in those he later recanted occurred in Uvalde. It was investigated by Jim's good friend, Ranger Joaquin Jackson.

Ranger Jackson interviewed Lucas about a girl abducted from a local 7-11 store by two men in a pickup truck. According to Jim, Lucas confessed to Jackson that he and Ottis Toole were driving down the street, looking for action, when they spied a pretty girl in her car. They followed her for about half a mile, and she turned into the parking lot of the 7-11 store.

"I wanted her," Lucas said, "so we pulled up. When she came out, we grabbed her. We went down a road and pulled off into the brush, going along that dirt road. Back in there, there was a tree lying down. We laid her over that tree and raped her. We killed her and left her hanging over that tree."

Lying over a tree was exactly how the young woman was found.

When Lucas was with Ranger Jackson recreating the crime scene, it was dark, and Jackson was driving about seventy miles per hour down the highway. Lucas, in the back seat of the Ranger car, suddenly yelled, "Wait. Wait. Right here. Right here. Back up."

Joaquin Jackson slammed on the brakes.

"Go down that road, that ravine there," Lucas said and pointed to a dark, dirt road barely discernible at that time of night. It was the obscure dirt road where the victim had been found lying over the tree.

"No way in the world could he have known where that place was--unless he'd been there," Joaquin Jackson reported later. "We pulled down there, and he showed us. You can't tell me that he didn't kill her."

"In my mind," said Jim, "he did two of those murders he claimed to have done here in Corpus Christi. He picked up photographs of the girl, and said, 'Yeah, I killed her.' He then told how he and Ottis took her to this place, had sex with her, and then shot her."

Henry Lee Lucas may not have killed more than 650 people, as he claimed, but in the minds of the hundreds of investigators from across the Nation, he did murder many times. The Lucas Task Force operated eighteen months, and during that time, investigators representing a thousand different law enforcement agencies from forty states and Canada questioned

Lucas about approximately three thousand homicides. Of that number, Lucas was considered a suspect in about 150 murders.

It seems hard to believe that Lucas killed only his mother, his teenage lover, and an old woman in North Texas, especially in light of his extensive travels. Also, no other suspects have ever been charged in any of the murders he once claimed. Maybe the only one who really knows for certain is Henry Lee Lucas.

THE RADIO MURDER CASE

Sometimes solving crimes involves a stroke of luck more than intensive investigation, and every investigator looks forward to such times. Although it never happens often, it always leaves the lawman feeling elated, no matter how heinous the crime. For Jim, one of his major "stroke-of-luck situations" happened when he was called in to investigate what he calls "the radio murder case." It happened in the city of Bayside.

Bayside is a tiny, fishing community in the middle of Aransas County. It has about 150 permanent population which fluctuates all year round as "snowbirds" escaping the freezing weather of the north in the winter, as well as other tourists wanting a little more seclusion than Padre Island or Port Aransas in the summer, flock to the area for fishing, boating, swimming, and other forms of amusing relaxation.

Early one morning, about two-and-a-half miles outside the town's city limits, authorities found a dead man on a deserted stretch of county road. It had rained all the previous night, and the victim was lying face down in a ditch, beaten and drowned. The only clues were bits of belt buckle, blood, and other evidence up on the road indicating that the dead man had put up a terrific struggle for his life before he died.

In searching the area for clues, officers followed a set of tire tracks four miles through the mud on the horseshoe-shaped road until the tracks emptied back out on the main highway, but they found no other items of evidence along the route. All they really had to go on was the fight scene on the road and, of course, the dead man in the ditch.

When the sheriff's deputies searched the body, they found only a tiny scrap of paper with a telephone number on it. There was absolutely nothing else. The dead man had no billfold, no identification, no visa or passport---nothing which would help the authorities to identify him. With so many tourists in the area all the time, chances were better than average that the man would remain unidentified, if someone didn't report him missing. The body was duly taken to the morgue, and authorities began the laborious task of trying to identify the victim and apprehend his killer using the meager scrap of clues that they had.

The first item on the agenda was the telephone number on the scrap of paper found on the body. It was a Corpus Christi number, and Aransas County Sheriff Bob Hewes dialed it. The woman who answered the phone said the dead man could be Fred Pavlecek. "He's staying with us," she said. "He came in from out of town, and he had a little room at the back of the house. He hasn't been here too long."

Sheriff Hewes immediately contacted Jim, and the two of them went to the house. They found only a young girl, about fourteen-years-old, at home. They questioned her about Fred, getting a description which matched the dead man in the morgue.

"Yeah," she said, "he left the other night, and he hasn't come back yet. He had just bought himself a new radio." She then went to Fred's room and found the receipt where Fred had purchased the radio. On the receipt was the radio's serial number.

Now the authorities knew Fred had a radio with him, but since it wasn't found at the murder scene, chances were that the murderer had taken it. If they could locate the radio, they might be able to apprehend the killer, or at least get a lead to the killer's identity. Jim also discovered that Fred had been seen getting into a car with two men in front of the City Bakery in town. And, that's where Fred's trail ended---until he showed up dead in the drainage ditch with his radio missing.

Days passed, and the authorities could do nothing without further leads. They were waiting for the radio to show up when Lady Luck lent a hand.

The city of Portland had a talkative drunk named Solly Soliz* in their jail. And Solly wanted to make points with the officers, hoping that he could win favors in return. He said to one of the guards, "I'm going to tell you something. My brother-in-law beat up a guy and stole his radio."

The Portland police knew that Jim and Aransas County Sheriff Bob Hewes were working together on a murder case where a man had been beaten to death and his radio stolen. The Portland police chief called Jim and gave him Solly's brother-in-law's name. Jim called Sheriff Hewes, and the two of them went to the brother-in-law's house, which was out in the country.

The brother-in-law wasn't at the farmhouse when the two officers arrived, but his wife was. Jim informed the man's wife that he had information which said that her husband might have a stolen radio. In no way did he want to alarm the woman, so he said nothing which would infer that her husband might have stolen the radio or that another man had been murdered. Jim also told her that he thought the radio might be on the premises and that he'd like to search the house. He asked for her consent to search. She gave her permission, and Jim had her sign a Consent to Search document.

"We searched the house up one side and down the other," Jim said, "and could find no trace of the radio. It wasn't out in plain sight or packed away in the back of some closet. We went through the kitchen cupboards, the pantry, everything, and we were just about to give up when I remember the hall closet. The house had a long hall, and she used the hall closet as a sort of clothes hamper. I had just looked in there and cursorily poked about, but now I decided to empty it out."

"I opened the door and dug around through the clothes, and there, under a pile of clothes about four feet deep was the radio. I matched the serial number, and it was the same one."

The woman told the lawmen that her husband would be home shortly. Jim and Sheriff Hewes decided to sit in the car and wait. When the suspect drove into the yard, Jim called him over to the car, put him in the back seat, and began to interrogate him.

"You've got this radio in your house, and it's stolen," Jim began. He then spelled out a scenario for the man, hoping to elicit a confession. "I know where you got it and how you got it. You and this friend picked up this old boy at the City Bakery that night around 10:00 p.m., and he had this radio with him. You drove around listening to the radio and drinking beer, and you went out to Bayside. You pulled up that country road out there, and you got into an argument, like all guys do. You stopped, and you got out, and you decided you'd settle it with fists, like men do.

"You probably hit him once or twice, and your friend beat him up. Then he fell in a ditch full of water, and your friend was so mad at him that he stood on him until he drowned. Is that the way it happened?"

"Yeah," the suspect stammered, "I only hit him one or two times."

"Ok. You're under arrest. You have the right to remain silent...."

The lawmen drove the suspect to Refugio, because they were in Refugio County, and put him in jail. They then drove over to the friend's house and said the same things to to the friend, only this time, Jim reversed the roles of the two suspects. Now, Jim told the story as if the man in the Refugio jail was the killer.

"Oh, yeah," the friend said, when confronted with the new story as Jim reconstructed it, "We beat him up, and he drowned him."

"We got confessions on both of them and solved the case," Jim said. "It only goes to show that if you give them an out, they don't realize that they are hanging themselves."

THE THREE RIVERS CAPER

Jim always appreciated advanced warnings from his informers about any planned crime, whether it happened or not, because it gave him time to get with the local officials and apprehend the perpetrators before something really ugly, like gunshots, could damper the day. Although not all stakeouts resulted in an arrest, over the years, he's saved untold numbers of lives in that fashion---officers, bystanders, and criminals alike.

Early one Monday morning in the early 1980's, one of Jim's informers approached him with the plans to burglarize a drug store for narcotics in the tiny community of Three Rivers. Three Rivers is located about an hour's drive north of Corpus Christi on Interstate 37 toward San Antonio. According to the informer, the crooks were going to drive a car to Three Rivers on Wednesday, and around 10:00 p.m. that night, they would throw a brick through the front glass door or through the window of the store to test for a burglar alarm. They would then drive down the street and wait for awhile to see if the police would investigate. If no one showed up, they would return, steal the narcotics, and leave.

Jim promptly got with Ranger Glenn Krueger from Beeville, the Sheriff of Live Oak County, and the Chief of Police of Three Rivers, and they planned a stakeout of the drug store. Since the drug store sits right by the busy interstate highway, offering an easy avenue for escape for the thieves, Jim and the Chief of Police settled in the city hall across from the drug store, and Ranger Krueger and the Sheriff were across the street leading to the interstate highway on the side of the building, opposite the side door. The Chief of Police also had a key to the front door of the store.

At about the appointed time of the burglary, a highway patrol officer showed up with a prisoner to be processed with the Justice of the Peace. Usually, it only took about ten or fifteen minutes for that type of arrest to be concluded, but that particular night it seemed to drag on forever. Jim began to think the officer might actually be enjoying a coffee break somewhere in the building. Everyone in the stakeout sat in nervous anticipation, waiting for the highway patrol officer to leave, all the while wondering if the planned burglary had been inadvertently compromised by the presence of the highway patrol vehicle parked on the street. Just as Jim entertained the idea of sending the police chief over to the building to shoo the officer back out on patrol, the patrolman returned, got in his car, and drove off.

Apparently everything was still "go" for the two crooks because shortly after the highway patrol cruiser drove off, the suspects drove by. They made one slow canvass past the front of the store, turned around at the end of the block, and slowly drove back past the store to the other end of the street. Seeing nothing suspicious, the crooks slowly drove back, stopped in front of the store, and one man got out. He threw a brick through the front window. The brick created a hole not much larger than a television screen, but it made a deafening noise in the still night when the glass broke. The brick thrower leaped back into the car, and they hightailed it to the end of the street, where they parked and waited for results.

After about thirty minutes, the two crooks walked nonchalantly past the building, peeped inside, kicked a little more glass out of the window, and continued walking on down the block as if nothing had happened. A few minutes later, they came back, bent down, and disappeared inside.

It was now time for the lawmen to react. The crooks were inside the drug store, and all the lawmen had to do was to enter the store and arrest them. Jim and the Chief of Police raced to the front of the store, and Ranger Krueger and the Sheriff ran to the side door, but when the Chief put the key to the front door lock, it wouldn't work.

Jim couldn't stand it. "I'm going in," he said, and bent over and zipped through the hole in the window. Holding his big .45 automatic in his hand, he walked cautiously down one dark aisle toward the back where the pharmaceuticals were located, until he could hear the robbers. He then announced in a loud, firm voice, "Texas Ranger! You're under arrest!"

The informer was supposed to escape as part of the deal for helping nab the other crook, and when Jim heard a slight commotion around the corner, he just assumed the noise was caused by the informer going out the side door like he was supposed to do. Rounding the corner, however, he was surprised to find that the noise had been caused by the other crook scrambling to locate a big bottle of paregoric which, when Jim saw him, he had pressed to his lips and was guzzling down in big gulps. The crook later told Jim that "when you said, 'Texas Ranger,' I just knew you were going to kill me, and I wanted to die happy, so I just gulped it all down."

Meanwhile, the others had difficulties. The Chief of Police still couldn't get the key to unlock the front door. He scrambled after Jim through the broken front window, ripping his shirt in the process. Hearing Jim's yell of "Texas Ranger," the informer tried to escape out the side door, but he couldn't get the door to open. And since he couldn't get the door open, Ranger Krueger and the Sheriff couldn't get in. The two lawmen had to beat the door down before they could enter and offer assistance. In kicking the door in, they stumbled over the informer and had to usher the man out in hushed tones to keep from compromising his undercover work.

The informer then returned to Corpus Christi. A couple of days later, he entered a store, stole a pair of boots, and left his old pair in the store. Jim recognized the old boots as belonging to the informer, and a warrant for arrest was promptly issued. Since the informer was already a two-time loser out on parole, he went back to prison for life.

"Crime just doesn't pay," Jim said with a big grin.

THE WARREN HOUSLOUER CRISIS

One of Jim's worst toe-to-toe standoffs with an armed and dangerous crook occurred in the early Spring of 1984. He had never before met anyone quite like Warren Hauslouer. The man was an expert shot with a pistol. He was also chronically ill with a medical condition that caused him to twitch and jerk, making Jim wonder if the loaded pistol the man held would accidentally go off with disastrous results. To further compound the situation, Warren Hauslouer was determined to die. His chosen method of execution? He wanted to shoot it out with police. It was Jim's duty to talk him out of it.

The crisis began when two sheriff's deputies tried to arrest Warren Hauslouer on a retaliation warrant.

"It's just up the street," San Patricio County Deputy Sheriff Bobby Mayfield radioed from his patrol car. "How do you want to handle it?"

"We'll just go in and get him," Chief Deputy Carl Perkins radioed back, "and if he gives us any trouble, we'll knock a little sense into him."

It was 1:30 p.m., April 26, 1984, and the two deputies were in separate patrol units, driving slowly down Sunset Street in Ingleside, searching the mailboxes for a house number or a name that would identify which home belonged to Warren Hauslouer. The wanted man had violated a restraining order, and the deputies had a warrant for retaliation arrest. They didn't expect any trouble---each had made hundreds of arrests in the past without difficulties---but it never hurt to be prepared for the worst.

It was Deputy Mayfield who finally spotted the modest, two-storied house near the corner on the left side of the street. Partially covering the left corner of the front porch and one of the two windows on that side of the house was a giant, white-blooming oleander bush in bad need of pruning. The yard also held one lone ornamental date palm with several unsightly dead fronds drooping down the trunk. But the remainder of the yard indicated that someone avidly interested in gardening lived there. Both the pittosporum hedge and the grass had a fresh, trimmed look to them, and the sidewalk and driveway on the right side of the house were neatly edged in decorative monkey grass.

Bobby Mayfield pulled his cruiser into the driveway, set the parking brake, and got out. Carl Perkins turned around in the intersection at the end of the block and returned to park parallel in the street. Mayfield waited for Perkins to join him on the front lawn before both deputies strode purposefully to the front door.

Warren Hauslouer was not only at home, he personally answered the knock at his door. He was not, however, happy to see the lawmen. He waited just long enough to hear Carl Perkins say, "We have a warrant for your arrest," before he turned and fled.

Bobby Mayfield was on him like a rooster on a June bug. "We can do this the easy way," Mayfield said through clenched teeth, as he and Perkins wrestled with the other man, "or we can do it your way."

Hauslouer appeared not to hear. He was so determined not to be arrested that he struggled fiercely with the two deputies. It took the combined strength of both lawmen to overpower him. During the fracas, he kicked Bobby Mayfield hard in the shin and bit Carl Perkins severely on the left arm.

The two deputies finally pinned Hauslouer to the floor and handcuffed his hands behind his back. Breathing heavily, they took a moment to refill their lungs before wrestling Hauslouer onto his feet and out to the patrol car. As Perkins gingerly surveyed his arm, Mayfield glanced around the room, rubbing his throbbing leg. A scatter rug lay shoved to one side at the foot of the stairs, and a lamp was knocked over onto the sofa, but the rest of the place didn't look too bad. He turned his stare to Perkins.

"Better get that looked at," he said, eyeing Perkins' bloody arm. "No telling what this guy had for lunch."

"Yeah," muttered Perkins, jerking the swearing Hauslouer to his feet, "probably need a rabies shot, too."

The deputies quickly searched the still-struggling and cussing Hauslouer before marching him out the door. Expertly and none too carefully, they forced the resisting man into the rear seat of Bobby Mayfield's patrol unit and slammed the door shut, just as Hauslouer's feet rose up to meet it. With a sigh of relief, Mayfield slipped behind the wheel, started the engine, and began to carefully back out the driveway.

Hauslouer, however, still wasn't done. Unknown to Mayfield, he had a surprise for the deputy. With his hands cuffed behind his back, Hauslouer squirmed and maneuvered until he found and pulled out the .38 caliber Smith and Wesson pistol, which he had hidden in his clothes and which the deputies did not find because he had squirmed and struggled so fiercely. Grunting in exertion and still muttering under his breath, he fired one shot through the right front seat of the patrol unit, hitting the dash.

With the sound of the unexpected gunshot reverberating in his ear and the smell of gunpowder in his nostrils, the deputy slammed on the brakes. Mayfield and Hauslouer each jumped out of the patrol car. The deputy dove for cover, and Hauslouer raced back into his residence, still armed with the revolver. Carl Perkins, tires squealing on the asphalt, pulled his car into the driveway and rejoined Bobby Mayfield. Unsheathing their weapons and using Mayfield's car as a shield, the two deputies discussed what to do next.

"Drop your weapon and come on out," Perkins finally yelled.

Almost as an afterthought, he added, "And let me see your hands!"

Warren Hauslouer refused. He called out that he would never surrender, that he could not stand to be put into jail again. "I'll die first," he yelled out in defiance to the officers. He then threatened to shoot anyone who tried to take him.

By 2:00 p.m., other officers from the San Patricio County Sheriff's Office, the Ingleside Police Department, and the Texas Department of Public Safety were on the scene to secure the area. Also called was Dr. C. H. Lewis. Hauslouer had a serious medical problem, and Dr. Lewis was treating him for it. After much discussion, the officers decided to let Dr. Lewis enter the house, hoping that the courageous doctor could talk Hauslouer into surrendering. It didn't work.

By 2:15 p.m., it was still a stand-off. Hauslouer wanted to shoot it out with the police, and the police, quite naturally, refused to accept such an insane plan. The police also had another problem. Many of the residents of Ingleside worked in the nearby chemical plants, and the shift was just about to change. With the prospect of dozens of spectators looming on the horizon, the police called for reinforcements. They called the Texas Ranger office in nearby Corpus Christi and asked for Jim.

By this time, Jim had been a twenty-seven-year veteran of law enforcement, and he knew exactly what sort of situation he would be facing in Ingleside. He received the message to assist the San Patricio County officers at 2:19 p.m., and fifteen minutes later, he was on the scene. It was every bit as grim as he imagined. Warren Hauslouer was holed up in his house with a loaded .38 caliber pistol, threatening to shoot any officer who came into view.

Jim conferred with the authorities for several moments, trying to get an idea, a "handle" that he could use in the situation. Doctor Lewis, who had been inside patiently trying to talk the barricaded man into surrendering, emerged and joined the conference. The news the doctor brought with him was not good. Warren Hauslouer refused to surrender. He wanted to die in a shootout and was determined to provoke one just as soon as the opportunity presented itself. He did, however, have one request---he wanted his wife brought to the scene.

While the police made arrangements to locate Hauslauer's wife, Jim handed Dr. Lewis his Ranger identification. He asked the doctor to take it inside to the barricaded man and explain that a Texas Ranger was outside and wanted to talk. "Tell him that I will come in unarmed."

Doctor Lewis went back into the residence. A few minutes later, Anita Hauslouer* arrived and went into the house to talk to her husband. The lawmen waited...and waited...and waited. A half hour later, at approximately 3:15 p.m., Dr. Lewis came out and said that Hauslouer had

199

finally agreed to talk to the Ranger. Jim then gave his pistol to Department of Public Safety officer Sergeant Hall, and he boldly walked up to the front door and into the house.

Squaring his shoulders, determined to put an end to the standoff, Jim looked around the room for Hauslouer. He found the armed man waiting for him, staring down from the top of the stairs with an almost maniacal look on his face. Hauslouer had the loaded pistol in one handcuffed hand, and he kept it pointed straight at Jim, cocked and ready to fire.

Warren Hauslouer was forty-six years old, and he had a medical condition which caused his whole body to jerk and twitch in uncontrollable spasms. Doctor Lewis had been treating him for the illness, but it was incurable and getting worse all the time. He had lost his job as a carpenter and, being unable to find other work, was deeply depressed. As he stood at the top of the stairs watching the tall Ranger, he continually changed hands with the gun, moving it back and forth while his body trembled and shook. Jim knew that with the hammer cocked, it was only a matter of time before it went off.

"I'm an expert with firearms, and I can hit what I want, even with my hands cuffed," Hauslouer warned.

"I don't want to hurt you," Jim responded, rapidly assessing the situation and deciding to use the 'good ole boy' approach. "I don't want you to hurt me or anyone else. I just want for us to talk."

At that moment, Anita Hauslouer came in from the kitchen and told Jim that she had some medication and water for her husband. She asked if she could give it to him. Normally, Jim wouldn't even entertain the idea of getting another person involved in a potential hostage-type situation, but the woman was the armed man's wife, and the medicine just might help control the man's jerking, twitching trigger finger. Jim nodded in approval, voicing that she go ahead and do it.

When Anita Hauslouer returned to the kitchen, Jim started slowly up the stairs, talking quietly as he went. He took one stair at a time, stopping and calculating Hauslouer's mental and physical conditions before advancing to the next step. He'd faced many armed and dangerous men in his career, but none quite like the man at the top of the stairs holding the loaded, cocked pistol with spasmodic fingers. How far up the staircase could he go before Hauslouer shot him?

Cautiously, carefully, Jim advanced, talking in deep, soothing tones. "I'm not here to hurt you," he said. "I'm here to help, but I can't do anything until you lower the gun. Put the gun down, Warren, and let's talk." Reaching the top stair, he slowly sat down, making sure his every movement could be clearly seen by the armed man.

"Why don't you sit down, too?" Jim suggested. His tone was not patronizing. It conveyed all the commitment of a friend talking to a friend. "I know you're getting tired of standing up there."

He watched Hauslouer jerk and twitch, continually cocking and uncocking the loaded pistol, moving it back and forth between his hands.

"I don't want either of us to get hurt. I have a family the same as you do."

"I won't shoot you, if you don't jump me," Warren Hauslouer finally said.

"Okay," replied Jim. "Let's just talk."

Warren Hauslouer sat down, and they began talking. Jim listened quietly as Hauslouer bared his soul, explaining how he wanted to die rather than live with the medical problems he now had. "I can't get a job. I can't support my family. I can't do anything. I might as well die." Several times he said, "Well, it's time I went out there and shot an officer so they will shoot me and kill me." Always, he kept cocking and uncocking the revolver, moving it from one hand to the other, alternately pointing it at Jim or the floor.

Each time Hauslouer threatened to shoot an officer, Jim patiently talked him out of it. Patience is one of Jim's specialties. Gifted with a magnificent amount of it, he's talked through many crisis situations during his career.

Every once in a while, Anita Hauslouer came in and talked to her husband. So, too, did the doctor, but Hauslouer refused to be swayed by their pleading. He adamantly refused to surrender. He kept blurting out, "Well, I want to die because of my critical handicap. I can't support my family any more. I'm going out and shoot an officer and have the officer kill me."

By this time, Jim had learned that Warren Hauslouer thought his family would collect double indemnity on an insurance policy if he allowed himself to be shot and killed in a shootout with the police. Jim attempted to straighten out the misconception for the armed man.

"If you go out there and shoot it out with the police, and you die in the exchange of gunfire, it's the same as committing suicide," Jim explained. "The insurance company will not pay off on suicide. Don't do it, Warren. Put down your gun and surrender to me. That way, no one will get hurt."

Hauslouer refused to surrender. He didn't really believe that shooting it out with the police was a form of suicide, but the Ranger's words did worry him. Although he still continued with his insane idea of wanting to provoke a gunfight, he began to show signs that the tall lawman sitting at the top of the stairs was getting through to him. Every once in a while when he'd say "time for me to go out and end it," he'd make no real effort to leave. He would wait, instead, for Jim to talk him out of it again.

Realizing that Warren Hauslouer was almost, but not quite, at the point of surrender, Jim decided on another approach, one that the spasmodic and twitching man was sure to understand. Jim told Hauslouer that if he shot a police officer and the officer was hurt, then the officer wouldn't be able to support his family. "Do you want that, Warren?" Jim asked. "Do you really want that man's family to suffer?"

That seemed to make a lot of sense to Hauslouer. The logic of it hit him right where he sat, and he winced as he thought it over. "All right," he finally said, "I won't shoot them. I'll just shoot their cars up."

Knowing he was making progress, Jim delivered the *coup de grace* with his customary finesse. "Let me explain something to you," he said. "You have four bullets left in that gun, and when you shoot that fourth bullet, they're going to come over here and straddle you. You'll probably get a knot on your head from somebody, and maybe worse. It's stupid, and you're too smart for that. Don't do it, Warren."

It was now about 4:30 p.m., and a justice of the peace had arrived. Jim told Hauslouer that he'd bring the magistrate inside and they could all talk over what would happen when Hauslouer surrendered. Warren Hauslouer agreed.

Jim carefully and slowly walked down the stairs and out of the house, aware of the cocked gun pointed at him as he left. He explained the situation to the peace officer and escorted the magistrate around to the back of the house and into the kitchen. Jim then brought the doctor and Hauslouer into the room. After the magistrate explained that Warren would be taken to the court house in Sinton where bond would be set and he would be released on bond, Warren Hauslouer surrendered to Jim.

"I was able to take the gun out of his hand," Jim said. "I unloaded the gun and handed it over to Sheriff Leroy Moody."

Warren Hauslouer was taken to Sinton, the county seat of San Patricio County, and released on a $15,000 bond for a retaliation warrant. On October 18, 1984, the charge of attempted murder of a police officer was changed to aggravated assault on a police officer. Hauslouer was tried in Sinton and received ten years probation.

Jim received a commendation from Department of Public Safety Director Colonel James Adams, who had risen to the number-two job in the FBI under J. Edgar Hoover before retiring and coming home to Texas. In part, it read, "...it is not easy to converse with a man holding a loaded, cocked pistol pointing at you, but in your usual fashion, you again demonstrated the courageous and competent demeanor which has made the Ranger Service the outstanding law enforcement organization it is."

For Jim, it was just another job well done. He had done it many times before and would do it again and again. For Warren Houslouer, however, the incident wasn't over. He was serious about wanting to die. After the trial, he went home and committed suicide by shooting himself in the head with a .357 magnum revolver.

THE KARNES CITY HOSTAGE CRISIS

Hostage situations were nothing new to Jim, although he always dreaded them. For one thing, there was absolutely no way of knowing how the criminal would react, no way of knowing what would happen when the crook finally realized that he could not escape. Jim always found himself fearing for the safety of the hostage. It was one reason that he always broke all speed records getting to the location.

June 25, 1985, began as just another day, and like all Rangers, Jim had more work than he could possibly handle. Eyeing the folders on the corner of the desk, he mentally ticked off the most pressing business, checked his messages, scanned his mail, and then headed out the door to begin the day. Three hours later, he was in the air in a DPS helicopter, on his way to a hostage crisis in Karnes City.

Karnes City is a tiny, hamlet about sixty miles north of Corpus Christi on Highway 181. It's an old city founded by the Mexicans and Spaniards in the late 1700's as St. Joe. By the mid-1850s, it was predominately central European, as hundreds of immigrants walked from Galveston to settle in and around St. Joe. In fact, Panna Maria, five miles outside town, is the oldest established Polish settlement in North America.

When the railroad pushed through St. Joe in 1894, the town's residents engineered an election, got the county seat moved from nearby Helena to St. Joe, and changed the town's name to Karnes City. It's grown very little since then, and visitors see it as a town frozen in time.

As the county seat of Karnes County, about the only modern building in town is the County Jail. Officials would have gladly kept the original jail, but new, strict jail standards enforced by the State had made it obsolete, resulting in the modern law enforcement facility.

At 10:05 a.m. that morning, jail inmate Roland Garcia took two sheriff's employees hostage in the holding cell of the jail. He had been bench-warranted back from the State Penitentiary in Huntsville to stand trial for car theft and had been in the jail about one week. While waiting in his cell, he managed to fashion a knife about eight inches long from one of the metal louvers of the air-conditioning vent.

Garcia was thirty-eight years old, stood five feet, nine inches tall, and weighed 225 pounds. He had been in and out of trouble most of his life and had finally wound up in the State Penitentiary, where he did a lot of weight lifting. His husky appearance was all muscle, not fat. He was very strong, and authorities considered him extremely dangerous.

Like most jails, the Karnes City jail had a phone for the inmates to use, which was located away from the general prison population. It was on the back wall of the holding cell. Around 10:00 a.m., Roland was let out of his cell to use the telephone. The moment he stepped into the holding cell, he took jailer Eddie Garcia hostage. Eddie Garcia, twenty years old and the father of a four-year-old son, was no relation to Roland.

Eddie Garcia immediately hollered for Daisy Villanueva, the secretary-dispatcher and mother of a two-year-old girl, to get help. Daisy, however, apparently did not understand. She got up from her post, walked back to the cell to seek clarification, and became Roland Garcia's second, terrified hostage.

Roland promptly locked himself and the hostages inside the holding cell. There was now no way to get to him because he now had all the keys. He then made his demands of Karnes County Sheriff Bobby Mutz.

First, Roland wanted a patrol car and two sets of handcuffs. He wanted Sheriff Mutz to let him escape with the two hostages. When the sheriff flatly refused, Garcia then decided he wanted to talk to his father in San Antonio. That was okay with the sheriff, and the arrangements were made. But if the sheriff thought the inmate's father would talk his son into surrendering, he was in for a surprise. Roland's father only said he would drive down from San Antonio to talk to his son---he would not tell him to surrender.

It turned out that Roland had some problems with the other prisoners in the Karnes County jail, which made him very unhappy about being incarcerated in the facility. When he found out he couldn't escape from the jail with the hostages in a patrol car, he wanted to go back to the State Penitentiary in Huntsville. Since he didn't trust the sheriff to make the necessary arrangements, he refused to surrender the knife or let Daisy go. He kept the knife to her throat at all times, saying, "If I don't get what I want, you'll see blood."

At 11:30 a.m., Ranger Captain Jack Dean contacted Jim and advised him to "hop-tail it to Karnes City" and see what he could do about the situation. Jim contacted Ranger Steve Black and then got a DPS helicopter, piloted by Gene Matocha, to fly them to Karnes City.

Once in the air, DPS Sergeant John Narramore contacted the helicopter and advised Jim to land out on the highway, not at the jail. "Garcia's already observed a news helicopter flying in the area, and he said he'd kill Daisy unless the helicopter left," he warned. "He also said that if any other officers, Texas Rangers, or the FBI arrives, he'd kill them both. You're gonna have to be invisible."

Pilot Matocha landed on the highway, out of sight of the jail at 12:30 p.m., and Sergeant Narramore met the Rangers and drove them into town to the jail. Sheriff Mutz met with the Rangers, told them the situation, and then advised Jim that, as the senior Ranger at the scene, he was in charge. Jim asked if the sheriff knew for sure that Roland would not talk to a Ranger.

"No, that's right," Sheriff Mutz replied, shaking his head negatively, his tone of voice holding conviction. "He won't talk to anybody else, except me and the dispatcher. He said he'd kill the girl if he so much as saw another officer."

"Where is the key to this door," Jim wanted to know, indicating the holding cell door around the corner.

"There is no key," replied the sheriff. "The jailer has all the keys, and the jailer's in the cell with him."

"Where were the jail cells made?"

"San Antonio Steel," replied the sheriff.

Jim had Sheriff Mutz call the company and have them immediately make a key to the cell door. He then asked Steve Black to fly to San Antonio in the helicopter. While Ranger Black and Pilot Matocha were in the air, Jim arranged for a DPS trooper to pick up the key from San Antonio Steel Company and meet the helicopter at the airport with it. In approximately one hour, Jim had a key to the jail cell.

Sheriff Mutz slipped around the corner to the cell, which was only about ten feet away, and tried the key in the door. It worked perfectly, and the Sheriff left the door unlocked.

Since Roland kept the knife to Daisy's throat all the time, the lawmen kept out of sight. The cell door was constructed with a looking glass about eighteen inches by six inches in size. There was also a round speaking hole for talking through the door. Anyone looking out had a fair view of the hall.

"Here's what we're going to do," Jim said to Sheriff Mutz. "We're going to stay right around this corner so anyone on the inside looking out cannot see us. We'll just stay right back here, and if he ever gets away from the girl, you yell, 'Go!' Then, I'll go in and protect the girl, Steve will go in right behind me and protect the jailer, and you and Sgt. Narramore will go in and get the prisoner."

It was a good plan, and it almost worked.

The holding cell was about twenty feet wide by fourteen feet deep. One end of the cell was the dispatcher side, which had the door the lawmen were going to use. Back in the left rear corner was the pay telephone that prisoners could use to make outside phone calls. It was the phone Roland had used to call his daddy in San Antonio. On the other end of the cell was a door leading back to the cells of the general prison population. Roland had placed a large desk against it.

As Sheriff Mutz kept his vigil at the glass, Roland made several phone calls from the pay phone, but he always kept the girl close to him. It was a tense standoff for the officers.

206

Finally, at 4:45 p.m., Roland went to the telephone, leaving the hostages. The sheriff hollered, "Go!" jerked the door open, and ten or twelve officers entered the room screaming, "Hands up! Hands down! Drop the knife! On the floor! On your feet! Sit down! Lie down! Hands behind your head! Hands on top your head!" Somewhere in the confused shouting voices was Jim's deep baritone booming, "Shut up! Shut up! Shut the hell up!"

In the onrush of bodies, Daisy Villanueva crawled out on all fours, screaming. Roland Garcia dropped the phone and lunged at the jailer, cutting him slightly on the cheek near the mouth. Jim got between Roland and the jailer and, at gunpoint, kept Roland from doing any further damage to Eddie Garcia. Sergeant Narramore and Ranger Black also had their weapons aimed at Roland, who froze. Although Roland and Jim were just a few feet apart, Roland still had the knife, and he refused to drop it.

When everything was quiet, Jim said, "I'm Texas Ranger Jim Peters."

"I know who you are," Roland Garcia said. "I'll talk to you. If you'll get up there by the cell, I'll talk to you."

"Everybody out of the cell," Jim commanded, his eyes never once leaving the armed man. When the other officers were outside, Jim shut the door and began to negotiate with Roland.

After about ten minutes of talking without convincing Roland to drop the knife, Jim suggested that they both take opposite sides of the cell. "Back up against the bars," Jim advised, "and I will back up against the bars over here before one of us gets hurt. It's not a very fair fight with you with a knife and me with a 9 mm with sixteen rounds in it."

Roland complied, and they talked for awhile longer, but Roland still wouldn't surrender. Although it appeared to anyone looking in through the glass in the cell door that Jim was getting nowhere with the talks, in reality, Jim had accomplished quite a bit. He is an astute judge of character, and when he determined that he had established a certain measure of rapport with Roland, he said, "My legs are getting tired. I'm going to sit down in this chair here. Why don't you sit down on that bench there by the telephone? I know you're tired, too."

Roland sat down, and when he did, he said, "If I was to give up my knife, then the sheriff won't let me see my daddy who's coming here from San Antonio, and he won't take me back to Huntsville." It was a question more than a statement, and his tone of voice held the sound of hope.

"The sheriff's going to let you see your father," Jim assured the man, "and he's going to have you sent back to Huntsville." As proof, Jim hollered for the sheriff. "Come on in here, Sheriff. Tell Garcia what you're going to do when he surrenders that knife."

Sheriff Mutz entered the cell. He'd been listening to the conversation from the other side of the door, and he knew what was happening. The sheriff said, "He surrenders the knife and when his father gets here, they visit. Then, I've got a car backed up here right outside the jail, and it will take him right straight back to Huntsville."

Roland thought about it a few minutes, and then tossed the knife on the floor to Jim. He gave Jim the keys to the jail. He had the jailer's billfold, which he took off the desk where he had laid it, and handed it over to Jim. The crisis was over. Jim once again had taken a dangerous situation and turned it around.

On December 4, 1985, Roland Garcia was tried for aggravated kidnapping in 218th District Court in Jourdanton, about thirty miles south of San Antonio and about the same distance west of Karnes City. He received seventy-five years in the Department of Corrections, in addition to the time he's already served.

Jim added yet another commendation to his impressive career record for his handling in the crisis.

EPILOGUE

After Jim retired, the Rangers revamped their organization, allowing women to join their ranks for the first time in the history of the force. And it's created quite an uproar ever since. Jim's not against seeing women Rangers assisting the local constabularies, but he does have reservations about the success of the venture.

"A Ranger is nowhere comparable to a police official," he said. "Police agencies have women in their ranks because the women serve a purpose---they live in their community and work for the betterment of that community. I've worked with some very capable, outstanding, women investigators in my career.

"But Rangers are not like any other investigative agency in the world. Rangers go everywhere in the State, living off the land, sometimes going days without rest. They have to function under all sorts of adverse conditions, and work with all sorts of despicable characters. I find it difficult to believe that a sheriff over in some county, who's having a problem with a dangerous criminal, who's calling for Ranger assistance, would be happy to see a woman Ranger drive up. I mean, if you were the crook and you had just given a big, burly sheriff a hard time, would you surrender to a woman? Most criminals would find the situation totally ludicrous. So do I.

"It all boils down to credibility. How much credibility would the woman Ranger have in the overall scheme of things? Would she come across as tough and no-nonsense? Maybe. Then again, maybe not. Go ahead and recruit her, but first make sure that she has the necessary skills for the job."

According to many Rangers from the Old School, the two women chosen in 1993 to be the first women Rangers ever in the organization really didn't have good investigative backgrounds. Cheryl Steadman was promoted from a clerical job that involved processing warrants. Marrie Garcia had spent the past several years in San Antonio's driver's license service. Neither woman had ever worked a criminal case in her life. A third woman, this time Black to supposedly meet the racial quotas, was hired in 1994. According to several Rangers, Christine Nix also did not have adequate criminal investigative experience. "I'm sure they're very nice ladies," the comments go, "but they're just inexperienced. What sort of help are they going to be in a hostage crisis situation or something along that nature?"

One woman who turned down a Ranger position three times is Lisa Sheppard, a Department of Public Safety criminal investigator with more than fifteen years under her belt. She's recognized and respected by law enforcement agencies all over Texas. Even before she became an officer, she used her remarkable skills as a forensic sketch artist to assist Jim during his hypnosis sessions. Not only is she a totally familiar figure to other investigative agencies, but these other agencies are proud to have her assistance. "Lisa Sheppard is undoubtedly the most qualified officer that I've seen in many, many years," said Alice Police Chief Jack Compton. "And I don't mean female---I mean officer."

So why did Lisa Sheppard turn down the Ranger position? It's because she felt insulted at being relegated to company headquarters like the other female Rangers. She wanted a field position in one of the openings at Beeville, Kingsville, or Corpus Christi, a position more in keeping with her experience as a criminal field investigator. She'd worked throughout South Texas with rural officials. "I'm at the point where I don't think of myself in terms of gender anymore. I'm an investigator," she said.

"The guys in the office would joke, 'The Rangers think you're less than zero because they'd rather have nobody in Beeville than to put you there.' It was professionally humiliating."

Alice Police Chief Jack Compton agrees. "I don't know about the other women. I don't know what their qualifications were. But I know Lisa Sheppard could do well on her own in a single Ranger station, which was what she expected."

"It's real hard for someone in law enforcement to feel victimized. We're the hunter, not the hunted," said Lisa. "I just decided to take my toys and go home."

During his twenty-one year career, Senior Ranger Maurice Cook, head of the 103-member Texas Rangers, knows of only three people who ever turned down a promotion to Ranger. Lisa was one of them. "There were so many years where there were no women in the Rangers," he said. "By and large, the Rangers are not dissatisfied. We certainly are not going to discriminate against employees based on race and sex. We intend to hire as many females, African-Americans, Hispanics as we can, based on their ability....When you've never had females compete, it's hard to hire females."

But many of the Old School feel betrayed. After all, the elite force of Texas officers has always had a hand in the State's biggest criminal cases. They've clashed with rustlers and renegades, killers and con men, bootleggers and bank robbers, drug lords and serial killers. They have always been in sync with Texas, even if they are at odds with the changing times. The Rangers were someone special, different, with a deep sense of honor. They KNEW how to get the job done---they were Rangers ALL THE TIME.

Many of Jim's Ranger friends are retired now, and most of them are glad to be gone before the new organization really shapes up. One good friend, Joaquin Jackson, seemed to be speaking for all when he said to a reporter, "I can see the brotherhood slipping. The government won't let us pick our own people. The ones we're recruiting are there strictly to meet federal standards. People who don't know 'come here' from 'sic 'em' about the Rangers are now sitting on the interview boards. Politics and law enforcement don't mix. They never did. A lot of us got tired of it. It just got to be too much." Jackson hung up his spurs after twenty-seven years of Rangering, most of it along the baddest and meanest trails of the Tex-Mex border.

A lot of good men retired in 1993. Along with Joaquin Jackson, there was Robert Steele, originally from the New York City Police Department. Steele was perhaps the only man on the force who became a Ranger without a Texas background. He had been worked over by the mob in a failed sting operation and been left to die on the Long Island Expressway. But he survived, relocated his family to San Antonio, then flew back to New York and testified against the mobsters at their trial. He'd been a hell of a Ranger for thirteen years.

Gone also was George Frasier, a fine investigator, on to be a preacher, and Bobby Prince and Clayton Smith who had headed the Henry Lee Lucas Task Force in 1984. Jack Dean, Captain of Company "D", retired, going on to become U. S. Marshal for the Southern District. And there's Joe Bailey Davis of Kerrville who, at the age of fourteen, had written then DPS Director Colonel Homer Garrison about becoming a Ranger....

There are still problems to be ironed out with women in the ranks. Cheryl Steadman resigned in 1994 in anger and humiliation, accusing the Rangers of "sexual harassment, discrimination and retaliation." She said "everything went to hell in a handbasket" when she refused to spend the night at a country retreat with "23 drunk Rangers," describing the retreat as a two-room cabin where she was told to peel potatoes, make a salad and perform other "womanly" chores.

Nevertheless, women Rangers will continue to be recruited. They are here to stay, in spite of the grumbling in the ranks. The Old School no longer exists anymore, and for some it's awfully hard to take. It's like putting tradition up on a shelf. "You can see it, but don't touch it," is the way one Ranger sums it up.

"Some things out to remain sacred," said retired Ranger Sid Merchant, "and the Rangers are one of them."

APPENDIX A ABBREVIATED SENTENCES

The Dallas County District Attorney's Office has furnished the following chart so that the public may be more aware of the actual time a person serves in the Texas Department of Corrections on sentences accessed by a judge or jury. The figures are based on the premise that a prisoner becomes a "trusty" at TDC and earns "good" time while he is incarcerated.

Also, it should be noted that the parole eligibility falls within the exclusive powers of the Governor of Texas acting through the Board of Pardons and Paroles. Neither the judge nor the jury has the power to determine a prisoner's release from the TDC.

Sentence	Parole Eligibility
2 years	3 months, 7 days
3 years	4 months, 26 days
4 years	6 months, 15 days
5 years	8 months, 3 days
6 years	9 months, 23 days
7 years	11 months, 10 days
8 years	1 year, 0 months, 28 days
9 years	1 year, 2 months, 18 days
10 years	1 year, 4 months, 6 days
20 years	2 years, 8 months, 13 days
30 years	4 years, 2 months, 0 days
40 years	5 years, 4 months, 27 days
50 years	6 years, 9 months, 3 days
60 years & life	8 years, 0 months, 10 days

APPENDIX B

THE UNITED STATES OF AMERICA
VS
JOSE MANUEL MIGUEL XAVIAR GONZALES

The following is a verbatim transcript of a sentence imposed upon a defendant convicted of murder in the United States District Court for the Territory of New Mexico in 1881 by a United States Judge, sitting at Taos in an adobe stable used as a temporary courtroom. It has erroneously been attributed to Judge Roy Bean, and although the legendary Judge did impose sentences very similar in nature---he once imposed a fine of $50 for Loitering to a dead man---he did not pass this judgment.

"To: JOSE MANUEL MIGUEL XAVIAR GONZALES:

Jose Manuel Miguel Xaviar Gonzales, in a few short weeks it will be spring. The snows of winter will flee away, the ice will vanish, and the air will become soft and balmy. In short, Jose Manuel Miguel Xaviar Gonzales, the annual miracle of the years will awaken and come to pass, but you won't be there.

The rivulet will run it soaring course to the sea, the timid desert flowers will put forth their tender shoots, the glorious valleys of this imperial domain will blossom as the rose. Still, you won't be here to see.

From every tree top some wild woods songster will carol his mating song, butterflies will sport in the sunshine, the busy bee will hum happy as it pursues its accustomed vocation. The gentle breeze will tease the tassels of the wild grasses, and all nature, Jose Manuel Miguel Xaviar Gonzales, will be glad, but you. You won't be here to enjoy it because I command the sheriff or some other officers of the country to lead you out to some remote spot, swing you by the neck from a knotting bough of some sturdy oak, and let you hang until you are dead.

And then, Jose Manuel Miguel Xaviar Gonzales, I further command that such officer or officers retire quickly from your dangling corpse, that vultures may descend from the heavens upon your filthy body until nothing shall remain but bare, bleached bones of a cold-blooded, copper-colored, blood-thirsty, throat-cutting, chili-eating, sheep-herding, murdering SON-0F-A-BITCH."

BIBLIOGRAPHY:

Bostic, Deane E. "Killer With a Bad Temper!" *Official Detective Stories*, April 1976.

Bostic, Deane E. "National Police Officer of the Month," *Master Detective*, July 1976.

Bostic, Deane E. "Ranger Trackdown of Texas' One-Man Crime Wave," *True Detective*, September 1976.

Bostic, Deane E. "Who Killed the Nicest Guy in the Coast Guard," *Startling Detective*, January 1977.

Bostic, Deane E. "Final Chapter for Texas' Rich Man-Poor Man," *True Police Cases*, April 1977.

Cartwright, Gary. "The Death of a Ranger," *Texas Monthly*, August 1978.

Cochran, Frances Bramlett. South of the Alamo. Corpus Christi: Coastal Bend Genealogical Society, 1992.

Corpus Christi Business Journal, August 14, 1987.

Corpus Christi Caller, "Ex-Convict Still at Large After 2nd Day of Manhunt," February 9, 1962.

— "Freer Manhunt Continues," February 12, 1962.

— "Richardson Main 'Positive,'" August 22, 1972.

— "Youth Identifies Hammond as Man Who Shot Richardson," August 23, 1972.

— "State Rests Case Against Hammond," August 29, 1972.

— "Defense Witnesses Testify Hammond Was in Fort Worth," August 30, 1972.

— "Jody's Death Came only Hours before a New Citation Arrived," June 14, 1974.

— "Inmate Takes Jailer Hostage," June 26, 1985.

Corpus Christi Times, "Texas Rangers 'Update' Themselves." November 21, 1969.

— "Mrs. Parr Was in Complicated Legal Wrangle," June 12, 1974.

— "Jody Parr Fatally Shot," June 13, 1974.

— "Gregarious Jody Spent Last Hours in Solitude," June 14, 1974.

— "Services Are Set for Mrs. Parr," June 14, 1974.

Corpus Christi Caller-Times, "S. Texans Fondly Remember Clint Peoples." June 23, 1992.

— "Killer is Put to Death for 9-Year-Old Slaying," April 1, 1994.

— "A Ranger in Spirit, Not Name," July 24, 1994.

— "Retiring Ranger is Modern Lawman," August 17, 1987.

— "Retired Texas Ranger Walter A. Russell Dies," 1976.

— "Infamous Box 13 Is not Forgotten," April 10, 1994.

Corpus Christi Magazine, "Texas Rangers: Tall Men, Tall Tales," February 1984.

Cox, Mike. The Confessions of Henry Lee Lucas. New York: Pocket Books, 1991.

Dillow, Gordon. "The Lone Ranger," *Philip Morris Magazine*, July-August, 1989

Draper, Robert. "The Twilight of the Texas Rangers." *Texas Monthly*, February 1994.

Durham, George. Taming the Nueces Strip: The Story of McNelly's Rangers. Austin: University of Texas Press, 1962.

Greensboro Daily News, "A Tall Texas Ranger from North Carolina," May 29, 1971.

Haley, James L. Texas: From the Frontier to Spindletop. New York: St. Martin's Press, 1991.

Hemphill, Jerry R. Colts from Texas and the Old West. Texas Colts, Blainsvills, Georgia, 1990.

Holder, Dennis. "One Riot, One Ranger," Family Weekly, June 30, 1985.

Paul, Lee. "Death Faced Straight Up," Wild West, August 1993.

San Antonio Sun, "Lone Man Disarms Deputy Sheriff then Fatally Shoots Officer and Wife," July 20, 1973.

----- Obituaries: William Carroll Nelson, September 12, 1993.

San Marcos Daily Record, "Kidnapping Suspect Is Captured," July 22, 1987.

The Thin Blue Line, "The Texas Rangers, the Pride Continues," Volume I, Number II, 1987.

Tulsa World, "Famed Texas Rangers Fighting Battle from Within," June 4, 1995.

About the Author:

Lee Paul is what the Original Texans call a "Transplanted Texan," having been born in South Dakota and living all over the United States before settling in Texas in 1968. After attending school at Texas Tech University, Lee moved to Corpus Christi in 1971, obtaining a Bachelor of Science degree from Texas A & I University in Kingsville. Upon graduation, Lee went to work in the oil fields of South Texas until retirement in 1991.

Lee has been writing professionally since 1968, earning writing awards in both fiction and nonfiction. Special interest categories are western lore, history, and American legends, the latter of which Lee feels is slowly being lost to the younger generation. For reading enjoyment, Lee likes biographies, true crime, and action-adventure novels. Some favorite authors are Philip MacDonald, Tony Hillerman, Alistar MacLean, Ann Rule, and John D. MacDonald. Hobbies include an impressive collection of juvenile series books ("I'm still looking for those last elusive Lone Ranger and Judy Bolton books..."), cookie jars, and postage stamp art.

Lee currently resides in Tulsa, Oklahoma, with her husband and many pets.